THE PSALTER OF THE CHURCH

THE PSALTER OF THE CHURCH

THE PRAYER BOOK VERSION OF THE PSALMS

WITH INTRODUCTION AND MARGINAL NOTES

BY

JAMES G. CARLETON, D.D.

LECTURER IN DIVINITY, TRINITY COLLEGE, DUBLIN;
CANON OF ST PATRICK'S, DUBLIN

Cambridge:
at the University Press
1909

CAMBRIDGE
UNIVERSITY PRESS

University Printing House, Cambridge CB2 8BS, United Kingdom

Cambridge University Press is part of the University of Cambridge.

It furthers the University's mission by disseminating knowledge in the pursuit of education, learning and research at the highest international levels of excellence.

www.cambridge.org
Information on this title: www.cambridge.org/9781107445765

First published 1909
First paperback edition 2014

A catalogue record for this publication is available from the British Library

ISBN 978-1-107-44576-5 Paperback

PREFACE

THIS handbook of the Prayer Book Psalter is designed to meet the case of the many Church people who would welcome help—if given in a concise and easily apprehended form—towards a better understanding of the Psalms, but for whom the study of elaborate and diffuse commentaries is out of the question. The special feature of the present book is the printing of the Psalter and the explanatory notes side by side in parallel columns. By this arrangement the reader is enabled to take in the meaning of a passage at a glance; and the weariness of carrying the eye to the foot of the page, or of turning to the end of the volume for the comment, is avoided.

I take this opportunity to acknowledge my obligation to the Syndics of the University Press for undertaking the publication of the book. I also desire to thank the Rev. H. J. Lawlor, D.D., Professor of Ecclesiastical History, University of Dublin, for his great kindness in reading the proofs, and for many valuable suggestions.

J. G. C.

June, 1909.

CONTENTS

'I will sing with the spirit, and I will sing with the understanding also.' 1 Cor. xiv. 15.

INTRODUCTION

I.

The Book of Psalms.

The Psalter formed a portion of the last of the three sections—named respectively 'the Law,' 'the Prophets' and 'the Writings' or 'the Sacred Writings'—into which the Old Testament, as we now call it, was popularly divided by the Jews before the Christian era. Our Lord referred to this threefold division when He summed up all Scripture as 'the Law of Moses, and the Prophets, and the Psalms' (St Luke xxiv. 44)—'the Psalms' here giving their name to 'the Writings' probably either because they were placed first in that section, or because the books which it contained were largely of a poetical character.

The five books of the Psalter

The Psalter itself was divided into five Books (now indicated for the English reader in the Revised Version), viz. Book I. Ps. i.—xli., Book II. Ps. xlii.—lxxii., Book III. Ps. lxxiii.—lxxxix., Book IV. Ps. xc.—cvi., Book V. Ps. cvii.—cl.

The end of each of the first four Books is marked by a doxology, Ps. cl. constituting the doxology at the end of Book V. and of the Psalter.

The gradual formation of the Psalter

An examination of the Psalter leads to the conclusion that it grew up gradually, and reached its present form by the combination of several collections of poems.

The division into Books is itself an indication of this. But besides, we observe that many of the Psalms have Titles which assign them to certain authors. In the first Book, for example, practically all the Psalms are attributed to David. It may reasonably be regarded as having once existed as a separate Psalm-book which was perhaps the nucleus of the future Psalter. Another collection of Psalms is suggested by the Title 'of the sons of Korah' (xlii.—xlix., lxxxiv., lxxxv., lxxxvii., lxxxviii.), another by that 'of Asaph' (l., lxxiii.—lxxxiii.) prefixed to each. A group of Psalms has the common inscription 'A Song of Ascents' (cxx.—cxxxiv.); another is marked by having the call to praise—'Hallelujah'—either at the beginning or end, or in both places (civ.—cvi., cxi.—cxiii., cxv.—cxvii., cxxxv., cxlvi.—cl.).

The use of Divine Names, also, bears witness to the composite character of the Psalter. In the first Book, 'Jehovah,' generally rendered 'the LORD' in our English Versions, is almost exclusively employed. In the second and third, 'Elohim,' translated 'God,' is mainly used until Ps. lxxxiv. is reached, when 'Jehovah' again becomes prominent, and continues so throughout the fourth and fifth Books.

Another fact which points to the original independence of various parts of the Psalter is the repetition of the same Psalm wholly or in part in different books. Thus Ps. xiv. and xl. 16 ff. in Book I. appear again as Ps. liii. and lxx. in Book II.; and Ps. lvii. 8—12 and lx. 5—12 in Book II. recur as Ps. cviii. in Book V. And it is noteworthy, as evidencing the revising hand of an editor, with regard to the Psalms which Book I. has in common with Book II., that where 'Jehovah' occurs in Ps. xiv. and xl. 16 ff., it has been changed into 'Elohim'—universally in Ps. liii., partially in Ps. lxx.

The frequent quotation of earlier in later Psalms, and evident additions to Psalms made at subsequent times, are significant in the same direction.

A further proof of compilation is the manifest grouping together of Psalms which are akin in subject-matter. Thus in Book I. the Psalms are chiefly of a personal character; they express the joys and sorrows and aspirations of individuals. In Books II. and III. the national element is foremost. We find here mainly prayers and thanksgivings which took their rise from public dangers and deliverances. And again in Books IV. and V., the Psalms are, generally speaking, of a liturgical character. They are specially suited for use in Divine worship, and many of them probably were composed for that purpose.

The Titles of the Psalms

The ascription of several of the Psalms in the Titles (retained in the Authorized and Revised, but not in the Prayer-Book Version) to David and others cannot be regarded as decisive of the question of authorship. Internal evidence proves that some of these Psalms could not have been composed by those to whom they are thus assigned. Psalms xx., xxi. and cx., for instance, though entitled Psalms of David, are plainly addressed to a king, and not written by a king: and Ps. lxix., likewise attributed to David, has allusions which make it impossible to date it earlier than the captivity.

At the same time we should not be justified in wholly dis regarding the Titles as if they gave no guidance at all in the question of authorship. It would be difficult to account for the tradition which ascribes so many of the Psalms to David—and it is with regard to him that the problem chiefly confronts us—if none or comparatively few were written by him. And we have independent witness to the truth of the Title in one instance. Psalm xviii. appears also in 2 Sam. xxii., and is assigned to David both in the Psalter and in the history.

The uniformity with which, as has been before noticed, all the Psalms in Book I. are ascribed to David has been explained in this way: namely that this Book originated in a collection of David's Psalms, to which others, not all by him, were added later on, and that the Title 'Psalms of David' which belonged to the original collection was subsequently prefixed in the singular to each Psalm.

We have here, in fact, the first stage of that extension of nomenclature by which eventually the entire Psalter became known as the Psalms of David—the name of the primary and principal author of the Psalter being given to the whole.

In this commentary the Title a 'Psalm of David' is quoted when it confirms what on other grounds seems to be the authorship: the historical notice also, peculiar to the 'Psalms of David,' of the special occasion on which the Psalm was composed, is cited when it appears to give help to the interpretation of the Psalm.

Hebrew poetry

The poetry of the ancient Hebrews, in the opinion of many scholars, was written in metre, based upon accent; but the laws of that metre are almost wholly conjectural, and it obviously cannot be represented in a translation. There is, however, a feature generally recognized as characterizing Hebrew poetry, namely a system of parallelism which, as it belongs to the meaning and not to the mode of expression, retains its essence when translated. This system admits of much flexibility and assumes various forms which are generally distributed into three typical classes.

1. *Synonymous parallelism.* Here clauses correspond one with another in such a way that the second repeats the sense of the first in different terms. Instances of this kind are of constant occurrence in the Psalter. Take for example Ps. xv.:

'LORD, who shall dwell in thy tabernacle:
Or who shall rest upon thy holy hill?'

and Ps. xxi. 1, 2:

'The king shall rejoice in thy strength, O LORD:
Exceeding glad shall he be of thy salvation.
Thou hast given him his heart's desire:
And hast not denied him the request of his lips.'

2. *Antithetic or contrasted parallelism.* Here the two lines are contrasted by an opposition of terms or sentiments or both. We have two instances in immediate succession in Ps. xx. 7, 8:

'Some put their trust in chariots, and some in horses:
But we will remember the Name of the LORD our God.

They are brought down, and fallen:
But we are risen, and stand upright.'

3. *Synthetic or constructive parallelism.* Here the parallelism consists only in the similar form of construction, the two parts of the couplet corresponding in respect of the shape and turn of the sentence, noun, for example, answering to noun, or verb to verb, or interrogative to interrogative. This kind of parallelism is not always easily discerned. A clear example may be found in Ps. cxlviii. 7—13:

'Praise the LORD upon earth:
Ye dragons, and all deeps;
Fire and hail, snow and vapours:
Wind and storm, fulfilling his word;
Mountains and all hills:
Fruitful trees and all cedars, &c.'

It can easily be seen that this feature in Hebrew poetry—the mutual relationship between each part of the couplet—may render valuable aid in the elucidation of obscure or ambiguous passages.

In the Revised Version, the Psalms and other poetic portions of the Old Testament are printed so as to exhibit the parallelism.

Alphabetical Psalms

A characteristic of some Psalms which cannot be preserved in a translation is the arrangement of the initial letters of the clauses or verses or pairs of verses, as the case may be, in the order of the alphabet.

This arrangement is, as a rule, found only in Psalms of a special kind, those, namely, that give expression to thoughts—bearing on a single topic, and presenting it in different lights—more or less loosely strung together. By the acrostic system an artificial bond of connection is supplied which serves as a help to the memory. In Ps. cxix. this system is carried out with greater elaboration than elsewhere (see note prefixed to that Psalm). The other alphabetical Psalms are ix., x., xxv., xxxiv., xxxvii., cxi., cxii., cxlv.

II.

THE PSALTER OF THE CHURCH.

The Version of the Psalms which finds place in the Book of Common Prayer is naturally the one with which English Church people are most familiar and which they love best. From their earliest years they have joined in the recitation of the Psalms in this Version as a part of Divine worship: it is connected in their minds with the most solemn associations; and has been a factor of inestimable importance in the building up of their spiritual life.

The Prayer Book Psalter of the present day is practically the same as that of the first English Prayer Book (1549), which was taken from the Authorized Version of that date, commonly called the 'Great Bible.'

In the 'Great Bible' (1539) although the translation of the other books was made from the original Hebrew or Greek, the Psalms were transferred, with some alterations, from Coverdale's Bible (1535) which was a translation 'out of Douche [i.e. German] and Latyn into English' as the title-page states. Hence it is that in many places, the rendering of the Prayer Book Version follows the Vulgate—the Latin Bible—where the latter differs from the Hebrew. In King James's Version (1611) now known as 'the Authorized,' the Psalms, like the other books, were translated directly from the original, and are, on the whole, more correctly rendered than in the Prayer Book Version. It should however be noted that, in several instances, the scholars who have given us the Revised Version (1885) have thought well to return to the Prayer Book renderings. At the final English Revision of the Prayer Book (1662), while the Epistles and Gospels were conformed to the Authorized Version, yet the old Version of the Psalms, having become familiar to worshippers, and being more rhythmical and better adapted for chanting than the new, was allowed to retain its position of honour.

A few words seem needed with reference to the Vulgate Psalter from which, as we have seen, the Prayer Book Psalms, in large measure, derive their origin. This was the Psalter used in the Church services at the time of the Reformation; and the Psalms being then popularly known by their first words in Latin, these were retained as headings in the English Version, furnishing an evidence, cognizable by all, of the connection between the former and the latter.

The Vulgate Psalter

The Psalter in the Vulgate together with the rest of that Version is the work of St Jerome (end of fourth century), but, unlike the other books, it is not a direct translation from the original. It is a revision of the Old Latin Psalter, which in St Jerome's days was hallowed in people's minds by use in private devotion and in public worship. This Psalter had in early Christian times been translated from the Septuagint, the Greek Version from which the quotations from the Old Testament in the New are generally taken, and which, with the Greek New Testament, formed the Bible of the primitive Greek-speaking Church. Hence it arises that in most cases in which the Prayer Book Version agrees with the Vulgate against the Hebrew, the rendering may ultimately be traced to the Septuagint. St Jerome made a subsequent translation of the Psalms from the Hebrew, but it was not admitted into the Vulgate, and, as happened in a later age in these countries, the old familiar Version maintained its place in Church worship and in popular affection.

The Prayer Book Psalter cannot claim to be a perfect Version; still, in the main, it fairly represents the original; and whatever inaccuracies it contains, we have means at hand in the Revised Version for their correction. To a large extent it is its own interpreter, and it has instructed and cheered the hearts of thousands who have sought no further guidance to its meaning than its own words afford them.

But while this is undoubtedly the case, it is likewise true that the Prayer Book Version is by no means in all parts easy to be understood; indeed, here and there, we meet with passages which are absolutely unintelligible. Some of these obscure places are peculiar to itself, some it shares with the Authorized and even with the Revised Version: for it occasionally happens that the most accurate rendering of the original needs explanation before its meaning can be grasped.

If then the worshipper is not content to utter words which are without signification to him, if he is desirous of 'singing with the understanding,' it is of essential consequence that he should seek external aid for the elucidation of the Psalter.

The object of the present work is to render this aid to those who through want of time or opportunity are unable to consult more detailed commentaries, or even to check the Prayer Book Psalter with the Revised Version.

An explanation of the plan adopted is given further on (see p. xxx).

There are some words of frequent occurrence in the Psalter which may conveniently be considered here.

Some words explained

'Godly,' 'holy,' 'saint.' These words, in many instances, translate a single Hebrew word, which, in the opinion of most modern scholars, should rather be explained according to the meaning given to it in the R.V. margin of Ps. iv. 3, 'one that he [the LORD] favoureth'—the reference being primarily not to the character of the person, but to his position of privilege as a member of the chosen race.

'Soul.' The Hebrew word thus translated frequently means 'self' or 'life,' and should be so understood when the context requires either of these senses.

'Poor.' There is little difference in the Hebrew between the word thus rendered and another word which is translated 'meek,' 'lowly' or 'humble': in fact the Hebrew margin frequently directs the one to be substituted for the other. The two words, therefore, may be regarded as practically interchangeable, and each may be interpreted according to the requirements of the passage.

'Hell,' 'the pit,' 'the grave.' These words represent the Hebrew 'Sheol' which is left untranslated in the Revised Version. 'Sheol' corresponds to the Greek 'Hades,' and signifies the under-world regarded as the abode of departed spirits.

'LORD' when thus printed represents 'Jehovah' in the original. The Jews, from feelings of reverence, shrank from pronouncing the Sacred Name, and substituted for it a word equivalent to the English 'Lord.' Their example was followed by the translators of the Septuagint; and from it the usage found its way through the Vulgate into the English Bible. In a few passages the word 'GOD' represents 'Jehovah' (see p. xxx).

'The Name of the LORD' expresses the complex notion of God's Person and character as He has revealed them in Exod. xxxiii. 19, xxxiv. 5—7 and elsewhere.

'Heard' is generally replaced in R.V. by 'answered' when the reference is to prayer granted. It has not been thought necessary to note this in the margin, as prayer 'heard' is equivalent to prayer 'answered.'

'Save,' 'salvation,' 'redeem,' 'redemption.' These words, as used by the Psalmists, primarily refer to temporal deliverance personal or national.

'People' frequently represents a Hebrew plural word meaning 'nations,' and in such cases the R.V. clears up the meaning by substituting 'peoples.'

'Heathen.' This word signifying in the original non-Israelitish peoples seems more expressive than the R.V. substitute 'nations.'

'Quicken.' The Hebrew word thus rendered varies in meaning between 'give new life to,' 'preserve alive,' and 'refresh.'

III.

SOME FEATURES OF THE SUBJECT-MATTER OF THE PSALMS.

Life beyond the grave

The Psalmists wrote before Christ 'abolished death and brought life and incorruption to light through the gospel' (2 Tim. i. 10). Little had been revealed to them about the existence that survives death. Thus while they have a vivid realization of communion with God, and absolute trust in His mercy, they generally write as those whose interests are confined to the present condition of things. When they refer to a future life it is usually in gloomy terms, as to a vague and shadowy state of being that hardly deserved the name of life when compared with the activity of 'the life which now is.' The dead are 'in the darkness' (cxliii. 3); they are 'no more' (xxxix. 15); they dwell 'in the land where all things are forgotten' (lxxxviii. 12); they are 'cast off' by God and 'remembered by Him no more' (lxxxviii. 4). 'The dust' cannot 'give thanks to God or declare His truth' (xxx. 10).

These despondent thoughts were the natural outcome of the teaching of the Law which restricted the scope of its rewards and penalties to the present world. The devout Israelite who recognized his call as one of the chosen race to carry out God s will, to bear witness for Him before the nations and prepare the way for the ultimate triumph of righteousness, knew of no other sphere than the life in the flesh in which he could fulfil his Divinely appointed destiny. He had no revelation of a further field of active service beyond the grave.

It is worthy of note that this class of passages is not without parallel in the New Testament. Our Lord's own words are, 'We must work the works of Him that sent Me, while it is day: the night cometh when no man can work' (St John ix. 4).

Even though the Christian is assured that when he dies, other and doubtless more important work will be provided for him, still he must recognize this world as the scene of the only kind of activity of which he has distinct knowledge.

But it would be wrong to regard the Psalms as devoid of all hope of a blissful immortality. We must put an unnatural interpretation on the following passages, among others, if we do not see in them this hope more or less distinctly expressed. 'Thou wilt shew me the path of life: in Thy presence is fulness of joy; in Thy right hand there are pleasures for evermore' (xvi. 12). 'As for me, I shall behold Thy face in righteousness: I shall be satisfied, when I awake, with Thy likeness' (xvii. 16). 'God will redeem my soul from the power of Sheol: for He shall receive me' (xlix. 15). 'Thou shalt guide me with Thy counsel, and afterward receive me to glory' (lxxiii. 23). The Psalmists had, now and again, visions of the future life with God which are lit up well-nigh with the brightness of the Christian revelation.

Imprecations on enemies

We find occasionally in the Psalms prayers for vengeance upon wicked enemies, and expressions of exultation on their fall, which sound out of harmony with the spirit of Christianity (see in particular xxxv. 4—8, xl. 17, 18, lviii. 6—8, lix. 11—15, lxix. 23—29, cix. 5—19).

This language has been explained by attributing it to the imperfect standard of morality of Old Testament times which our Lord, in the Sermon on the Mount and elsewhere, has contrasted with the higher requirements He expects from His followers.

But to leave the matter there would be to do an injustice to the Psalmists.

There are certain considerations to which we must give due weight before we can form a just estimate of these Imprecatory Psalms, as they are generally called.

They are not prompted by feelings of irritation or desire for personal revenge. The appeal for vengeance is made to God and judgement is left in His hands. Side by side, too, with the strongest denunciations we find sentiments of kindliness and goodwill towards the offender (see xxxv. 13, 14, cix. 3, 4). The motive of the Psalmists is essentially zeal for God's righteousness, the triumph of which was delayed so long as wickedness had the upper hand. The Psalmists had not the clear revelation, made to us, of a future state of retribution. Here or not at all, they believed, punishment would overtake the ungodly. When, then, in this world they saw might prevailing against right, the wicked persecuting the good, was it not, from their point of view, an imperative duty to implore God to vindicate His honour and manifest His righteous rule over the world in the only way in which, in their opinion, this could be effected, namely by the visible overthrow of the wicked?

And this duty must have seemed all the plainer when the enemies who oppressed them were foreigners; for Israel was the people of Jehovah, and its foes were His. If the chosen race were subjected to the tyranny of strangers, it would appear that Jehovah was unable to protect His own: His promises would seem to have failed, and the cause of truth and righteousness to be in jeopardy.

But again, we have been taught more distinctly than those under the Old Covenant to distinguish between wrong and the wrong-doer, to hate the one and love the other; and yet we are far from concluding that this duty forbids us in all cases to desire that the sinner may receive the due reward of his deeds. The state enacts penalties against transgressors; the magistrate condemns not merely crimes but criminals, and we approve. If we hear of some vile act of iniquity, we earnestly hope that justice will overtake the offender; we rejoice when the supremacy of the law is vindicated by his punishment.

It should moreover be borne in mind that the disorganized state of society in which the Psalmists lived prevented them from relying, as we can, on the orderly working of the law to bring criminals to account. They had to commit the maintenance of their just cause solely to God, the Supreme Judge, and implore Him to check the wicked in their career of violence.

And if they pray for the overthrow of foreign oppressors, we should reflect that we also feel justified in praying that our king may 'vanquish and overcome all his enemies'; though we, unlike the Psalmists, suppress all reference to the horrors which success in war implies.

Instead of apologizing for these Psalms we should rather earnestly take to heart and profit by the practical lesson they have to teach us. Their authors by their righteous hatred of sin as an offence against God impress upon Christians the truth, to which the New Testament also distinctly testifies, that the stern side of religion is as real as the merciful; that God's compassion is not exercised by an indiscriminate benevolence; that His salvation cannot reach the impenitent; that the wicked are in rebellion against Him, and unless they sue for peace a fearful retribution awaits them. These Psalms are a standing protest, needful at all times, against lack of moral earnestness, and the danger of thinking lightly of sin.

Claims to integrity

Another feature in the Psalms which sometimes causes perplexity is the presence in them of assertions of uprightness and of obedience to the commandments, also confident appeals to God to judge the hearts of the writers, which seem to savour of self-righteousness. The chief passages of this kind are vii. 8, xvii. 3—5, xviii. 20—24, xxvi., xxxii. 7, lxiv. 4, lxxxvi. 2, ci. 3, cxix. 101, 110, 128, 168.

In some cases where these sentiments occur the context proves that the Psalmist is merely protesting his innocence of some specific charge brought against him (see vii. 3, 4). But, in general, before taking upon ourselves to pass adverse criticism upon the Psalmists, we should make sure that we do not misinterpret or press beyond their due significance the moral terms that they apply to themselves.

We have seen above (p. xvi) that the word translated 'holy,' 'godly,' 'saint,' is now given by most scholars the meaning 'one favoured by God.' Such epithets as 'righteous,' 'perfect,' 'clean,' 'innocent,' need not be taken as implying more than honesty of purpose, a right direction of the will, the character of the man who is sincerely desirous of serving God. They are declarations of integrity which may be paralleled with St Paul's assertions, 'I have lived before God in all good conscience until this day' (Acts xxiii. 1), 'I know nothing against myself' (1 Cor. iv. 4). They are Old Testament claims to the possession of the 'honest and good heart' of the Parable of the Sower (St Luke viii. 15). They are not declarations of sinlessness; for the Psalter is pervaded by a sense of sin, and of the need of pardon and renewal; and sometimes in the same Psalms which contain protestations of rectitude we find humble confession of guilt and prayer for mercy (see xxvi. 11, xxxii. 6, lxxxvi. 2, 16, cxix. 25, 176).

Nevertheless, it should not be forgotten that the Psalmists living, as they did, before the Holy Ghost came in His fulness to 'convict the world in respect of sin and of righteousness,' to enlighten the conscience and reveal the spiritual demands of God's law, would find it easier than we should to satisfy themselves that they had fulfilled God's requirements. Thus we may shrink from employing, as our own, words of self-approval which they were able to use with all sincerity, and which from their stand-point betokened no lack of humility. But we need not think that this impairs the value of these passages for us Christians or makes them less suited for our lips. The deepest consecration which the Psalms possess for us is that they were used by Christ during His earthly life, that He made their words His own. Any difficulty we have of interpreting them, any scruple about employing them in worship, vanishes when we regard them as His utterances. The more ample the assertions of innocence and integrity, the more worthy are they of the Perfect Man.

Predictions of Christ

Of all the books of the Old Testament the Psalter is most frequently quoted in the New as pointing forward to Christ and His Church. Our Lord has repeatedly appealed to the testimony of the Psalms to Himself. The foreshadowing of Christ in the Psalter takes, to speak generally, one of four forms. He is set forth as a King, as a Sufferer, as the Son of Man, as God—the supreme Judge of the world.

Christ as King. (Ps. ii., xviii., xx., xxi., xlv., lxi., lxxii., lxxxix., cx., cxxxii.) These Royal Psalms, as they have been named, usually have for their immediate subject the reigning king, either David or one of his successors, and they are generally called forth by some critical event in the history of the nation. Their authors have before their minds the Divine promise made to David and his house through the Prophet Nathan: 'I took thee from the sheepcote...that thou shouldest be prince over my people, over Israel...When thy days be fulfilled, and thou shalt sleep with thy fathers, I will set up thy seed...and I will establish the throne of his kingdom for ever. I will be his father, and he shall be my son: if he commit iniquity, I will chasten him with the rod of men...but my mercy shall not depart from him....And thine house and thy kingdom shall be made sure for ever before thee: thy throne shall be established for ever' (2 Sam. vii. 8—16).

This promise, the charter of the Davidic line, the Psalmists treat of and develop as circumstances prompt them. They dwell on the predestined glories of the house of David—often sharply contrasted with present abasement: they lament the apparent failure of the promise, and appeal to God to grant fulfilment of it: they see visions of a future period when the king of David's line will reign victoriously over all nations of the world. Although the Psalmists themselves may not have been conscious of it, we see that they claimed for David and his house such powers and prerogatives, and for his kingdom such extent and duration, as were destined to be realized only in the Divine Son of David, and in His universal and everlasting dominion.

In other parts of the Psalter, besides the Royal Psalms, the kingdom of Israel is identified with that of God, and the incorporation with it of all the peoples is predicted. In particular may be mentioned the series of triumphal Psalms which were probably composed on the occasion of the overthrow of Sennacherib's host in the reign of Hezekiah. (Ps. xlvi.—xlviii., lxvi., lxxv., lxxvi.)

Christ as Sufferer. Passages from the following Psalms are quoted in the New Testament as having been fulfilled in certain details of our Lord's sufferings, xxii., xxxv., xli., lxix., cix.

These Psalms bear, in themselves, plain evidences of having been written to describe the personal experiences of men passing through severe bodily and spiritual anguish. But they were servants of God unjustly afflicted, and being such, their afflictions, unknown to themselves, foreshadowed those of the Great Servant of the Lord, the Man of Sorrows. And besides this, it was divinely ordered that certain features in their sufferings should prefigure some of the circumstances which attended Christ's Passion, and even that what the Psalmists evidently meant to be metaphorical descriptions of their trials should come literally true in the details of the Crucifixion. The words of the Psalmists were thus, according to the New Testament phrase, 'fulfilled,' that is they received a new and deeper meaning.

Christ as the Son of Man. Psalms which emphasize the dignity of man and attribute to him universal dominion (viii.), which delineate the perfect human character (xv.), which picture the ideal fellowship with God (xvi.), which proffer, on the part of man, unreserved surrender to God's will (xl.)—these reach forward for their adequate fulfilment to the Son of Man, the Sinless, who is one with the Father, and unto whom all authority hath been given in heaven and on earth.

Christ as God. In other Psalms (chiefly l., lxviii., xciii., xcv.—c.) the visible appearance of Jehovah upon earth is announced as a Conqueror to confound His enemies, as a Judge to vindicate the righteous, as a Saviour to deliver the oppressed. His reign of righteousness and joy is proclaimed. All peoples are bidden to worship and obey Him. Here we have witness borne to the Advent of Christ under yet another aspect—the aspect which regards it as the Coming of God Himself in visible form. These visions of the Psalmists whatever they meant for them, to Christian readers speak plainly of the Incarnation of the Son of God.

Mystical interpretation

In considering the testimony which the Psalms bear to Christ, it would be unreasonable to confine our attention to the passages quoted in this sense in the New Testament. Our Lord said of the Hebrew Scriptures, 'these are they which bear witness of Me' (St John v. 39); and His words authorize us to read those Scriptures with the conviction that He is to be found everywhere in them. Thus the references to the Psalms which occur in the New Testament are to be regarded merely as specimens of the rich store of Messianic allusion which Christians may expect to find in the Psalter.

And in making this use of the Psalms we are but continuing what has been the practice of Christians from the commencement. They have always followed the example set them by the New Testament writers in looking beyond the original purport of the Psalms, and discerning in them a meaning fuller and more spiritual than the literal—a meaning which must have transcended the thoughts of the authors, because it needed for its elucidation the light of the Gospel.

It may, indeed, be truly said that the Psalms were written rather for Christians than for God's ancient people. The Psalter passed as an inspired Hymn-book from the Temple to the Church. Was not this divinely foreseen event providentially arranged for? Must we not believe that the Psalmists were supernaturally guided to make their utterances such as would be patient of a higher interpretation than that of which they themselves were conscious; so that after the passing of the few centuries still allotted to the dispensation of 'Israel after the flesh,' those utterances might be fitted, throughout all subsequent ages, to express the devotional thoughts, the aspirations, the prayers and praises of the 'Israel of God'?

The Church of Christ is the successor of the Jewish, the inheritor of her privileges, traditions and titles of honour. This fact gives us the key to the Christian interpretation of the Psalms. We see that the hopes which centred in David and his line and kingdom received their fulfilment in his Divine Son, the King of Kings. We see that what is said of Israel or Jacob, must be applied, on the principle of continuity, to the wider family into which Israel developed, to those who in Christ are 'Abraham's seed, heirs according to promise.' The names 'Sion' and 'Jerusalem' describe for us the Catholic Church in its militant or triumphant stage. 'Saints,' 'redemption,' 'salvation,' and many another term are glorified with their higher Gospel meaning. The undefined sense of fellowship with God is exalted into participation in the Divine Nature through membership with Christ.

The use to which the Church puts the Psalter in Divine worship is the most prominent assertion of her right to understand the Psalms mystically, that is, to interpret them from the standpoint of her higher knowledge of things spiritual. The Church has claimed these Hebrew poems, composed under the dim light of an imperfect revelation, as her own, she has made them the expression of her public devotions. She has ordered their daily recitation, and, by appending the *Gloria Patri* to each, has intimated the sense in which she would have them understood. And further, by her system of Proper Psalms she has given detailed guidance in spiritual interpretation. For by assigning fixed Psalms for use on the Great Days that commemorate the cardinal events of redemption, she testifies that these hymns of the Ancient Church are invested in her mind with special Christian meanings, that they proclaim truths which their authors—'prophets and righteous men' of old—'desired to see' and yet 'saw not.'

IV.

TABLES OF PROPER AND SPECIAL PSALMS.

PROPER PSALMS.

	Matins.	Evensong.
Christmas Day	19, 45, 85	89, 110, 132
*Ash Wednesday	6, 32, 38	102, 130, 143
Good Friday	22, 40, 54	69, 88
Easter Day	2, 57, 111	113, 114, 118
Ascension Day	8, 15, 21	24, 47, 108
Whitsunday	48, 68	104, 145

Additional in American Prayer Book.

Advent Sunday	8, 50	96, 97
Circumcision	40, 90	65, 103
Epiphany	46, 47, 48	72, 117, 135
Purification	20, 86, 87	84, 113, 134
Annunciation	89	131, 132, 138
Easter Even	4, 16, 17	30, 31
Trinity Sunday	29, 33	93, 97, 150
Transfiguration	27, 61, 93	84, 99, 133
St Michael's	91, 103	34, 148
All Saints' Day	1, 15, 146	112, 121, 149

* The Psalms appointed for Ash Wednesday, including the 51st (in the Commination Service), have from very early times been known as the Penitential Psalms.

SPECIAL PSALMS AT MATINS AND EVENSONG AND IN OCCASIONAL OFFICES.

Matins: 95, Invitatory; 148, second alternative for Te Deum [Ireland]; 100, alternative for Benedictus.

Evensong: 98, alternative for Magnificat; 92, *vv.* 1—4, second alternative for Magnificat [America]; 67, alternative for Nunc Dimittis; 103, *vv.* 1—4, 21, 22, second alternative for Nunc Dimittis [America].

Matrimony: 128 or 67.

Visitation of the Sick: 71 [130 America].

Burial of the Dead: 39, 90.

Churching of Women: 116 or 127.

Commination: 51.

Forms of Prayer to be used at Sea—Thanksgiving after a storm: 66, 107.

King's Accession: 20, 101, 121.

Service for the first Sunday on which a minister officiates in a new cure [Ireland]: 84, 122, 132.

Office of Institution [America]: 122, 132, 133, 68 or 26.

Harvest Thanksgiving [Ireland]: 65, 67, 103, 104, 145, 147. (Two or more to be used.)

Consecration of a Church [English Convocation, 1712, Ireland, America]: 24, 84, 122, 132.

Consecration of a Graveyard [Ireland]: 49 or 115.

PSALTER AND COMMENTARY

PLAN OF COMMENTARY.

The notes are placed side by side with the text.

When the comment is simply in the words of the Revised Version (often identical with the Authorized, in which case the letters R.V. are not prefixed), or of the R.V. margin, it is printed in italics, the passage corrected in the text being indicated by small brackets. When the comment is other than, or supplementary to, the Revised Version, it appears in Roman type.

In passages where the Prayer Book Version, though not a literal translation, is a fair paraphrase of the meaning, and also where a slight inaccuracy does not materially affect the sense, it has not been thought necessary to give the Revised Version.

The text is printed as it appears in the Prayer Book with the following exceptions. 'LORD' or 'GOD,' when either word represents 'Jehovah' in the original (see p. xvii), is distinguished, as in the Authorized and Revised Versions, and in the American Psalter, by small capitals. The usage of R.V. has also been adopted in the removal of initial capitals in cases where they might mislead the reader; and in printing the more accurate 'cherubim' for 'cherubims.' Besides, a few alterations have been made in punctuation and by the insertion of parentheses, when needed by the sense of the passage.

A short introduction has been prefixed to each Psalm describing its theme, and, in some cases, the circumstances under which it was probably written, the Title being quoted in whole or in part where it seemed to throw light on these points (see pp. xi, xii.)

Quotations from Holy Scripture are made according to the Revised Version.

Abbreviations.—A.V. = Authorized Version, R.V. = Revised Version, A.R.V. = Authorized and Revised Versions, P.B.V. = Prayer Book Version, mg. = margin, Vulg. = Vulgate Sept. = Septuagint.

THE PSALMS OF DAVID

THE FIRST DAY

Morning Prayer

PSALM I. *Beatus vir, qui non abiit &c.*

GENERAL PREFACE TO THE PSALTER

Contrast between the blessedness of the righteous and the misery of the wicked.

Proper on All Saints' Day [America].

BLESSED is the man that hath not walked in the counsel of the ungodly, nor stood in the way of sinners : and hath not sat in the seat of the scornful.

Negative description of the righteous man. He avoids association with the wicked. The threefold parallelism, 'walk,' 'stand,' 'sit'; 'counsel,' 'way,' 'seat,' marks a steady progression in wickedness.

2 But his delight is in the law of the LORD : and in his law will he [a]⌜exercise himself⌝ day and night.

Positive side of the righteous man's character. Glad obedience to the law and continuous study of it.

[a] *meditate.*

3 And he shall be like a tree planted by the water-side : that will bring forth [b]his fruit in due season.

[b] R.V. *its.*

4 His leaf also shall not wither : and look, whatsoever he doeth, it shall prosper.

5 As for the ungodly, it is not so with them : but they are like the chaff, which the wind scattereth away [1]⌜from the face of the earth⌝.

The threshing-floors of the East are on elevated places exposed to the wind which blows away the chaff when the winnower with his fan (shovel) throws the grain into the air. St Matt. iii. 12.

6 Therefore the ungodly shall not be able to stand in the judgement : neither the sinners in the congregation of the righteous.

'the righteous' here = the ideal Israel which shall be manifested at the judgement, when the LORD'S 'people shall be all righteous.' Is. lx. 21.

7 But the LORD knoweth the way of the righteous : and the way of the ungodly shall perish.

'knoweth,' i.e. regardeth with loving care.

[1] Not in A.R.V., added in P.B.V. from Vulg.

PSALM II. *Quare fremuerunt gentes?*

Vassal princes threaten a revolt, destined to result in their own utter discomfiture, against some king of David's line, perhaps Solomon. Mystically the Psalm points forward to the contest between the world and Christ, remarkably evidenced at His Passion by the combination of Caiaphas and Pilate, Jews and Gentiles against Him. Acts iv. 25—28.

Proper on Easter Day.

WHY do the heathen so furiously rage together : and why do the [a]people imagine a vain thing?

[a]R.V. *peoples.*

2 The kings of the earth stand up, and the rulers take counsel together : against the LORD, and against his anointed.

'his anointed' = the king of David's house, the type of the coming Messiah (anointed one). From this verse and *v.* 7 are taken two titles given by the Jews to the expected Deliverer viz. Messiah and Son of God. St Matt. xxvi. 63; St John i. 49.

3. The confederates speak.

3 Let us break their bonds asunder : and cast away their cords from us.

'their bonds...their cords,' i.e. those of the LORD and His anointed.

4 He that dwelleth in heaven shall laugh them to scorn : the Lord shall have them in derision.

5 Then shall he speak unto them in his wrath : and [b]vex them in his sore displeasure.

[b]A.R.V. mg. *trouble.*

6. The LORD's words.

6 Yet have I set my king : upon my holy hill of Sion.

7—9. The king speaks, quoting the LORD's promise to him.

7 [c]⌜I will preach the law, whereof the LORD hath said unto me⌝:

[c]R.V. *I will tell of the decree: The LORD said unto me.*

Thou art my son, this day have I begotten thee.

i.e. I have declared thee My son by placing thee on thy royal throne. The allusion is to God's promise to David and his heirs through Nathan. 'I will be his father, and he shall be my son.' 2 Sam. vii. 14. These words received their complete fulfilment when Christ 'born of the seed of David...was declared to be the Son of God...by the resurrection of the dead.' Rom. i. 3, 4. See Acts xiii. 33.

8 Desire of me, and I shall give thee the heathen for thine inheritance : and the utmost parts of the earth for thy possession.

9 'Thou shalt bruise them with a rod of iron : and break them in pieces like a potter's vessel.

'bruise,' Sept. has 'rule,' and is followed in Rev. ii. 27, xii. 5, xix. 15.

10 Be wise now therefore, O ye kings : be learned, ye that are judges of the earth.

11 Serve the LORD in fear : and rejoice [1]⌜unto him⌝ with reverence.

10—12. The Psalmist speaks. He exhorts the insurgent rulers to shew true wisdom by submitting to Jehovah in the person of His anointed son.

12 [2] Kiss the son, lest he be angry, and so ye perish [a]⌜from the [1] right way : if his wrath be kindled, (yea, but a little,)⌝ blessed are all they that put their trust in him.

Give him the kiss of homage; see 1 Sam. x. 1; 1 Kings xix. 18; Hos. xiii. 2.

[a] R.V. *in the way* [i.e. in your expedition], *for his wrath will soon be kindled.*

PSALM III. *Domine, quid multiplicati?*

'A Psalm of David when he fled from Absalom his son' (Title). The morning prayer (see *v.* 5) of one who, in the midst of danger, put his trust in God.

LORD, how are they increased that trouble me : many are they that rise against me.

'The LORD hath avenged thee this day of all them that rose up against thee.' Words of the Cushite in announcing to David the victory over Absalom. 2 Sam. xviii. 31, 32.

2 Many one there be that say of my soul : There is no help for him in his God.

They say that God as well as man has turned against me.

[1] Not in A.R.V., added in P.B.V. from Vulg.
[2] 'Kiss the son.' Two other translations preferred by many scholars are given in R.V. mg. viz. *Lay hold of* (or, *Receive*) *instruction*, and *Worship in purity.*

3 But thou, O LORD, art [a]⌜my defender⌝ : thou art my [b]worship, and the lifter up of my head.

[a] R.V. *a shield about me.* Cp. Gen. xv. 1.

[b] 'worship' = *glory*.

4 I did call upon the LORD with my voice : and he heard me out of his holy hill.

'his holy hill' = Sion where Jehovah specially manifested His Presence.

5 I laid me down and slept, and rose up again : for the LORD sustained me.

6 I will not be afraid for ten thousands of the people : that have set themselves against me round about.

The hosts on the side of Absalom.

7 [c]⌜Up, LORD⌝, and help me, O my God : for thou smitest all mine enemies upon the cheek-bone; thou hast broken the teeth of the ungodly.

[c] *Arise, O LORD.* The first words of the cry raised when the ark set forward in the wilderness, Num. x. 35. They frequently occur in the Psalter. The complete formula appears in Ps. lxviii. 1.

They are like wild beasts made helpless by the breaking of the jaw.

8 Salvation belongeth unto the LORD : [d]⌜and thy blessing is⌝ upon thy people.

[d] R.V. *Thy blessing be.* David prays for the whole nation including those that have set themselves against him.

PSALM IV. *Cum invocarem.*

'A Psalm of David' (Title). An evening hymn (see *v.* 9), probably written like the previous Psalm during the flight from Absalom.

Proper on Easter Even [America].

HEAR me when I call, O God of my righteousness : thou hast set me at liberty when I was in trouble; have mercy upon me, and hearken unto my prayer.

God who knows my righteousness and will vindicate it.

Former deliverances embolden me now to plead to Thee for help.

2 O ye sons of men, how long will ye blaspheme mine honour : and have such pleasure in vanity, and seek after [e]leasing?

'sons of men.' The Hebrew phrase here means 'men of high rank.' See Ps. xlix. 2, lxii. 9. The Psalmist is addressing the rebellious leaders.

[e] 'leasing' = (R.V.) *falsehood.* The rebellion of Absalom was founded on intrigue and misrepresentation. 2 Sam. xv. 2—6.

3 Know this also, that the LORD hath chosen to himself [a]⌜the man that is godly⌝ : when I call upon the LORD, he will hear me.

[a] R.V. mg. *one that he favoureth.*

4 [1]⌜Stand in awe⌝, and sin not : commune with your own heart, and in your chamber, and be still.

'Stand in awe' of God and the king, and break with your sin of rebellion.

Meditate on these truths in the silence of the night, and cease from your enterprise.

5 Offer the [b]sacrifice of righteousness : and put your trust in the LORD.

[b] *sacrifices* of righteousness are those offered with a right disposition.

6 There be many that say : Who will shew us any good?

The desponding words of David's faint-hearted adherents.

7 LORD, lift thou up : the light of thy countenance upon us.

David's prayer combines two petitions of the priestly benediction, 'The LORD make his face to shine upon thee,' 'the LORD lift up his countenance upon thee and give thee peace' (see *v.* 9). Num. vi. 24—26.

8 Thou hast put gladness in my heart : [c]⌜since the time that⌝ their corn, and wine, [2]⌜and oil⌝, increased.

9 I will lay me down in peace, and take my rest : for it is thou, LORD, only, that makest me dwell in safety.

[c] R.V. *more than they have when.* David's God-given gladness in this time of his trouble is greater than that of his enemies in this time of their prosperity.

PSALM V. *Verba mea auribus.*

'A Psalm of David' (Title) when in peril from treacherous foes. A morning hymn (*v.* 3).

PONDER my words, O LORD : consider my meditation.

'meditation' = silent or scarcely audible prayer like Hannah's. 1 Sam. i. 13.

2 O hearken thou unto the voice of my calling, my King, and my God : for unto thee will I make my prayer.

David, the king, acknowledges the supreme Kingship of God.

[1] R.V. mg. *Be ye angry*, after Sept. The verse is so quoted Eph. iv. 26. With this rendering the primary meaning of the words is 'Be ye angry with my rule, if you must, but do not sin by rebelling against it.'

[2] Not in A.R.V., added in P.B.V. from Vulg.

3 My voice shalt thou hear betimes, O LORD : early in the morning will I [a]direct my prayer unto thee, and will [b]⌜look up⌝.

[a]R.V. *order.* It is the word used (Lev. i. 7, 8) of the priest's arranging the wood &c. for the sacrifice. David compares his morning devotions to the daily morning offering.

[b]R.V. *keep watch* for an answer to my prayer.

4 For thou art the God that hast no pleasure in wickedness : neither shall any evil dwell with thee.

4—6. The wicked are excluded from God's presence.

5 [c]⌜Such as be foolish⌝ shall not stand in thy sight : for thou hatest all [d]⌜them that work vanity⌝.

[c]R.V. *The arrogant.*

[d]*workers of iniquity.*

6 Thou shalt destroy them that speak [e]leasing : the LORD will abhor both the bloodthirsty and deceitful man.

[e]'leasing' = (R.V.) *lies.*

7 But as for me, I will come into thine house, even upon the multitude of thy mercy : and in thy fear will I worship toward thy holy temple.

The Psalmist, through the divine favour, will draw near to God.

8 Lead me, O LORD, in thy righteousness, because of mine enemies : make thy way plain before my face.

God's righteousness is pledged to protect His true worshippers.

'thy way,' i.e. the way Thou hast appointed for me.

9 For there is no faithfulness in [f]his mouth : their inward parts are very wickedness.

[f]*their.*

10 Their throat is an open sepulchre : they flatter with their tongue.

11 [g]⌜Destroy thou them⌝, O God; let them perish through their own imaginations : cast them out in the multitude of their ungodliness; for they have rebelled against thee.

[g]R.V. *Hold them guilty.*

The enemies of David are rebels against God whose vicegerent he is.

12 And let all them that put their trust in thee rejoice : they shall ever [h]⌜be giving of thanks⌝, because thou defendest them; they that love thy Name shall be joyful in thee;

[h]*shout for joy.*

God's Name Jehovah (LORD) here and elsewhere stands for His character as He has revealed it to His people.

13 For thou, LORD, wilt give thy blessing unto the righteous : and with thy favourable kindness wilt thou defend him as with a shield.

Evening Prayer

PSALM VI. *Domine, ne in furore.*

The Psalmist is suffering from severe illness aggravated by the taunts of enemies.

The first of the Penitential Psalms.

Proper on Ash Wednesday.

O LORD, rebuke me not in thine indignation : neither chasten me in thy displeasure.

The Psalmist regards his illness as a proof of God's displeasure.

2 Have mercy upon me, O LORD, for I am [a]weak : O LORD, heal me, for my bones are vexed.

[a]R.V. *withered away.*

3 My soul also is sore troubled : but, LORD, how long wilt thou punish me?

Words used by our Lord on the eve of His Passion, 'Now is my soul troubled.' St John xii. 27; see Ps. xlii. 6.

4 Turn thee, O LORD, and deliver my soul : O save me for thy mercy's sake.

5 For in death no man remembereth thee : and who will give thee thanks in [b]⌜the pit⌝?

The general O.T. conception of death as a cheerless existence cut off from communion with God; cp. Is. xxxviii. 18.

[b]R.V. *Sheol* = the world beyond the grave.

6 I am weary of my groaning; every night wash I my bed : and water my couch with my tears.

7 [c]⌜My beauty is gone⌝ for very trouble : [d]⌜and worn away⌝ because of all mine enemies.

[c]R.V. *Mine eye wasteth away.* The eye reveals the ravages of disease.

[d]*it waxeth old.*

Sudden change of note from depression to exultation: the Psalmist's prayer is heard, his enemies will be discomfited.

8 [e]⌜Away from me, all ye that work vanity⌝ : for the LORD hath heard the voice of my weeping.

[e]*Depart from me, all ye workers of iniquity.* Words appropriated by our Lord as His final sentence on the wicked. St Matt. vii. 23.

9 The LORD hath heard my petition : the LORD will receive my prayer.

10 All mine enemies shall be confounded, and sore vexed : they shall be turned back, and put to shame suddenly.

PSALM VII. *Domine, Deus meus.*

'[1] Shiggaion of David, which he sang unto the LORD, concerning the words of Cush a Benjamite' (Title). Cush was probably a follower of Saul and foremost among the calumniators of David.

O LORD my God, in thee have I put my trust : save me from all them that [a]persecute me, and deliver me;

[a] R.V. *pursue.*

2 Lest he devour my soul, like a lion, and tear it in pieces : while there is none to help.

'he' = Cush or Saul himself.

3 O LORD my God, if I have done any such thing : or if there be any wickedness in my hands;

Cp. David's words when he protests his innocence to Saul. 1 Sam. xxiv. 11, xxvi. 18.

4 If I have rewarded evil unto him that dealt friendly with me : (yea, I have delivered him that without any cause is mine enemy;)

So far was David from wantonly injuring his friends, that he saved the life of Saul his enemy when in his power. 1 Sam. xxiv. 4ff., xxvi. 8ff.

5 Then let mine enemy [b]persecute my soul, and take me : yea, let him tread my life down upon the earth, and lay [c]⌜mine honour⌝ in the dust.

[b] R.V. *pursue.*

[c] R.V. *my glory*, poetical for 'soul,' as being the noblest part of man; see Ps. xvi. 10; Gen. xlix. 6.

6 Stand up, O LORD, in thy wrath, and lift up thyself, because of the indignation of mine enemies : arise up for me in the judgement that thou hast commanded.

David calls upon God to take His place as Judge and vindicate his innocence.

7 And so shall the congregation of the [d]people come about thee : [e]⌜for their sakes therefore lift up thyself again⌝.

[d] R.V. *peoples.* In David's vision all nations will be gathered together to hear his acquittal pronounced.

[e] R.V. *and over them return thou on high*, i.e. after Thy visit to earth to gather the peoples, take again the seat of judgement which Thou hast seemed to abandon for a time.

8 The LORD shall judge the [f]people; give sentence with me, O LORD : according to my righteousness, and according to the innocency that is in me.

[f] R.V. *peoples.*

[1] 'Shiggaion' probably means a poem of irregular structure and emotional character.

9 O let the wickedness of the ungodly come to an end : but [a]guide thou the just.

[a] *establish.*

10 For the righteous God : trieth the very hearts and reins.

'The heart' in the O.T. is the seat of thought and determination; 'the reins' (=kidneys) of the emotions.

11 My help cometh of God : who preserveth them that are true of heart.

12 God is a righteous Judge, [1]⌜strong, and patient⌝ : and God is provoked every day.

13 If a man will not turn, he will whet his sword : he hath bent his bow, and made it ready.

14 He hath prepared for him the instruments of death : he [b]⌜ordaineth his arrows against the persecutors⌝.

[b] R.V. *maketh his arrows fiery shafts*, i.e. the lightning-flashes.

15—17. The wicked man brings destruction on himself as the natural consequence of his own doings.

15 Behold, he travaileth with mischief : he hath conceived sorrow, and brought forth [c]ungodliness.

[c] *falsehood.*

16 He hath [d]graven and digged up a pit : and is fallen himself into the [e]destruction that he made for other.

[d] 'graven'=digged.

[e] *ditch.*

'other' is the old plural for 'others.'

17 For his travail shall come upon his own head : and his wickedness shall fall on his own pate.

18 I will give thanks unto the LORD, according to his righteousness : and I will praise the Name of the LORD most High.

[1] Not in A.R.V., added in P.B.V. from Vulg.

PSALM VIII. *Domine, Dominus noster.*

'A Psalm of David' (Title). The greatness of man as lord of creation—fully realized when man in Christ was exalted to be Ruler of the universe. Heb. ii. 6 ff.

Proper on Ascension Day and on Advent Sunday [America].

O LORD our Governour, how excellent is thy Name in all the world : thou that hast set thy glory [a]above the heavens!

'our,' i.e. He is Lord not of David only, but of all Israel (i.e. mankind from the Christian point of view).

'excellent' formerly meant 'pre-eminent,' 'excelling.'

[a]R.V. *upon.*

The glory of God is confessed even by children whose lisping praises put to silence the hostility of the wicked. Our Lord quotes the words in accepting the Hosannas of the children in the temple. St Matt. xxi. 16; see xi. 25; 1 Cor. i. 27.

2 Out of the mouth of very babes and sucklings hast thou ordained strength, because of thine enemies : that thou mightest still the enemy, and the avenger.

'ordained strength,' Sept. 'perfected praise,' so quoted St Matt. xxi. 16.

'avenger' = revengeful. Ps. xliv. 17.

3 For I will consider thy heavens, even the works of thy fingers : the moon and the stars, which thou hast ordained.

4 What is man, that thou art mindful of him : and the son of man, that thou visitest him?

'visitest,' i.e. with love and providential care.

5 Thou madest him [b]⌜lower than the angels⌝ : to crown him with glory and [c]worship.

[b]So Sept., Vulg. and Heb. ii. 7. R.V. *but little lower than God.* 'God created man in his own image.' Gen. i. 27.

[c]'worship' = *honour.*

6 Thou makest him to have dominion of the works of thy hands : and thou hast put all things in subjection under his feet;

Gen. i. 26.

Man's dominion reached its climax in the universal rule of the Son of Man. Heb. ii. 9.

7 All sheep and oxen : yea, and the beasts of the field;

8 The fowls of the air, and the fishes of the sea : and whatsoever walketh through the paths of the seas.

9 O LORD our Governour : how excellent is thy Name in all the world!

'excellent'; see *v.* 1.

THE SECOND DAY

Morning Prayer

[1] PSALM IX. *Confitebor tibi.*

'A Psalm of David' (Title). A triumphant thanksgiving on the defeat of external enemies.

An alphabetical Psalm.

I WILL give thanks unto thee, O LORD, with my whole heart : I will speak of all thy marvellous works.

2 I will be glad and rejoice in thee : yea, my songs will I make of thy Name, O thou most Highest.

3 While mine enemies are driven back : they shall fall and perish at thy presence.

4 For thou hast maintained my right and my cause : thou art set in the throne that judgest right.

God has intervened on David's behalf.

5 Thou hast rebuked the heathen, and destroyed the ungodly : thou hast put out their name for ever and ever.

6 [a]⌜O thou enemy, destructions are come to a perpetual end : even as the cities which thou hast destroyed⌝, their memorial is perished with them.

[a]R.V. *The enemy are come to an end, they are desolate for ever; and the cities which thou hast overthrown.*

i.e. the memorial (remembrance) of the enemy. Cp. Exod. xvii. 14, 'I will utterly blot out the remembrance of Amalek from under heaven.'

[1] This Psalm and the next form a single Psalm in Sept. and Vulgate. Each pair of verses of Ps. ix begins with the earlier letters of the Hebrew alphabet in successive order; and the arrangement is continued irregularly in Ps. x.

7 But the LORD [a]⌜shall endure⌝ for ever : he hath also prepared his [b]seat for judgement.

[a] R.V. *sitteth as king.*

[b] *throne.*

8 For he shall judge the world in righteousness : and minister true judgement unto the [c]people.

[c] R.V. *peoples.*

9 The LORD also will be a [d]defence for the oppressed : even a [d]refuge in [1]due time of trouble.

[d] R.V. *high tower.*

10 And they that know thy Name will put their trust in thee : for thou, LORD, hast never failed them that seek thee.

11 O praise the LORD which dwelleth in Sion : shew the [e]people of his doings.

[e] R.V. mg. *peoples*, i.e. the Gentile nations.

12 For, [f]⌜when he maketh inquisition for blood, he remembereth them⌝ : and forgetteth not the complaint of the poor.

[f] R.V. *he that maketh inquisition for blood* (i.e. demandeth a reckoning for bloodshed) *remembereth them* (i.e. 'the poor' in next clause).

'the poor' here = the nation of Israel oppressed by foreign tyrants.

13 Have mercy upon me, O LORD; consider the trouble which I suffer of them that hate me : thou that liftest me up from the gates of death ;

14 That I may shew all thy praises within the [g]ports of the daughter of Sion : I will rejoice in thy salvation.

[g] *gates*, the places of public concourse.

'daughter of Sion' = Jerusalem personified.

15 The heathen are sunk down in the pit that they made : in the same net which they hid privily, is their foot taken.

16 The LORD [h]⌜is known to execute judgement⌝ : the ungodly is trapped in the work of his own hands.

[h] R.V. *hath made himself known, he hath executed judgement.*

17 The wicked shall [i]⌜be turned into hell⌝ : and all the [k]people that forget God.

[i] R.V. *return to Sheol*, i.e. die, here = perish prematurely; the allusion is to Gen. iii. 19, 'Dust thou art, and unto dust shalt thou return.'

[k] *nations.*

[1] Not in A.R.V., added in P.B.V. from Vulg.

18 For the poor shall not alway be forgotten : the patient abiding of the meek shall not perish for ever.

19 Up, LORD, and let not man have the upper hand : let the heathen be judged in thy sight.

20 Put them in fear, O LORD : that the heathen may know themselves to be but men.

PSALM X. *Ut quid, Domine?*

A plaintive appeal to Jehovah to assert Himself and protect the nation from domestic tyrants.

An alphabetical Psalm. See Ps. ix. footnote, p. 11.

WHY standest thou so far off, O LORD : and hidest thy face in the [1]needful time of trouble?

2 [a]⌜The ungodly for his own lust doth persecute the poor⌝ : let them be taken in the crafty wiliness that they have imagined.

[a]R.V. *In the pride of the wicked the poor is hotly pursued.*

P.B.V. 'lust' = strong desire.

3 For the ungodly hath made boast of his own heart's desire : [b]⌜and speaketh good of the covetous, whom GOD abhorreth⌝.

[b]R.V. *and the covetous renounceth, yea, contemneth the LORD.*

4 [c]⌜The ungodly is so proud, that he careth not for God : neither is God in all his thoughts⌝.

[c]R.V. *The wicked, in the pride of his countenance, saith, He will not require it. All his thoughts are, There is no God.*

5 His ways are alway [d]grievous : thy judgements are far above out of his sight, and therefore defieth he all his enemies.

[d]R.V. *firm*, i.e. not subject to the fluctuations of fortune, prosperous. 'Far above' &c., i.e. he thinks of God as so distant that he may safely disregard Him.

6 For he hath said in his heart, Tush, I shall never be cast down : there shall no harm happen unto me.

[1] Not in A.R.V., added in P.B.V. from Vulg.

7 His mouth is full of cursing, deceit, and fraud : under his tongue is ungodliness and vanity.

'under his tongue,' i.e. like a delicious morsel retained in his mouth; cp. Job xx. 12; Cant. iv. 11.

8 He sitteth lurking in the thievish corners of the streets : and privily in his lurking dens doth he murder the innocent; his eyes are set against the poor.

Such acts of brigandage were common in those unsettled times; cp. Prov. i. 10—18; Hos. vi. 9.

9 For he lieth waiting secretly, even as a lion lurketh he in his den : that he may [a]ravish the poor.

The wicked man compared to (9) a lion, (10) a hunter, (11) a lion again.

[a]*catch.*

10 He doth [a]ravish the poor : when he getteth him into his net.

P.B.V. 'ravish' = seize with violence.

11 [b]⌜He falleth down, and humbleth himself : that the congregation of the poor may fall into the hands of his captains⌝.

[b]R.V. *He croucheth, he boweth down* (the attitude of a lion in wait for his prey), *and the helpless fall by his strong ones* (i.e. his claws).

12 He hath said in his heart, Tush, God hath forgotten : he hideth away his face, and he will never see it.

13 Arise, O LORD God, and lift up thine hand : forget not the poor.

14 Wherefore should the wicked [c]blaspheme God : while he doth say in his heart, Tush, thou [1]God [d]⌜carest not for it⌝.

[c]*contemn.*

[d]*wilt not require it.*

15 Surely thou hast seen it : for thou beholdest ungodliness and wrong.

16 That thou mayest take the matter into thine hand : the poor committeth himself unto thee; for thou art the helper of the [e]friendless.

[e]*fatherless.*

17 Break thou the power of the ungodly and malicious : [f]⌜take away his ungodliness, and thou shalt find none⌝.

[f]*seek out his wickedness till thou find none*, i.e. make ungodliness ultimately to vanish. 'To seek and not to find' is a Biblical phrase for the entire disappearance of some object; see Ps. xxxvii. 37; Is. xli. 12; St John vii. 34.

[1] Not in A.R.V.

18 The LORD is King for ever and ever : and the heathen are perished out of [a]the land.

[a] *his*, God's land, primarily Canaan, ultimately the world when it shall be subdued unto Him.

19 LORD, thou hast heard the desire of the poor : thou preparest their heart, and thine ear hearkeneth thereto ;

20 To help the fatherless and poor unto their right : that the man of the earth [b]⌜be no more exalted against them⌝.

[b] R.V. *may be terrible no more.*

PSALM XI. *In Domino confido.*

'A Psalm of David' (Title). Written by him when in great danger of life, probably at the court of Saul, and urged by his friends to seek safety in flight.

IN the LORD put I my trust : how say ye then to my soul, [c]⌜that she should flee as a bird unto the hill⌝?

[c] *Flee as a bird to your mountain.* The words of timid friends of David, continued in *vv.* 2, 3. The hill-country was the natural place of refuge for those in danger; see Judg. vi. 2; 1 Sam. xiv. 22, xxiii. 14.

2 For lo, the ungodly bend their bow, and make ready their arrows [d]⌜within the quiver⌝ : that they may privily shoot at them which are true of heart.

[d] *upon the string.*

3 [e]⌜For the foundations will be cast down : and what hath the righteous done⌝?

[e] *If the foundations* (of society) *be destroyed, what can the righteous do?*

4 The LORD is in his holy temple : the LORD'S seat is in heaven.

4—8. David's reply.

5 His eyes consider [1]⌜the poor⌝ : and his eye-lids try the children of men.

6 The LORD [f]alloweth the righteous : but the ungodly, and him that delighteth in wickedness doth his soul abhor.

[f] *trieth.* P.B.V. 'alloweth' = approveth on trial; see Rom. xiv. 22 (A.V.).

[1] Not in A.R.V., added in P.B.V. from Vulg.

7 Upon the ungodly he shall rain snares, fire and brimstone, storm and tempest : this shall be their portion to drink.

As He destroyed Sodom and Gomorrah. Gen. xix. 24.

8 For the righteous LORD loveth righteousness : [a]⌜his countenance will behold the thing that is just⌝.

[a]R.V. *The upright shall behold his face.* An anticipation of the Gospel revelation, 'we shall see him even as he is.' 1 St John iii. 2; see Rev. xxii. 4. P.B.V. follows Vulg.

Evening Prayer

PSALM XII. *Salvum me fac.*

A prayer for help in a time of general corruption and hypocrisy.

HELP me, LORD, for there is not one godly man left : for the faithful are minished from among the children of men.

2 They [b]⌜talk of vanity⌝ every one with his neighbour : they do but flatter with their lips, and dissemble in their double heart.

[b]*speak vanity*, i.e. falsehood.

3 The LORD shall root out all deceitful lips : and the tongue that speaketh proud things;

4 Which have said, With our tongue will we prevail : [c]⌜we are they that ought to speak⌝, who is lord over us?

[c]*our lips are our own.*

5 Now for the comfortless troubles' sake of the needy : and because of the deep sighing of the poor,

6 I will up, saith the LORD : and will help every one from him that swelleth against him, and will set him at rest.

God will intervene to set things right.

7 The words of the LORD are pure words : even as the silver, which from the earth is tried, and purified seven times in the fire.

8 Thou shalt keep them, O LORD: thou shalt preserve him from this generation for ever.

'them,' i.e. the needy and poor, *v.* 5. 'him,' i.e. each sufferer.

9 The ungodly walk on every side : [a]⌜when they are exalted, the children of men are put to rebuke⌝.

i.e. arrogantly pursue their evil way without opposition.

[a]R.V. ***when vileness is exalted among the sons of men***, i.e. when wickedness is honoured and successful.

PSALM XIII. *Usque quo, Domine?*

The author is passing through a period of extreme danger and perplexity.

HOW long wilt thou forget me, O LORD, for ever : how long wilt thou hide thy face from me?

The confused question, 'How long... for ever?' indicates a state of mind wavering between hope and despair.

2 How long shall I seek counsel in my soul, and be so vexed in my heart : how long shall mine [b]enemies triumph over me?

[b]*enemy* as in *v.* 4; one foe in particular is before the Psalmist's mind.

3 Consider, and hear me, O LORD my God : lighten mine eyes, that I sleep not in death.

i.e. revive my strength and spirits. The eyes reflect the state of health; see Ps. vi. 7, xxxviii. 10; 1 Sam. xiv. 27, 29.

4 Lest mine enemy say, I have prevailed against him : for if I be cast down, they that trouble me will rejoice at it.

5 But my trust is in thy mercy : and my heart is joyful in thy salvation.

6 I will sing of the LORD, because he hath dealt [c]⌜so lovingly⌝ with me : [1]⌜yea, I will praise the Name of the LORD most Highest⌝.

[c]*bountifully.*

[1] Not in A.R.V., added in P.B.V. from Vulg. which borrows from vii. 18.

PSALM XIV. *Dixit insipiens.*

The Psalmist looks out upon a world utterly godless and corrupt. The righteous few are the prey of the wicked. The days of Babel and Sodom are revived.

THE fool hath said in his heart : There is no God.

'The fool,' so the Bible describes the man who has forsaken the fear of God; see Ps. lxxiv. 19, 23; 2 Sam. xiii. 12, 13.

2 They are corrupt, and become abominable in their doings : there is none that doeth good, [1]⌜no not one⌝.

3 The LORD looked down from heaven upon the children of men : to see if there were any that would understand, and seek after God.

So at Babel, 'The LORD came down to see,' Gen. xi. 5; and before the destruction of Sodom, 'The LORD said...I will go down now and see,' Gen. xviii. 20, 21.

4 But they are all gone out of the way, they are altogether become abominable : there is none that doeth good, no not one.

5 [2][a]⌜Their throat is an open sepulchre, with their tongues have they deceived⌝ : [b]⌜the poison of asps is under their lips⌝.

[a] Ps. v. 10.

[b] Ps. cxl. 3.

6 [c]⌜Their mouth is full of cursing and bitterness⌝ : [d]⌜their feet are swift to shed blood⌝.

[c] Ps. x. 7.

[d] Is. lix. 7.

7 [e]⌜Destruction and unhappiness is in their ways, and the way of peace have they not known⌝ : [f]⌜there is no fear of God before their eyes⌝.

[e] Is. lix. 7, 8.

[f] Ps. xxxvi. 1.

8 Have they no knowledge, that they are all such workers of mischief : eating up my people as it were bread, and call not upon the LORD?

God speaks.

'My people,' i.e. God's faithful ones, called 'the generation of the righteous' in *v.* 9, 'the poor' in *v.* 10.

[1] Not in A.R.V., added in P.B.V. from Vulg. which borrows from *v.* 4.

[2] *Vv.* 5—7 do not occur in the Hebrew, and have no place in A.R.V. In Rom. iii. 10—12, St Paul freely quotes *vv.* 2—4 from the Sept., and then adds citations from other parts of the O.T. This series of passages was transferred from the Epistle to some MSS. of the Sept., whence it passed into the Vulgate and P.B.V.

9 There were they brought in great fear, [1]⌜even where no fear was⌝ : for God is in the generation of the righteous.

The effect which God's words will have upon the wicked.

10 As for you, ye have made a mock at the counsel of the poor : because he putteth his trust in the LORD.

11 [a]⌜Who shall give salvation unto Israel out of Sion?⌝ When the LORD turneth the captivity of his people : then shall Jacob rejoice, and Israel shall be glad.

[a] *Oh that the salvation of Israel were come out of Zion!* where God dwells among men. Ps. iii. 4.

'turneth the captivity,' probably metaphorical for 'reverseth the misfortune' as in Job xlii. 10 and elsewhere.

THE THIRD DAY

Morning Prayer

PSALM XV. *Domine, quis habitabit?*

'A Psalm of David' (Title). The character of the servant of God worthy of being admitted to His Presence is perfectly realized only in the human life of Christ.

Proper on Ascension Day and on All Saints' Day [America].

LORD, who shall dwell in thy tabernacle : or who shall rest upon thy holy hill?

2 Even he, that leadeth an uncorrupt life : and doeth the thing which is right, and speaketh the truth from his heart.

3 He that hath used no deceit in his tongue, nor done evil to his neighbour : and hath not slandered his neighbour.

4 He that setteth not by himself, but is lowly in his own eyes : and maketh much of them that fear the LORD.

'set by' = esteem, value.

[1] Not in A.R.V., added in P.B.V. from Vulg. which borrows from the sister Psalm liii. 6.

5 He that sweareth unto his neighbour, and disappointeth him not : [1]⌜though it were to his own hindrance⌝.

6 He that hath not given his money upon usury : nor taken reward against the innocent.

The taking of usury, i.e. interest, was forbidden by the Law; but the only case contemplated was the lending of money to relieve distress. Exod. xxii. 25; Lev. xxv. 35—37.

7 Whoso doeth these things : shall never fall.

PSALM XVI. *Conserva me, Domine.*

'[2]Michtam of David' (Title). The LORD Himself is the glorious inheritance and unfailing support of His people.

Proper on Easter Even [America].

PRESERVE me, O God : for in thee have I put my trust.

2 O my soul, thou hast said unto the LORD : Thou art my God, [a]⌜my goods are nothing unto thee⌝.

[a]R.V. *I have no good beyond thee.* P.B.V. from Vulg.

3 All my delight is upon the saints, that are in the earth : and upon such as excel in virtue.

'the saints,' i.e. the nation of Israel set apart for God's service.

4 But they that run after another god : shall have great trouble.

'they that run &c.,' i.e. the heathen nations and apostate Israelites.

5 Their drink-offerings of blood will I not offer : neither make mention of their names within my lips.

'of blood,' i.e. offered with blood-stained hands, or as loathsome as though they consisted of blood.

'their names,' i.e. the names of their gods: in obedience to the command, 'Make no mention of the name of other gods.' Exod. xxiii. 13.

6 The LORD himself is the portion of mine inheritance and of my cup : thou shalt maintain my lot.

'the portion &c.'; the allusion is to the promise made to the tribe of Levi, 'I am thy portion and thine inheritance,' Numb. xviii. 20,—a promise shared by the whole nation which was unto God 'a kingdom of priests.' Exod. xix. 6.

'my cup.' The LORD is the Psalmist's spiritual sustenance, as the gifts consecrated to Jehovah were the food of the Levites. Deut. xviii. 1.

[1] Not in A.R.V., added in P.B.V. from Vulg.
[2] 'Michtam' is probably a musical term, but its meaning is unknown.

7 The [a]⌜lot is⌝ fallen unto me in a fair ground : yea, I have a goodly heritage.

[a]*lines are.* The allusion is to the measuring lines by which plots of land were marked out.

8 I will thank the LORD for giving me [b]warning : my reins also [c]chasten me in the night season.

[b]*counsel.*

[c]*instruct.* 'reins' (kidneys), put for man's emotional part; see Ps. vii. 10.

9 I have set GOD always before me : for he is on my right hand, therefore I shall not fall.

'on my right hand,' the position of a champion.

10 Wherefore my heart was glad, and my glory rejoiced : my flesh also shall [d]⌜rest in hope⌝.

'glory' = soul, so called as being man's noblest part; see Ps. vii. 5 ; xxx. 13.

[d]R.V. *dwell in safety.* P.B.V. and A.V. follow Vulg.

11 For why? thou shalt not leave my soul [e]⌜in hell⌝ : neither shalt thou suffer thy [f]holy one to see corruption.

[e]R.V. *to Sheol,* i.e. Thou wilt not give up my life to the unseen world. The next clause has the same meaning.

[f]R.V. mg. *godly* or *beloved.* It is the same word which in Ps. iv. 3 R.V. mg. is translated *one that he favoureth.* David's confident words that God would preserve him from death were obviously not realized in his own case; they were fulfilled in the Son of David's victory over the grave. Acts ii. 25—31, xiii. 35—37.

12 Thou shalt shew me the path of life ; in thy presence is the fulness of joy : [g]⌜and at⌝ thy right hand there [h]⌜is pleasure⌝ for evermore.

[g]R.V. *in,* i.e. pleasures for evermore are in God's possession and gift.

[h]*are pleasures.*

PSALM XVII. *Exaudi, Domine.*

'A Prayer of David' (Title). A cry to God for help from a persecuted soul, confident in its integrity.

Proper on Easter Even [America].

HEAR the right, O LORD, consider my complaint : and hearken unto my prayer, that goeth not out of feigned lips.

2 Let my sentence come forth from thy presence : and let thine eyes look upon [i]⌜the thing that is equal⌝.

[i]R.V. *equity.*

3 Thou hast proved and visited mine heart in the night-season; thou hast tried me, and shalt find no wickedness in me : for I am utterly purposed that my mouth shall not offend.

The Psalmist fearlessly offers his thoughts, words and deeds (*v.* 4) to the test of God's scrutiny.

4 [a]⌜Because of men's works, that are done against the words of thy lips : I have kept me from the ways of the destroyer⌝.

[a] R.V. *As for the works of men, by the word of thy lips I have kept me from the ways of the violent*, i.e. By making God's word my rule of conduct, I have avoided the lawless ways of worldly men.

5 [b]⌜O hold thou up my goings in thy paths : that my footsteps slip not⌝.

[b] R.V. *My steps have held fast to thy paths, my feet have not slipped.* P.B.V. and A.V. follow Vulg.

6 I have called upon thee, O God, for thou shalt hear me : incline thine ear to me, and hearken unto my words.

7 Shew thy marvellous loving-kindness, thou that art the Saviour of them which put their trust in thee : from such as resist thy right hand.

i.e. God saves them which trust in Him from such as resist Him.

8 Keep me as the apple of an eye : hide me under the shadow of thy wings,

See Deut. xxxii. 10, 11; Prov. vii. 2; Zech. ii. 8.

9 From the ungodly that trouble me : mine enemies compass me round about to take away my soul.

10 They are inclosed in their own fat : and their mouth speaketh proud things.

Their worldly and luxurious life has made them arrogant and unfeeling.

11 They lie waiting in our way on every side : [c]⌜turning their eyes down to the ground⌝;

[c] R.V. *They set their eyes to cast us down to the earth.*

12 Like as a lion that is greedy of his prey : and as it were a lion's whelp, lurking in secret places.

13 Up, LORD, disappoint him, and cast him down : deliver my soul from the ungodly, [d]⌜which is a sword of thine⌝;

[d] R.V. *by thy sword.* P.B.V. means that God employs the agency even of the wicked to carry out His purposes; see Is. x. 5; but this truth is not in place here.

14 [a]⌜From the men of thy hand, O LORD, from the men, I say, and from the evil world⌝: which have their portion in this life, whose bellies thou fillest with thy hid treasure.

[a]R.V. *From men, by thy hand, O LORD, from men of the world.* In P.B.V. 'of thy hand' means 'who are Thy agents' as in *v.* 13.

'The LORD Himself is the portion' of the righteous. Ps. xvi. 6.

Cp. the words addressed to Dives, 'Thou in thy lifetime receivedst thy good things.' St Luke xvi. 25.

15 They have children at their desire : and leave the rest of their substance for their babes.

16 But as for me, I will behold thy [b]presence in righteousness : [c]⌜and when I awake up after thy likeness, I shall be satisfied with it⌝.

[b]*face.*

[c]*I shall be satisfied, when I awake, with thy likeness.* 'when I awake' in the world beyond the grave.

Evening Prayer

PSALM XVIII. *Diligam te, Domine.*

'A Psalm of David...who spake unto the LORD the words of this song in the day that the LORD delivered him from the hand of all his enemies, and from the hand of Saul' (Title). These words reappear in 2 Sam. xxii. 1 introducing the same Psalm.

I WILL love thee, O LORD, my strength ; the LORD is my stony rock, and my [d]defence : my Saviour, my God, and my [e]might, in whom I will trust, my buckler, the horn also of my salvation, and my [f]refuge.

The figures are suggested by the natural features of Palestine whose mountains and rocks had served David for strongholds when pursued by Saul.

[d]*fortress.*

[e]R.V. *strong rock.*

[f]*high tower.*

2 I will call upon the LORD, which is worthy to be praised : so shall I be safe from mine enemies.

3 [1]The [g]sorrows of death compassed me : and the overflowings of ungodliness made me afraid.

[g]R.V. *cords.* P.B.V. and A.V. follow Sept. (as also Acts ii. 24) and Vulg.

[1] 2 Sam. xxii. 5 has 'the waves of death' which agrees better with the parallel clause 'the overflowings (*floods*) of ungodliness.'

4 The [a]⌜pains of hell⌝ came about me : the snares of death overtook me.

5 In my trouble I [b]⌜will call⌝ upon the LORD : and [c]complain unto my God.

6 [d]⌜So shall he hear⌝ my voice out of his [1]holy temple : [e]⌜and my complaint shall come before him, it shall enter even into his ears⌝.

7 [f]⌜The earth⌝ trembled and quaked : the very foundations also of the hills shook, and were removed, because he was wroth.

8 There went a smoke out [g]⌜in his presence⌝ : and a consuming fire out of his mouth, so that coals were kindled at it.

9 He bowed the heavens also, and came down : and it was dark under his feet.

10 He rode upon the cherubins, and did fly : he came flying upon the wings of the wind.

11 He made darkness his [h]secret place : his pavilion round about him with dark water, and thick clouds to cover him.

12 At the brightness of his presence his clouds removed : hail-stones, and coals of fire.

13 The LORD also thundered out of heaven, and the Highest [i]⌜gave his thunder⌝ : hail-stones, and coals of fire.

14 He sent out his arrows, and scattered them : he cast forth lightnings, and destroyed them.

15 The springs of waters were seen, and the foundations of the [2]round world were [k]discovered, at thy chiding, O LORD : at the blasting of the breath of thy [l]displeasure.

[a] R.V. *cords of Sheol.* 'Sheol' and 'death' (*v.* 3) are likened to hunters snaring their prey.

[b] *called.* Here and in the next verse David is recounting his past experience.

[c] *cried.*

[d] *He heard.*

His temple in heaven.

[e] R.V. *and my cry before him came into his ears.*

7—16. Jehovah intervened to deliver His servant, manifesting His presence by earthquake and thunderstorm.

[f] *Then the earth.*

[g] *of his nostrils.*

[h] R.V. *hiding.*

i.e. The reflection of His glory divided the clouds, which then sent forth hail and lightning.

[i] R.V. *uttered his voice.*

'them,' i.e. the foes of David and Jehovah.

[k] R.V. *laid bare.* P.B.V. and A.V. 'discovered' is archaic for 'uncovered.'

[l] *nostrils.*

[1] Not in A.R.V., added in P.B.V. from Vulg.
[2] Not in A.R.V., suggested by the Vulg. *orbis terrarum.*

16 He [a]⌜shall send down⌝ from on high [b]⌜to fetch⌝ me : [c]⌜and shall take⌝ me out of many waters.

[a] *sent.*
[b] *he took.*
[c] *he drew.*

17 He [d]⌜shall deliver⌝ me from my strongest enemy, and from them which [e]hate me : for they [f]are too mighty for me.

[d] *delivered.*
Perhaps Saul is meant.
[e] *hated.*
[f] *were.*

18 They [g]prevented me in the day of my trouble : but the LORD was my upholder.

[g] R.V. *came upon.*

19 He brought me forth also into a place of liberty : he brought me forth, even because he had a favour unto me.

See Ps. xli. 11.

20 The LORD [h]⌜shall reward⌝ me after my righteous dealing : according to the cleanness of my hands [i]⌜shall he recompense⌝ me.

[h] *rewarded.*
[i] *hath he recompensed.*

21 Because I have kept the ways of the LORD : and have not forsaken my God, as the wicked doth.

22 For [k]⌜I have an eye unto all his laws⌝ : and [l]⌜will not cast out⌝ his commandments from me.

[k] *all his judgements were before me.*
[l] R.V. *I put not away.*

23 I was also uncorrupt before him : and eschewed mine own wickedness.

24 Therefore [m]⌜shall the LORD reward⌝ me after my righteous dealing : and according unto the cleanness of my hands in his eyesight.

[m] *hath the LORD recompensed.*

25, 26. God deals with men according to their characters; see 1 Sam. ii. 30, 'Them that honour me, I will honour' &c.

25 [n]⌜With the holy thou shalt be holy⌝ : and with a perfect man thou shalt [o]be perfect ;

[n] *With the merciful thou wilt shew thyself merciful;* see St Matt. v. 7.
[o] *shew thyself.*

26 With the clean thou shalt be clean : and with the froward thou shalt [p]⌜learn frowardness⌝.

[p] *shew thyself froward.*

27 For thou shalt save the people that are in adversity : and shalt bring down the high looks of the proud.

28 Thou also shalt light my candle : the LORD my God shall make my darkness to be light.

The lighted lamp in a house is a symbol of the continued life and prosperity of the family; see 1 Kings xi. 36; Job xviii. 6.

29 For in thee I shall discomfit an host of men : and with the help of my God I shall leap over the wall.

David's physical strength is a gift to him from God.

30 The way of God is an undefiled way : the word of the LORD also is tried in the fire; he is the defender of all them that put their trust in him.

31 For who is God, but the LORD: or who [a]⌜hath any strength⌝, except our God?

[a] *is a rock*; see Deut. xxxii. 4, 15, 18.

32 It is God, that girdeth me with strength [1]⌜of war⌝ : and maketh my way perfect.

33 He maketh my feet like harts' feet : and setteth me [b]⌜up on high⌝.

[b] *upon my high places*, i.e. Sion and other mountain fastnesses which came into David's possession.

34 He teacheth mine hands to fight : and mine arms [c]⌜shall break even⌝ a bow of steel.

[c] R.V. *do bend.*

35 Thou hast given me the [d]defence of thy salvation : thy right hand also [e]⌜shall hold⌝ me up, and thy [f]⌜loving correction⌝ [g]⌜shall make⌝ me great.

[d] *shield.*

[e] *hath holden.*

[f] R.V. mg. *condescension*; see Ps. cxiii. 5.

[g] *hath made.*

36 Thou shalt make room enough under me for to go : that my footsteps shall not slide.

37 I will follow upon mine enemies, and overtake them : neither will I turn again till I have destroyed them.

38 I will smite them, that they shall not be able to stand : but fall under my feet.

39 Thou hast girded me with strength unto the battle : thou [h]⌜shalt throw down⌝ mine enemies under me.

[h] *hast subdued.*

[1] Not in A.R.V.

40 Thou hast made mine enemies also to turn their backs upon me : [a]⌜and I shall destroy⌝ them that hate me.

[a] R.V. *that I might cut off.*

41 They [b]⌜shall cry⌝, but there [c]⌜shall be⌝ none to help them : yea, even [d]⌜unto the LORD shall they cry, but he shall not hear them⌝.

[b] *cried.*

[c] *was.*

[d] *unto the LORD, but he answered them not.*

42 [e]⌜I will⌝ beat them as small as the dust before the wind : I [f] will cast them out as the clay in the streets.

[e] *Then did I.*

[f] *did.*

43 Thou [g]⌜shalt deliver⌝ me from the strivings of the people : and thou [h]⌜shalt make⌝ me the head of the [i] heathen.

[g] *hast delivered.*

[h] *hast made.*

[i] R.V. *nations.* God had brought David safely through conflicts at home (the strivings of the people) in order to give him dominion over the neighbouring nations.

44 A people whom I have not known : shall serve me.

44—46. David's forecast of future successes.

45 As soon as they hear of me, they shall obey me : but the [k]⌜strange children shall dissemble with me⌝.

[k] R.V. mg. *strangers* (i.e. foreigners) *shall yield feigned obedience unto me.* Heb. *lie*, i.e. pay me the insincere allegiance of the vanquished. Ps. lxvi. 2, lxxxi. 16.

46 The [l]⌜strange children⌝ shall fail : and [m]⌜be afraid out of their prisons⌝.

[l] *strangers.*

[m] R.V. *shall come trembling out of their close places*, i.e. strongholds.

47 The LORD liveth, and blessed be my [n]⌜strong helper⌝ : and praised be the God of my salvation ;

[n] *rock.*

48 Even the God that seeth that I be avenged : and subdueth [o]⌜the people⌝ unto me.

[o] R.V. *peoples.*

49 It is he that delivereth me from my cruel enemies, and setteth me up above mine adversaries : thou [p]⌜shalt rid⌝ me from the wicked man.

[p] R.V. *deliverest.*

50 For this cause will I give thanks unto thee, O LORD, among the [q] Gentiles : and sing praises unto thy Name.

Quoted in Rom. xv. 9 as proving that Christ's salvation includes the Gentiles. David's rule over the nations prefigured the all-embracing Kingdom of his Son.

[q] R.V. *nations.*

51 Great prosperity giveth he unto his king : and sheweth loving-kindness unto David his anointed, and unto his seed for evermore.

An allusion to God's promise to David through Nathan, 2 Sam. vii. 12—16, which received its ultimate fulfilment in Christ.

THE FOURTH DAY

Morning Prayer

PSALM XIX. *Cœli enarrant.*

God's twofold revelation of Himself, in Nature and in His Law. The Incarnation is the crowning revelation of God for which the earlier revelations prepared the way.

Proper on Christmas Day.

THE heavens declare the glory of God : and the firmament sheweth his handywork.

2 [a]⌜One day telleth another : and one night certifieth another⌝.

3 There is neither speech nor language : [b]⌜but their voices are heard among them⌝.

4 Their [c]sound is gone out into all lands : and their words into the ends of the world.

5 In them hath he set a tabernacle for the sun : which cometh forth as a bridegroom out of his chamber, and rejoiceth as a [d]giant to run his course.

6 It goeth forth from the uttermost part of the heaven, and runneth about unto the end of it again : and there is nothing hid from the heat thereof.

1—6. God's revelation of Himself in Nature.

[a] *Day unto day uttereth speech, and night unto night sheweth knowledge,* i.e. Each day transmits its tidings to the next, each night to its successor. The day's testimony to God's glory differs from the night's, and so day and night are mentioned separately.

[b] R.V. *Their voice cannot be heard,* i.e. The utterance of the heavens, though so expressive, is inaudible.

P.B.V. and A.V. mean, The voices of the heavens are heard by people of every language.

[c] *line,* i.e. measuring cord which marks boundaries. The word may mean harp-string, hence P.B.V. which follows Vulg. This verse is quoted in Rom. x. 18 as mystically referring to the spread of the Gospel.

[d] *strong man.*

7 The law of the LORD is [a]⌜an undefiled law⌝, [b]converting the soul : the testimony of the LORD is sure, and giveth wisdom unto the simple.

[1]7—11. God's revelation of Himself in His Law. This revelation being made specially to Israel, the Covenant name Jehovah 'the LORD' is used.

[a]*perfect.*

[b]R.V. *restoring.*

8 The statutes of the LORD are right, and rejoice the heart : the commandment of the LORD is pure, and giveth light unto the eyes.

9 The fear of the LORD is clean, and endureth for ever : the judgements of the LORD are true, and righteous altogether.

'The fear of the LORD'; another name for the Law, regarded in its effect upon the heart; see Gen. xx. 11.

10 More to be desired are they than gold, yea, than much fine gold : sweeter also than honey, and the honey-comb.

11 Moreover, by them is thy servant taught : and in keeping of them there is great reward.

12 Who can [c]⌜tell how oft he offendeth⌝ : O cleanse thou me from [2]my secret faults.

[c]R.V. *discern his errors*, i.e. sins committed unwittingly, the 'secret faults' of the parallel clause; see Lev. iv. 2 ff.; Numb. xv. 28.

13 Keep thy servant also from presumptuous sins, lest they get the dominion over me : so shall I be undefiled, and innocent from [d]⌜the great offence⌝.

'presumptuous,' i.e. done 'with an high hand.' Numb. xv. 30.

[d]R.V. *great transgression.*

14 Let the words of my mouth, and the meditation of my heart : be [3]alway acceptable in thy sight,

'acceptable.' Sacrifice favourably received is said to be accepted before the LORD. Lev. i. 3, 4. Prayer is a sacrifice of the heart. Ps. cxli. 2; Hos. xiv. 2.

15 O LORD : my strength, and my redeemer.

[1] On account of the difference of subject and style and the change in the Divine Name many scholars regard *vv.* 7—15 as a supplement added to the Psalm by a later writer.

[2] Not in A.R.V., added in P.B.V. from Vulg.

[3] 'alway' not in A.R.V., it is added in P.B.V. from Vulg. If rightly inserted it may have been suggested by the continual daily sacrifice. Exod. xxix. 38.

PSALM XX. *Exaudiat te Dominus.*

A Psalm designed to be sung at the sacrifice which the king offers before going to war.

Proper on King's Accession and on Purification of B.V.M. [America].

THE LORD hear thee in the day of trouble : the Name of the God of Jacob defend thee ;

1—5. The supplication of the congregation for the king during the sacrifice.

Perhaps an allusion to Jacob's words, Gen. xxxv. 3, 'God, who answered me in the day of my distress.'

2 Send thee help from the sanctuary : and strengthen thee out of Sion ;

3 Remember all thy offerings : and accept thy burnt sacrifice ;

'offerings,' i.e. the meal-offering which accompanied the burnt-sacrifice. A portion of it was directed to be burnt as a memorial before God; see Lev. ii. 1, 2: hence the word 'Remember' here.

4 Grant thee thy heart's desire : and fulfil all thy mind.

5 We will rejoice in thy salvation, and triumph in the Name of [1]⌜the LORD⌝ our God : the LORD perform all thy petitions.

'thy salvation,' i.e. the deliverance which the king would bring his people.

6 Now know I, that the LORD helpeth his anointed, and will hear him from his holy heaven : even with the [a]wholesome strength of his right hand.

6—8. A single priest or the king himself announces the acceptance of the sacrifice.

Not merely from His earthly sanctuary, *v.* 2.

[a]*saving.*

7 Some put their trust in chariots, and some in horses : but we will [b]remember the Name of the LORD our God.

[b]R.V. *make mention of.*

8 They are brought down, and fallen : but we are risen, and stand upright.

9 [c]⌜Save, LORD, and hear us, O King of heaven : when we call upon thee⌝.

The concluding prayer of the congregation.

[c]R.V. mg. *O LORD save the king; and answer us when we call*, following Vulg. Hence the versicle and response at Matins and Evensong.

[1] Not in A.R.V.

PSALM XXI. *Domine, in virtute tua.*

A companion Psalm to the preceding. A thanksgiving on the king's return after victory.

Proper on Ascension Day and on King's Accession.

THE king shall rejoice in thy strength, O LORD : exceeding glad shall he be of thy salvation.

1—7. The congregation praise Jehovah for the king's safety and victory.

'thy salvation,' i.e. the deliverance which Thou hast vouchsafed to him.

The prayer of *v.* 4 of the preceding Psalm has been granted.

2 Thou hast given him his heart's desire : and hast not denied him the request of his lips.

3 For thou [a]⌜shalt prevent⌝ him with the blessings of goodness : and [b]⌜shalt set⌝ a crown of pure gold upon his head.

[a] *preventest,* i.e. goest to meet.

'goodness' = good fortune.

[b] *settest.*

i.e. crownest him again, renewest him in his kingdom.

4 He asked life of thee, and thou gavest him a long life : even for ever and ever.

Cp. the usual salutation, 'Let the king live for ever.' 1 Kings i. 31; Neh. ii. 3. The words are applicable in the highest sense only to the Son of David, the eternal King.

5 His honour is great in thy salvation : glory and great worship [c]shalt thou lay upon him.

'thy salvation'; see *v.* 1.

[c] R.V. *dost.*

'lay' = bestow. Ps. lxxxix. 20.

6 For thou [d]⌜shalt give him everlasting felicity⌝ : and [e]make him glad with the joy of thy countenance.

[d] R.V. *makest him most blessed for ever.*

[e] R.V. *makest.*

7 And why? because the king putteth his trust in the LORD : and in the mercy of the most Highest he shall not miscarry.

8 All thine enemies shall feel thy hand : thy right hand shall find out them that hate thee.

8—12. The king himself is addressed.

9 Thou shalt make them like a fiery oven in time of thy wrath : the LORD shall destroy them in his displeasure, and the fire shall consume them.

10 Their fruit shalt thou root out of the earth : and their seed from among the children of men.

'fruit,' i.e. children. Ps. cxxxii. 12; Lam. ii. 20.

11 For they intended mischief against thee : and imagined such a device as they are not able to perform.

12 Therefore shalt thou put them to flight : and the strings of thy bow shalt thou make ready against the face of them.

13 Be thou exalted, LORD, in thine own strength : so will we sing, and praise thy power.

The concluding prayer of the congregation.

Evening Prayer

PSALM XXII. *Deus, Deus meus.*

An agonising cry for succour by a servant of Jehovah who is undergoing inhuman persecution; followed by a thanksgiving for deliverance. The Psalmist's sufferings were divinely ordered so as to foreshadow those of Christ.

Proper on Good Friday.

MY God, my God, [1]⌜look upon me⌝; why hast thou forsaken me : and art so far from my health, and from the words of my complaint?

These words in the then dialect of Palestine (Aramaic) were made His own by our Lord when on the cross. St Matt. xxvii. 46.

'health' = welfare.

2 O my God, I cry in the daytime, but thou hearest not : and in the night-season also I take no rest.

3 And thou continuest holy : O thou [a]⌜worship of Israel⌝.

God's holiness is a pledge that He will be faithful to His own.

[a] R.V. mg. *that art enthroned upon the praises of Israel.* A spiritual form of the expression 'that sittest upon the cherubim.' Ps. lxxx. 1, xcix. 1.

4 Our fathers hoped in thee : they trusted in thee, and thou didst deliver them.

5 They called upon thee, and were holpen : they put their trust in thee, and were not confounded.

6 But as for me, I am a worm, and no man : a very scorn of men, and the outcast of the people.

[1] Not in A.R.V., added in P.B.V. from Vulg.

7 All they that see me laugh me to scorn : they shoot out their lips, and shake their heads, saying,

8 He trusted in GOD, that he would deliver him : let him deliver him, [a]⌜if he will have him⌝.

9 But thou art he that took me out of my mother's womb : thou [b]⌜wast my hope⌝, when I hanged yet upon my mother's breasts.

10 I have been left unto thee ever since I was born : thou art my God even from my mother's womb.

11 O go not from me, for trouble is hard at hand : and there is none to help me.

12 Many oxen are come about me : [c]fat bulls of Basan close me in on every side.

13 They gape upon me with their mouths : as it were a ramping and a roaring lion.

14 I am poured out like water, and all my bones are out of joint : my heart also in the midst of my body is even like melting wax.

15 My strength is dried up like a potsherd, and my tongue cleaveth to my gums : and thou shalt bring me into the dust of death.

16 For [1]many dogs are come about me : and the [d]council of the wicked layeth siege against me.

17 [2]⌜They pierced⌝ my hands and my feet ; I may tell all my bones : they stand staring and looking upon me.

'The people stood beholding. And the rulers also scoffed at him.' St Luke xxiii. 35. 'They that passed by railed on him, wagging their heads.' St Matt. xxvii. 39.

'He trusteth on God; let him deliver him now, if he desireth him.' St Matt. xxvii. 43.

[a] R.V. *seeing he delighteth in him.*

[b] R.V. *didst make me trust.* P.B.V. from Vulg.

The Psalmist's enemies are like furious bulls.

[c] *strong.*

Bashan was a rich pasture-land; see Deut. xxxii. 14; Ezek. xxxix. 18.

'Thou.' The sufferer looks beyond his persecutors to God who uses their agency; see Acts ii. 23.

The persecutors are like the fierce wild dogs of the east.

[d] *assembly.* P.B.V. from Vulg.

17, 18. The Psalmist describes his sufferings in figurative or proverbial terms which were literally fulfilled at our Lord's crucifixion.

'tell' = count.

'they' = my persecutors.

1 Not in A.R.V., added in P.B.V. from Vulg.

2 'They pierced.' R.V. mg. has 'So the Sept., Vulg. and Syr. According to other ancient versions, *They bound.* The Hebrew text as pointed reads, *Like a lion.*' With the latter reading, 'coming about me' must be understood from *v.* 16.

18 They part my garments among them : and cast lots upon my vesture.

'They said therefore...Let us...cast lots for it...that the scripture might be fulfilled which saith, They parted my garments among them, and upon my vesture did they cast lots.' St John xix. 24.

19 But be not thou far from me, O LORD : thou art my succour, haste thee to help me.

20 Deliver my soul from the sword : [a]⌜my darling⌝ from the power of the dog.

21 Save me from the lion's mouth: thou hast heard me also from among the horns of the [b]unicorns.

[a]A.R.V. mg. *my only one*, i.e. as the parallel clause shews, 'my soul' or 'life'; so called because one life only is allotted to man; see Ps. xxxv. 17.

Phrase used by St Paul of his own deliverance from great peril. 2 Tim. iv. 17.

[b]R.V. *wild-oxen*. P.B. and A.V. from Vulg.

22 I will declare thy Name unto my brethren : in the midst of the congregation will I praise thee.

22—26. The Psalmist's thanksgiving for deliverance.

In Heb. ii. 12, these words are made the utterance of Christ, avowing His kinship with His earthly brethren.

23 O praise the LORD, ye that fear him : magnify him, all ye of the seed of Jacob, and fear him, all ye seed of Israel;

24 For he hath not despised, nor abhorred, the [c]⌜low estate of the poor⌝ : he hath not hid his face from him, but when he called unto him he heard him.

[c]*affliction of the afflicted.*

25 [d]⌜My praise is of thee⌝ in the great congregation : my vows will I perform in the sight of them that fear him.

[d]R.V. *Of thee cometh my praise*, i.e. It is the LORD that giveth me cause for praise.

'vows,' i.e. the thank-offering which I vowed in my affliction.

26 The [e]poor shall eat, and be satisfied : they that seek after the LORD shall praise him; [f]⌜your heart shall live for ever⌝.

[e]*meek*. The sacrifice of thanksgiving (*v.* 25) was eaten by the offerer. Lev. vii. 15, 16. Here the meek are invited to take part in the feast.

[f]R.V. *Let your heart live for ever*. The entertainer's blessing upon his guests.

27 All the ends of the world shall remember themselves, and be turned unto the LORD : and all the kindreds of the nations shall worship before him.

27 to end. Prediction of the future extension of God's kingdom.

In Ps. ix. 17, the nations are said to have forgotten God.

28 For the kingdom is the LORD'S: and he is the [a]⌜Governour among the people⌝.

[a] R.V. *ruler over the nations.*

29 All such as be fat upon earth: [b]⌜have eaten, and worshipped⌝.

[b] *shall eat and worship.*

The guests at the eucharistic banquet are (1) the rich and powerful, 'such as be fat upon earth,' *v.* 29, (2) the poor, 'that cannot keep his soul alive,' *v.* 30.

30 All they that go down into the dust shall kneel before him: [c]⌜and no man hath quickened his own soul⌝.

i.e. they that through poverty and misery are ready to perish as explained by the parallel clause.

[c] R.V. *even he that cannot keep his soul alive.*

31 [d]⌜My seed⌝ shall serve him: [e]⌜they shall be counted unto the Lord for a generation⌝.

[d] *A seed.* P.B.V. 'my' from Vulg.

[e] R.V. *It shall be told of the Lord unto the next generation*, i.e. the knowledge of God's righteousness (*v.* 32) declared by His deliverance of His servant will be handed down from father to son.

32 They shall come, and [1]⌜the heavens⌝ shall declare his righteousness: unto a people that shall be born, [f]⌜whom the Lord hath made⌝.

[f] R.V. *that he hath done it.* P.B.V. from Vulg.

PSALM XXIII. *Dominus regit me.*

'A Psalm of David' (Title). The shepherd king towards the close of his life reviews God's goodness to him in the past.

THE LORD is my shepherd: therefore can I lack nothing.

1—4. Jehovah the Good Shepherd.

2 He [g]⌜shall feed me⌝ in a green pasture: [h]⌜and lead⌝ me forth beside the waters of comfort.

[g] *maketh me to lie down.*

[h] *He leadeth.*

3 He [i]⌜shall convert⌝ my soul: [k]⌜and bring me forth⌝ in the paths of righteousness, for his Name's sake.

[i] *restoreth*, see Ps. xix. 7. P.B.V. from Vulg.

[k] R.V. *He guideth me.*

i.e. not for my worthiness, but as proving that He is merciful and gracious as His Name implies; see Exod. xxxiv. 5, 6.

4 Yea, though I walk through the valley of the shadow of death, I will fear no evil: for thou art with me; thy rod and thy staff comfort me.

'the shadow of death.' A figurative expression for *deep darkness*, the R.V. mg. rendering, which follows another pointing of the Hebrew.

The shepherd's crook serves both as a rod with which he guides and protects his sheep, and as a staff upon which he leans while he watches over them.

5 Thou shalt prepare a table before me [a]⌜against them that trouble me⌝: thou hast anointed my head with oil, and my cup [b]⌜shall be full⌝.

5, 6. Jehovah the Psalmist's Host.
[a]*in the presence of mine enemies.*
'with oil,' as an honoured guest at a banquet; see Ps. xlv. 8; St Luke vii. 46.
[b]*runneth over.*

6 But [1]thy loving-kindness and mercy shall follow me all the days of my life: and I will dwell in the house of the LORD for ever.

'for ever.' R.V. mg. *for length of days.* The Psalmist, it may be, looks forward simply to a long life spent in communion with God. To the Christian his words speak also of eternal blessedness in the heavenly sanctuary.

THE FIFTH DAY

Morning Prayer

PSALM XXIV. *Domini est terra.*

'A Psalm of David' (Title). The ascent of Jehovah to His Sanctuary, and the character of the man who may ascend with Him.

Probably sung on the occasion of the triumphant removal of the ark to mount Sion.

Proper on Ascension Day. Special in Form of Consecration of a Church [Convocation (1712); Ireland; America].

[2]THE earth is the LORD'S, and all that therein is: [3]⌜the compass of⌝ the world, and they that dwell therein.

1, 2. Sung by the whole choir in procession.

2 For he hath founded it upon the seas: and [c]prepared it upon the floods.

The earth rising above the waters is pictured as supported by them.
[c]*established.*

3 Who shall ascend into the hill of the LORD: or who shall [d]⌜rise up⌝ in his holy place?

A single voice puts the question.
[d]*stand.*

4 Even he that hath clean hands, and a pure heart: and that hath not lift up his mind unto vanity, nor sworn to deceive his neighbour.

Another voice replies.

'vanity' = falsehood, here whatever is opposed to the truth of God.

[1] Not in A.R.V., added in P.B.V. from Vulg.
[2] 'The earth is the LORD'S' &c. Quoted in 1 Cor. x. 26 to prove the lawfulness of eating 'whatsoever is sold in the shambles' without distinction.
[3] Not in A.R.V., suggested by the Vulg. *orbis terrarum.*

5 He shall receive the blessing from the LORD : and righteousness from the God of his salvation.

5, 6. The whole choir join in.

6 This is the generation of them that seek him : even of them that seek thy face, [a]⌜O Jacob⌝.

[a] R.V. *O God of Jacob.*

7 Lift up your heads, O ye gates, and be ye lift up, ye everlasting doors : and the King of glory shall come in.

The summons of the choir as the procession reaches the city gates.
'everlasting,' i.e. of hoary antiquity.

8 Who is the King of glory : it is the LORD strong and mighty, even the LORD mighty in battle.

Challenge of the priests and levites from within the walls, and reply of the choir.

9 Lift up your heads, O ye gates, and be ye lift up, ye everlasting doors : and the King of glory shall come in.

The summons repeated.

10 Who is the King of glory : even the LORD of hosts, he is the King of glory.

Challenge and reply as before.
'hosts' = the armies of heaven, the angels.

PSALM XXV. *Ad te, Domine, levavi.*

The Psalmist is passing through a time of trouble : he prays for instruction, pardon and deliverance.

An alphabetical Psalm.

UNTO thee, O LORD, will I lift up my soul ; my God, I have put my trust in thee : O let me not be confounded, neither let mine enemies triumph over me.

2 For all they that hope in thee shall not be ashamed : but such as transgress without a cause shall be [b]⌜put to confusion⌝.

[b] *ashamed.*

3 Shew me thy ways, O LORD : and teach me thy paths.

A prayer of Moses. Exod. xxxiii. 13.

4 Lead me forth in thy truth, and learn me : for thou art the God of my salvation ; in thee hath been my hope all the day long.

'learn' = teach.

5 Call to remembrance, O LORD, thy tender mercies : and thy loving-kindnesses, which have been ever of old.

6 O remember not the sins [a]⌜and offences of my youth⌝ : but according to thy mercy think thou upon me, O LORD, for thy goodness.

[a] *of my youth, nor my transgressions* of later years.

7 Gracious and righteous is the LORD : therefore will he teach sinners in the way.

8 Them that are meek shall he guide in judgement : and such as are gentle, them shall he learn his way.

'judgement' = right rule of conduct; see Prov. i. 3.

9 All the paths of the LORD are mercy and truth : unto such as keep his covenant, and his testimonies.

10 For thy Name's sake, O LORD: be merciful unto my sin, for it is great.

The LORD who had proclaimed His Name as 'a God full of compassion and gracious, slow to anger,' etc. Exod. xxxiv. 6.

11 What man is he, that feareth the LORD : him shall he teach in the way that he shall choose.

i.e. the way that the LORD chooses for him.

12 His soul shall dwell at ease : and his seed shall inherit the land.

13 The secret of the LORD is among them that fear him : and he will shew them his covenant.

They shall be admitted to God's inner counsels and to His confidential communion; see Prov. iii. 32.

14 Mine eyes are ever looking unto the LORD : for he shall pluck my feet out of the net.

15 Turn thee unto me, and have mercy upon me : for I am desolate, and in misery.

16 The sorrows of my heart [b]⌜are enlarged : O⌝ bring thou me out of my troubles.

[b] R.V. mg. *relieve thou, and.*

17 Look upon my adversity and misery : and forgive me all my sin.

18 Consider mine enemies, how many they are : and they bear a tyrannous hate against me.

19 O keep my soul, and deliver me : let me not be confounded, for I have put my trust in thee.

20 Let perfectness and righteous dealing [a]⌜wait upon⌝ me : for my hope hath been in thee.

[a] *preserve.*

21 Deliver Israel, O God : out of all his troubles.

A concluding prayer for the whole nation. It may have been added when the Psalm was appointed for use in public worship. Note the word 'God' (Elohim) here, not 'LORD' (Jehovah) as elsewhere in the Psalm.

PSALM XXVI. *Judica me, Domine.*

The Psalmist pleads his uprightness and zeal for God's House, and prays that he may not share the fate of the wicked.

Special in Office of Institution of Ministers [America].

BE thou my Judge, O LORD, for I have walked innocently: my trust hath been also in the LORD, [b]⌜therefore shall I not fall⌝.

[b] R.V. *without wavering.*

2 Examine me, O LORD, and prove me : try out my reins and my heart.

The reins (kidneys) were regarded as the seat of the affections; the heart, of the thought and will. Combined they sum up the whole inner man.

3 For thy loving-kindness is ever before mine eyes : and I [c]⌜will walk⌝ in thy truth.

[c] *have walked.*

4 I have not dwelt with vain persons : neither will I have fellowship with the deceitful.

5 I have hated the congregation of the wicked : and will not sit among the ungodly.

6 I will wash my hands in innocency, O LORD : and so will I go to thine altar;

As the priests did in symbolic act before ministering. Exod. xxx. 17—21.

7 That I may shew the voice of thanksgiving : and tell of all thy wondrous works.

8 LORD, I have loved the habitation of thy house : and the place where [a]⌜thine honour⌝ dwelleth.

Cp. *v.* 5, 'I have hated the congregation of the wicked.'

[a] R.V. *thy glory.*

9 O shut not up my soul with the sinners : nor my life with the blood-thirsty;

i.e include me not with the wicked in their fate.

10 In whose hands is wickedness : and their right hand is full of [b]gifts.

[b] *bribes.*

11 But as for me, I will walk innocently : O deliver me, and be merciful unto me.

12 My foot standeth [c]right : I will praise the LORD in the congregations.

[c] *in an even place*, i.e. on the level open plain,—in security. In the full assurance of faith the Psalmist regards his prayer as already granted.

Evening Prayer

PSALM XXVII. *Dominus illuminatio.*

The first part (1—7) is a confident assertion of unfailing trust in God who has saved and will save from enemies. The second part 8—16 is an earnest intreaty for help in a time of gloom and extremity. Perhaps the latter portion was added subsequently.

Proper on Transfiguration [America].

THE LORD is my light, and my salvation; whom then shall I fear : the LORD is the strength of my life; of whom then shall I be afraid?

'My light.' This name is applied to God here only in the O.T.

2 When the wicked, even mine enemies, and my foes, came upon me to eat up my flesh : they stumbled and fell.

My enemies are as savage as wild beasts.

3 Though an host of men were laid against me, yet shall not my heart be afraid : and though there rose up war against me, yet will I put my trust in him.

4 One thing have I desired of the LORD, which I will require : even that I may dwell in the house of the LORD all the days of my life, to behold the [a]⌜fair beauty⌝ of the LORD, and to [b]visit his temple.

[a]R.V. mg. *pleasantness*, i.e. not merely the outward beauty of the sanctuary and its worship but also the gracious character of Him who is worshipped.

[b]*inquire in*, i.e. meditate in. P.B.V. from Vulg.

5 For in the time of trouble he shall hide me in his tabernacle : yea, in the secret place of his dwelling shall he hide me, and set me up upon a rock of stone.

6 And now shall he lift up mine head : above mine enemies round about me.

7 Therefore will I offer in his dwelling an oblation with great gladness : I will sing, and speak praises unto the LORD.

8 Hearken unto my voice, O LORD, when I cry unto thee : have mercy upon me, and hear me.

9 [c]⌜My heart hath talked of thee, Seek ye my face : Thy face, LORD, will I seek⌝.

[c]*When thou saidst, Seek ye my face; my heart said unto thee, Thy face, LORD, will I seek.*

10 O hide not thou thy face from me : nor cast thy servant away in displeasure.

11 Thou hast been my succour : leave me not, neither forsake me, O God of my salvation.

12 When my father and my mother forsake me : the LORD taketh me up.

A proverbial way of expressing extreme desolation.

13 Teach me thy way, O LORD : and lead me in [d]⌜the right way⌝, because of mine enemies.

[d]*a plain path*, i.e. level and free from obstruction.

14 Deliver me not over into the will of mine adversaries : for there are false witnesses risen up against me, and such as [a]⌜speak wrong⌝.

[a] *breathe out cruelty.*

15 I should utterly have fainted : but that I believe verily to see the goodness of the LORD in the land of the living.

16 O tarry thou the LORD'S leisure : be strong, and [b]⌜he shall comfort thine heart⌝; and put thou thy trust in the LORD.

[b] R.V. *let thine heart take courage.*

PSALM XXVIII. *Ad te, Domine.*

A cry to God for help against enemies, and a thanksgiving for anticipated deliverance.

UNTO thee will I cry, O LORD my [c]strength : [d]⌜think no scorn of me⌝; lest, if thou make as though thou hearest not, I become like them that go down into the pit.

[c] *rock.*

[d] R.V. *be not thou deaf unto me.*

2 Hear the voice of my humble petitions, when I cry unto thee : when I hold up my hands towards the mercy-seat of thy holy temple.

The gesture of prayer. Ps. lxiii. 5; 1 Tim. ii. 8.

3 O pluck me not away, neither destroy me with the ungodly and wicked doers : which speak friendly to their neighbours, but imagine mischief in their hearts.

4 Reward them according to their deeds : and according to the wickedness of their [e]⌜own inventions⌝.

[e] R.V. *doings.* P.B.V. from Vulg.

5 Recompense them after the work of their hands : pay them that they have deserved.

6 For they regard not in their mind the works of the LORD, nor the operation of his hands : therefore shall he break them down, and not build them up.

7 Praised be the LORD : for he hath heard the voice of my humble petitions.

The faith of the Psalmist assures him that his prayer has been heard.

8 The LORD is my strength, and my shield; my heart hath trusted in him, and I am helped : therefore my heart danceth for joy, and in my song will I praise him.

9 The LORD is [a]my strength : and he is the wholesome defence of his anointed.

[a]*their*, i.e. the strength of the people mentioned in *v.* 10.
The LORD's anointed = the king.

10 O save thy people, and give thy blessing unto thine inheritance : feed them, and set them up for ever.

'O LORD, save thy people: and bless thine heritage.' Te Deum and versicles at Matins and Evensong.

PSALM XXIX. *Afferte Domino.*

Jehovah who manifests Himself in the terrors of the thunderstorm speaks peace to His people.

Proper on Trinity Sunday [America].

[b]⌜BRING unto the LORD, O ye mighty, bring young rams unto the LORD : ascribe unto the LORD worship and strength⌝.

[b]R.V. *Give unto the LORD, O ye sons of the mighty, Give unto the LORD glory and strength.* 'The sons of the mighty' (or '*of God*' R.V. mg.) are the angels (see Ps. lxxxix. 7) who are called upon to praise Jehovah for the manifestation of His glory in the thunderstorm. P.B.V. from Vulg.

2 Give the LORD the honour due unto his Name : worship the Lord [c]⌜with holy worship⌝.

[c]R.V.mg. *in holy array.* The angels are regarded as vested like the priests in the earthly temple; see Ps. xcvi. 9.

3 [a]⌜It is the LORD, that commandeth the waters : it is the glorious God, that maketh the thunder⌝.

[a] *The voice of the LORD is upon the waters: the God of glory thundereth.* 'The voice of the LORD' seven times repeated indicates successive peals of thunder; cp. the 'seven thunders' of Rev. x. 3 ff.

4 [b]⌜It is the LORD, that ruleth the sea⌝; the voice of the LORD is mighty in operation : the voice of the LORD is a glorious voice.

[b] R.V. *even the LORD upon many waters.* 'The waters' are either the sea or the rain-charged clouds.

5 The voice of the LORD breaketh the cedar-trees : yea, the LORD breaketh the cedars of Libanus.

6 He maketh them also to skip like a calf : Libanus also, and Sirion, like a young [c]unicorn.

Mts. Lebanon and Sirion (=Mt. Hermon, Deut. iii. 9) are in the north, Kadesh (*v.* 7) in the south of Palestine. The storm sweeps through the whole land.

[c] R.V. *wild-ox.* P.B.V. from Vulg.

7 The voice of the LORD divideth the flames of fire; the voice of the LORD shaketh the wilderness : yea, the LORD shaketh the wilderness of [d]Cades.

i.e. the lightning.

[d] *Kadesh.* P.B.V. from Vulg.

8 The voice of the LORD maketh the hinds to bring forth young, and [e]⌜discovereth the thick bushes⌝ : in his temple [f]⌜doth every man speak of his honour⌝.

[e] R.V. *strippeth the forests bare.* P.B.V. and A.V. 'discovereth' is archaic for 'uncovereth.'

[f] R.V. *every thing saith, Glory,* i.e. the angelic worshippers respond to the call of the Psalmist in *vv.* 1, 2.

9 [g]⌜The LORD sitteth above the water-flood : and the LORD remaineth a King for ever⌝.

[g] R.V. *The LORD sat as king at the Flood: Yea, the LORD sitteth as king for ever,* i.e. He who of old presided over the Deluge still rules and controls the convulsions of Nature.

10 The LORD shall give strength unto his people : the LORD shall give his people the blessing of peace.

A portion of the priestly blessing. Num. vi. 26. See Ps. iv. 7, xxxi. 18.

THE SIXTH DAY

Morning Prayer

PSALM XXX. *Exaltabo te, Domine.*

A thanksgiving after recovery from a dangerous illness.

Proper on Easter Even [America].

I WILL magnify thee, O LORD, for thou hast [a]set me up: and not made my foes to triumph over me.

[a]R.V. *raised.*

The Psalmist's enemies would have exulted had his illness proved fatal.

2 O LORD my God, I cried unto thee : and thou hast healed me.

3 Thou, LORD, hast brought my soul out of [b]hell : thou hast kept my life from them that go down to the pit.

i.e. Thou hast preserved me when in great peril of death ; see parallel clause.

[b]R.V. *Sheol.*

4 Sing praises unto the LORD, O ye saints of his : and give thanks [c]⌜unto him for a remembrance of his holiness⌝.

[c]R.V. *to his holy name* (R.V. mg. *memorial*). God's Name (Jehovah), is His memorial, because it sets forth His character as He has revealed it. Exod. iii. 15, xxxiv. 5—7.

5 For his wrath endureth but the twinkling of an eye, and in [1]⌜his [d]pleasure is life⌝ : [e]⌜heaviness may endure for a night⌝, but joy cometh in the morning.

[d]*favour.*

i.e. 'life which is life indeed.' 1 Tim. vi. 19.

[e]R.V. mg. *Weeping may come in to lodge at even.*

6 And in my prosperity I said, I shall never be removed : thou, LORD, of thy goodness hast made my hill so strong.

'my hill.' The stronghold of Sion is a type of security.

7 Thou didst [f]⌜turn thy face from me⌝ : and I was troubled.

[f]*hide thy face.* P.B.V. from Vulg.

8 Then cried I unto thee, O LORD: and gat me to my LORD right humbly.

[1] R.V. mg. '*His favour is for a life time*' may give the true meaning.

9 What profit is there in my blood : when I go down to the pit?

9, 10. The Psalmist's prayer. He regards death as a state which allows no scope for active service to God; see Ps. vi. 5; Is. xxxviii. 18.

10 Shall the dust give thanks unto thee : or shall it declare thy truth?

11 Hear, O LORD, and have mercy upon me : LORD, be thou my helper.

12 Thou hast turned my heaviness into joy : thou hast put off my sackcloth, and girded me with gladness :

The Psalmist's prayer is granted.

13 [a]⌜Therefore shall every good man sing of thy praise without ceasing⌝: O my God, I will give thanks unto thee for ever.

[a] *To the end that my glory may sing praises to thee, and not be silent.* 'My glory' = my soul; see Ps. vii. 5, xvi. 10.

PSALM XXXI. *In te, Domine, speravi.*

The Psalmist passing through sore persecution is sustained by his trust in God.

Proper on Easter Even [America].

IN thee, O LORD, have I put my trust : let me never be put to confusion, deliver me in thy righteousness.

'O LORD, in Thee have I trusted: let me never be confounded.' Te Deum.

God's righteousness is a pledge that he will succour His servant.

2 Bow down thine ear to me : make haste to deliver me.

3 And be thou my strong rock, and house of defence : that thou mayest save me.

Show Thyself to be that which I know Thou art (*v.* 4).

4 For thou art my strong rock, and my castle : be thou also my guide, and lead me for thy Name's sake.

5 Draw me out of the net, that they have laid privily for me : for thou art my [b]strength.

[b] R.V. *stronghold.*

6 Into thy hands I commend my spirit : for thou hast redeemed me, O LORD, thou God of truth.

i.e. I entrust myself to Thee for safety. Our Lord gave a higher sense to these words when He used them to express the surrender of His human Life to God. St Luke xxiii. 46.

'redeemed,' i.e. preserved me amid temporal troubles; see 2 Sam. iv. 9. In the N.T. the word 'redeem' is sanctified to a deeper meaning.

7 I have hated them that [a]⌜hold of superstitious vanities⌝ : and my trust hath been in the LORD.

[a] *regard lying vanities*, i.e. false gods and other worthless objects of trust. Jonah ii. 8.

8 I will be glad, and rejoice in thy mercy : for thou hast considered my trouble, and hast known my soul in adversities.

8, 9. God's former mercies to the Psalmist give him confidence.

'considered,' i.e. regarded with loving care; see Ps. i. 7; xxxvii. 18.

9 Thou hast not shut me up into the hand of the enemy : but hast set my feet in a large [b]room.

[b] R.V. *place*, i.e. Thou hast (in the past) given me freedom and security. Ps. xviii. 19.

10 Have mercy upon me, O LORD, for I am in trouble : and mine eye is consumed for very heaviness; yea, my soul and my body.

The eye reveals the ravages of disease; see Ps. vi. 7, xiii. 3, xxxviii. 10.

11 For my life is waxen old with heaviness : and my years with mourning.

'waxen'=grown.

12 My strength faileth me, because of mine iniquity : and my bones are consumed.

The Psalmist acknowledges that his troubles have their root in his own sin.

13 I [c]⌜became a reproof⌝ among all mine enemies, but especially among my neighbours : and they of mine acquaintance were afraid of me; and they that did see me without conveyed themselves from me.

[c] R.V. *am become a reproach.*

14 I am clean forgotten, as a dead man out of mind : I am become like a broken vessel.

i.e. thrown away and forgotten.

15 For I have heard the [d]⌜blasphemy of the multitude⌝ : and fear is on every side, while they conspire together against me, and take their counsel to take away my life.

[d] R.V. *defaming of many.*

16 But my hope hath been in thee, O LORD : I have said, Thou art my God.

17 My time is in thy hand; deliver me from the hand of mine enemies : and from them that persecute me.

18 [a]⌜Shew thy servant the light of thy countenance⌝ : and save me for thy mercy's sake.

[a] *Make thy face to shine upon thy servant.* A part of the priestly blessing. Num. vi. 25; see Ps. iv. 7, xxix. 10.

19 Let me not be confounded, O LORD, for I have called upon thee : let the ungodly be put to confusion, and be put to silence in [b]⌜the grave⌝.

[b] R.V. *Sheol.*

20 Let the lying lips be put to silence : which cruelly, disdainfully, and despitefully, speak against the righteous.

21 O how plentiful is thy goodness, which thou hast laid up for them that fear thee : and that thou hast prepared for them that put their trust in thee, even before the sons of men!

21 to end. Thanksgiving for prayer answered.

22 [c]⌜Thou shalt hide them privily by thine own presence from the provoking of all men⌝ : thou shalt keep them secretly in thy tabernacle from the strife of tongues.

[c] R.V. *In the covert of thy presence shalt thou hide them from the plottings of man.*

23 Thanks be to the LORD : for he hath shewed me marvellous great kindness in a strong city.

i.e. His protection encompasseth me like a fortified city.

24 [d]⌜And when I made haste, I said : I am cast out of the sight of thine eyes⌝.

[d] R.V. *As for me, I said in my haste, I am cut off from before thine eyes.* A reminiscence of former impatience.

25 Nevertheless, thou heardest the voice of my prayer : when I cried unto thee.

26 O love the LORD, all ye his saints : for the LORD preserveth them that are faithful, and plenteously rewardeth the proud doer.

27 Be strong, and [a]⌜he shall establish your heart⌝: all ye that put your trust in the LORD.

[a]R.V. *let your heart take courage.*

Evening Prayer

PSALM XXXII. *Beati, quorum.*

'A Psalm of David' (Title). David, penitent after his great sin, records the relief which his confession of it brought to his soul.

The second of the Penitential Psalms.

Proper on Ash Wednesday.

[1] 1 BLESSED is he whose [b]unrighteousness is forgiven : and whose sin is covered.

[b]*transgression.*

2 Blessed is the man unto whom the LORD imputeth [c]⌜no sin⌝: and in whose spirit there is no guile.

[c]*not iniquity.*

'guile,' i.e. deceitfulness. God's forgiveness can reach the sinner only when his repentance is sincere.

3 For while I held my tongue : my bones consumed away through my [d]⌜daily complaining⌝.

3, 4. David's sufferings, in which he recognizes God's hand, before he confessed his sin.

'held my tongue,' i.e. kept silence as to my sin.

[d]*roaring all the day long.*

4 For thy hand [e]is heavy upon me day and night : and my moisture [f]⌜is like the drought in summer⌝.

[e]*was.*

'moisture,' figurative for bodily vigour; cp. Ps. xxii. 15.

[f]R.V. *was changed as with the drought of summer.*

5 I [g]⌜will acknowledge⌝ my sin unto thee : and mine unrighteousness have I not hid.

[g]*acknowledged.*

6 I said, I will confess my sins unto the LORD : and so thou forgavest the wickedness of my sin.

[1] 1, 2 quoted Rom. iv. 7, 8. In the Hebrew of these two verses three words are used for 'misdoing' with the meanings: 1. Breaking loose from God (transgression); 2. Falling short of the mark (sin); 3. Perversion of soul (iniquity). Also the divine pardon of sin is expressed in three ways, viz: 1. Taking away (forgiven); 2. Covering; 3. Not imputing or reckoning.

7 For this shall every one that is godly make his prayer unto thee, in a time when thou mayest be found : [a]⌜but in the great water-floods they shall not come nigh him⌝.

[a] R.V. *surely when the great waters* (of God's judgements) *overflow they shall not reach unto him.*

8 Thou art a place to hide me in, thou shalt preserve me from trouble : thou shalt compass me about with songs of deliverance.

'Your life is hid with Christ in God.' Col. iii. 3.

9 I will inform thee, and teach thee in the way wherein thou shalt go : and I will guide thee with mine eye.

9—12. David, penitent and pardoned, out of his own experience proceeds to instruct others.

10 Be ye not like to horse and mule, which have no understanding : whose mouths must be held with bit and bridle, [b]⌜lest they fall upon thee⌝.

[b] R.V. *else they will not come near unto thee.*

11 [c]⌜Great plagues remain for the ungodly⌝ : but whoso putteth his trust in the LORD, mercy embraceth him on every side.

[c] *Many sorrows shall be to the wicked.*

12 Be glad, O ye righteous, and rejoice in the LORD : and be joyful, all ye that are true of heart.

PSALM XXXIII. *Exultate, justi.*

The providence of God rules the world which He has made. The Psalmist has probably some signal deliverance of Israel from heathen foes before his eyes.

Proper on Trinity Sunday [America].

REJOICE in the LORD, O ye righteous : for it becometh well the just to be thankful.

2 Praise the LORD with harp : sing praises unto him with the lute, and instrument of ten strings.

3 Sing unto [a]⌜the LORD⌝ a new song : sing praises lustily [1]⌜unto him⌝ with a good courage.

[a] *him.*

'a new song.' The occasion calls for a fresh expression of thanksgiving.

4 For the word of the LORD is true : and all his works are faithful.

5 He loveth righteousness and judgement : the earth is full of the goodness of the LORD.

4, 5. Jehovah is to be praised on account of His moral attributes.

6 By the word of the LORD were the heavens made : and all the hosts of them by the breath of his mouth.

7 He gathereth the waters of the sea together, as it were upon an heap : and layeth up the deep, as in a treasure-house.

8 Let all the earth fear the LORD : stand in awe of him, all ye that dwell in the world.

6—9. Jehovah is to be praised on account of His creative acts.

'the word,' i.e. the fiat of creation, again referred to in *v.* 9.

'the hosts of them,' i.e. the heavenly bodies. Gen. ii. 1.

9 For he spake, and it was done : he commanded, and it stood fast.

'And God said.' Gen. i. 3, 6, 9 &c.

10 The LORD bringeth the counsel of the heathen to nought : and maketh the [b]devices of the [b]people to be of none effect, [1]⌜and casteth out the counsels of princes⌝.

10—18. Jehovah is to be praised on account of His providential rule of the world, especially (12, 17, 18) for His care of His chosen people.

[b]R.V. *thoughts. peoples.*

11 The counsel of the LORD shall endure for ever : and the thoughts of his heart from generation to generation.

In contrast with the counsel and the thoughts of the heathen peoples which the LORD bringeth to nought (*v.* 10).

12 Blessed are the people, whose God is the LORD [2]Jehovah : and blessed are the folk, that he hath chosen to him to be his inheritance.

13 The LORD [c]looked down from heaven, and [d]beheld all the children of men : from the habitation of his dwelling he considereth all them that dwell on the earth.

[c]*looketh.*
[d]*beholdeth.*

[1] Not in A.R.V. added in P.B.V. from Vulg.
[2] Not in A.R.V.

14 He fashioneth all the hearts of them : and understandeth all their works.

15 There is no king that can be saved by the multitude of an host : neither is any mighty man delivered by much strength.

15, 16. The futility of reliance upon merely human resources.

16 A horse is counted but a vain thing to save a man : neither shall he deliver any man by his great strength.

17 Behold, the eye of the LORD is upon them that fear him : and upon them that put their trust in his mercy;

18 To deliver their soul from death : and to feed them in the time of dearth.

19 Our soul hath patiently tarried for the LORD : for he is our help, and our shield.

20 For our heart shall rejoice in him : because we have hoped in his holy Name.

21 Let thy merciful kindness, O LORD, be upon us : like as we do put our trust in thee.

PSALM XXXIV. *Benedicam Domino.*

A celebration of God's moral government, especially as regards His protection of the righteous.

An alphabetical Psalm.

Proper on St Michael and all Angels [America].

I WILL alway give thanks unto the LORD : his praise shall ever be in my mouth.

2 My soul shall make her boast in the LORD : the humble shall hear thereof, and be glad.

3 O praise the LORD with me : and let us magnify his Name together.

4 I sought the LORD, and he heard me : yea, he delivered me out of all my fear.

5 They [a]⌜had an eye⌝ unto him, and were lightened : and their faces were not ashamed.

'They.' The experience of others agrees with that of the Psalmist. The meaning is 'all who look unto Him are lightened,' i.e. brightened and cheered.

[a] *looked.*

6 Lo, the poor crieth, and the LORD heareth him : yea, and saveth him out of all his troubles.

7 The angel of the LORD [b]tarrieth round about them that fear him : and delivereth them.

[b] *encampeth.*

'The Angel of the LORD,' i.e. the special representative of Jehovah; see Gen. xvi. 7; Exod. xxiii. 20 ff. &c.; mentioned in Psalter only here and in xxxv. 5, 6.

8 O taste, and see, how gracious the LORD is : blessed is the man that trusteth in him.

Quoted by St Peter (1 St Pet. ii. 3) for whom the LORD is Christ, 'If ye have tasted that the Lord is gracious.'

9 O fear the LORD, ye that are his saints : for they that fear him lack nothing.

10 The lions do lack, and suffer hunger : but they who seek the LORD shall want no manner of thing that is good.

11 Come, ye children, and hearken unto me : I will teach you the fear of the LORD.

Affectionate address as of a teacher to his disciples; see Prov. iv. 1; 1 St John ii. 1, 12 &c.

12 What man is he that lusteth to live : and would fain see good days?

'lusteth'=desireth.

13 Keep thy tongue from evil : and thy lips, that they speak no guile.

14 [c]Eschew evil, and do good : seek peace, and [d]ensue it.

[c] *Depart from.*

[d] *pursue.*

15 The eyes of the LORD are over the righteous : and his ears are open unto their prayers.

16 The countenance of the LORD is against them that do evil : to root out the remembrance of them from the earth.

17 The righteous cry, and the LORD heareth them : and delivereth them out of all their troubles.

18 The LORD is nigh unto them that are of a contrite heart : and will save such as be of an humble spirit.

19 Great are the troubles of the righteous : but the LORD delivereth him out of all.

20 He keepeth all his bones : so that not one of them is broken.

This figurative description of God's watchful care, together with the direction about the paschal lamb, Exod. xii. 46, is probably referred to by St John (xix. 36) as literally fulfilled in one circumstance of Christ's Passion, 'A bone of him shall not be broken.'

21 But misfortune shall slay the ungodly : and they that hate the righteous shall be [a]desolate.

[a] R.V. *condemned.*

22 The LORD delivereth the souls of his servants : and all they that put their trust in him shall not be [b]destitute.

[b] R.V. *condemned.*

THE SEVENTH DAY

Morning Prayer

PSALM XXXV. *Judica, Domine.*

'A Psalm of David' (Title). An appeal to Jehovah for help against active and malicious enemies. Perhaps written by David when pursued by Saul.

PLEAD thou my cause, O LORD, with them that strive with me : and fight thou against them that fight against me.

2 Lay hand upon the shield and buckler : and stand up to help me.

3 Bring forth the spear, [1]and stop the way against them that [a]persecute me : say unto my soul, I am thy salvation.

[a] R.V. *pursue.*

4 Let them be confounded, and put to shame, that seek after my soul : let them be turned back, and brought to confusion, that imagine mischief for me.

5 Let them be as [b]⌜the dust⌝ before the wind : and the angel of the LORD scattering them.

5, 6. A word-picture of a headlong rout.

[b] *chaff.*

'the angel of the LORD'; see note on Ps. xxxiv. 7.

6 Let their way be dark and slippery : [c]⌜and let⌝ the angel of the LORD [d]persecute them.

[c] R.V. *and.*

[d] R.V. *pursuing.*

7 For they have privily laid their net to destroy me without a cause : yea, even without a cause have they made a pit for my soul.

8 Let a sudden destruction come upon him unawares, and his net, that he hath laid privily, catch himself : that he may fall into his own mischief.

'him.' The singular is used collectively, or some individual enemy is referred to.

9 And, my soul, [e]be joyful in the LORD : it shall rejoice in his salvation.

[e] *shall be.*

10 All my bones shall say, LORD, who is like unto thee, who deliverest the poor from him that is too strong for him : yea, the poor, and him that is in misery, from him that spoileth him?

'All my bones,' i.e. The joy of my soul (*v.* 9) will throb through every member of my body.

11 False witnesses did rise up : they laid to my charge things that I knew not.

12 They rewarded me evil for good : to the great discomfort of my soul.

[1] For 'and stop the way,' R.V. mg. has '*and the battle axe*' following some modern commentators.

13 Nevertheless, when they were sick, I put on sackcloth, and humbled my soul with fasting : and my prayer shall turn into mine own bosom.

My prayer for mine enemies will bring *me* the blessings which I asked on their behalf.

14 I behaved myself as though it had been my friend, or my brother : I went heavily, as one that mourneth for his mother.

15 But in mine adversity they rejoiced, and gathered themselves together : yea, the very abjects came together against me unawares, [a]⌜making [1]mouths at⌝ me, and ceased not.

The lowest of the rabble join the ranks of my persecutors.

[a] *they did tear.*

16 [b]⌜With the flatterers were busy mockers : who⌝ gnashed upon me with their teeth.

[b] R.V. *Like the profane mockers in feasts, they,* i.e. Like professional buffoons who earned their dinners by making sport for the guests.

17 LORD, how long wilt thou look upon this : O deliver my soul from the calamities which they bring on me, and [c]⌜my darling⌝ from the lions.

[c] A.R.V. mg. *my only one,* i.e. my soul, or life, as the parallel clause shews; see Ps. xxii. 20.

'the lions' = my savage assailants.

18 So will I give thee thanks in the great congregation : I will praise thee among much people.

19 O let not them that are mine enemies triumph over me [d]ungodly : neither let them wink with their eyes that hate me without a cause.

[d] *wrongfully.*

'wink' &c. i.e., make gestures to express their joy at my calamity.

Words quoted by our Lord as fulfilled in His own case; St John xv. 25. They occur again Ps. lxix. 4.

20 And why? their communing is not for peace : but they imagine deceitful words against them that are quiet in the land.

21 They gaped upon me with their mouths, and said : [e]⌜Fie on thee, fie on thee, we saw it with our eyes⌝.

[e] *Aha, aha, our eye hath seen it,* i.e. thy misfortune.

[1] 'Mouths' in present P.B.V. has been substituted for 'mowes,' i.e. grimaces, which appeared in the early editions.

22 This thou hast seen, O LORD : hold not thy tongue then, go not far from me, O Lord.

23 [a]⌜Awake, and stand up to judge my quarrel⌝ : avenge thou my cause, my God, and my Lord.

[a] *Stir up thyself and awake to my judgement.* P.B.V. 'quarrel' formerly meant 'complaint,' as in Col. iii. 13 (A.V.).

24 Judge me, O LORD my God, according to thy righteousness : and let them not triumph over me.

25 Let them not say in their hearts, There, there, so would we have it : neither let them say, We have devoured him.

26 Let them be put to confusion and shame together, that rejoice at my trouble : let them be clothed with rebuke and dishonour, that boast themselves against me.

27 Let them be glad and rejoice, that favour my righteous dealing : yea, let them say alway, Blessed be the LORD, who hath pleasure in the prosperity of his servant.

28 And as for my tongue, it shall be talking of thy righteousness : and of thy praise all the day long.

PSALM XXXVI. *Dixit injustus.*

The wickedness of the ungodly in contrast with the faithfulness and loving-kindness of the LORD.

MY heart sheweth me the wickedness of the ungodly : that there is no fear of God before his eyes.

2 For he flattereth himself in his own sight : [b]⌜until his abominable sin be found out⌝.

[b] R.V. *that his iniquity shall not be found out and be hated.*

3 The words of his mouth are unrighteous, and full of deceit : he hath left off to behave himself wisely, and to do good.

4 He imagineth mischief upon his bed, and hath set himself in no good way : neither doth he abhor any thing that is evil.

5 Thy mercy, O LORD, reacheth unto the heavens : and thy faithfulness unto the clouds.

6 Thy righteousness standeth like the [a]⌜strong mountains⌝ : thy judgements are like the great deep.

[a] R.V. *mountains of God*, i.e. which God hath reared; cp. Ps. civ. 16.

7 Thou, LORD, [b]⌜shalt save both⌝ man and beast; How excellent is thy mercy, O God : and the children of men [c]⌜shall put their trust⌝ under the shadow of thy wings.

[b] *preservest.*

'excellent' formerly meant 'surpassing,' 'excelling.'

[c] R.V. *take refuge.*

8 They shall be satisfied with the plenteousness of thy house : and thou shalt give them drink of thy pleasures, as out of the river.

Jehovah regarded as a gracious host; see Ps. xxiii. 5.

9 For with thee is the well of life : and in thy light shall we see light.

'The water that I shall give him shall become in him a well of water springing up unto eternal life'; St John iv. 14.

'In him was life; and the life was the light of men'; St John i. 4.

10 O continue forth thy loving-kindness unto them that know thee : and thy righteousness unto them that are true of heart.

11 O let not the foot of pride come against me : and let not the hand of the ungodly [d]⌜cast me down⌝.

[d] R.V. *drive me away*, i.e. into exile from the LORD's land.

12 There are they fallen, all that work wickedness : they are cast down, and shall not be able to stand.

The vision of faith which sees the wicked already overthrown.

Evening Prayer

PSALM XXXVII. *Noli æmulari.*

The apparent prosperity of the wicked should not make men lose faith in the righteous government of God.

An alphabetical Psalm.

FRET not thyself because of the ungodly : neither be thou envious against the evil-doers.

'the evil-doers.' Our Lord's words in His explanation of the parable of the tares, 'them that do iniquity,' St Matt. xiii.41, are identical with the Sept. here.

2 For they shall soon be cut down like the grass : and be withered even as the green herb.

3 Put thou thy trust in the LORD, and be doing good : dwell in the land, and [a]⌜verily thou shalt be fed⌝.

To dwell in the LORD's land, i.e. Canaan, was a duty of the Israelite with which his prosperity was bound up; see 9, 11, 22, 30, 35.

[a] R.V. *follow after faithfulness.*

4 Delight thou in the LORD : and he shall give thee thy heart's desire.

5 Commit thy way unto the LORD, and put thy trust in him : and he shall bring it to pass.

6 He shall make thy righteousness as clear as the light : and thy just dealing as the noon-day.

7 Hold thee still in the LORD, and abide patiently upon him : but grieve not thyself at him, whose way doth prosper, against the man that [b]⌜doeth after evil counsels⌝.

[b] *bringeth wicked devices to pass.*

8 Leave off from wrath, and let go displeasure : fret not thyself, else shalt thou be moved to do evil.

9 Wicked doers shall be rooted out : and they that patiently abide the LORD, those shall inherit the land.

i.e. Canaan, *v.* 3.

10 Yet a little while, and the ungodly shall be clean gone : thou shalt look after his place, and he shall be away.

11 But [a]⌜the meek-spirited shall possess the earth⌝ : and shall be refreshed in the multitude of peace.

[a] R.V. *the meek shall inherit the land*, i.e. Canaan. The words are quoted with a larger meaning by our Lord in the Sermon on the Mount. St Matt. v. 5.

12 The ungodly seeketh counsel against the just : and gnasheth upon him with his teeth.

13 The Lord shall laugh him to scorn : for he hath seen that his day is coming.

i.e. the day of retribution.

14 The ungodly have drawn out the sword, and have bent their bow : to cast down the poor and needy, and to slay such as are of a right conversation.

'conversation'=manner of life.

15 Their sword shall go through their own heart : and their bow shall be broken.

16 A small thing that the righteous hath : is better than great riches of the ungodly.

17 For the arms of the ungodly shall be broken : and the LORD upholdeth the righteous.

18 The LORD knoweth the days of the godly : and their inheritance shall endure for ever.

'knoweth,' i.e. regardeth with loving care; see Ps. i. 7, xxxi. 8.

An 'inheritance,' as it has since been revealed, 'that fadeth not away' (1 St Pet. i. 4), in the kingdom that shall have no end.

19 They shall not be confounded in the perilous time : and in the days of dearth they shall have enough.

20 As for the ungodly, they shall perish; and the enemies of the LORD shall [b]⌜consume as the fat of lambs⌝ : yea, even as the smoke, shall they consume away.

[b] R.V. *be as the excellency of the pastures; they shall consume.* The wicked are compared to grass, which is often used in Palestine for fuel; see St Matt. vi. 30, 'the grass of the field, which to-day is, and to-morrow is cast into the oven.'

21 The ungodly borroweth, and payeth not again: but the righteous is merciful, and liberal.

The ungodly is driven by stress of poverty to borrow money and cannot pay it back: the righteous has enough not only for his own needs but for those of others.

22 Such as are blessed of God shall possess the land: and they that are cursed of him shall be rooted out.

i.e. Canaan, *v.* 3.

23 The LORD ordereth a good man's going: and maketh his way acceptable to himself.

'himself,' i.e. the LORD.

24 Though he fall, he shall not be cast away: for the LORD upholdeth him with his hand.

25 I have been young, and now am old: and yet saw I never the righteous forsaken, nor his seed begging their bread.

26 The righteous is ever merciful, and lendeth: and his seed is blessed.

27 Flee from evil, and do the thing that is good: and dwell for evermore.

28 For the LORD loveth the thing that is right: he forsaketh not his that be godly, but they are preserved for ever.

29 [1]⌜The unrighteous shall be punished⌝: as for the seed of the ungodly, it shall be rooted out.

30 The righteous shall inherit the land: and dwell therein for ever.

i.e. Canaan, *v.* 3.

31 The mouth of the righteous is exercised in wisdom: and his tongue will be talking of judgement.

32 The law of his God is in his heart: and his goings shall not slide.

[1] Not in A.R.V., added in P.B.V. from Vulg.

33 The ungodly [a]seeth the righteous : and seeketh occasion to slay him.

[a] *watcheth.*

34 The LORD will not leave him in his hand : nor condemn him when he is judged.

Though man may condemn, the LORD will acquit.

35 Hope thou in the LORD, and keep his way, and he shall promote thee, that thou shalt possess the land : when the ungodly shall perish, thou shalt see it.

i.e. Canaan, *v.* 3.

36 I myself have seen the ungodly in great power : and flourishing like a green bay-tree.

37 I went by, and lo, he was gone : I sought him, but [b]⌜his place⌝ could no where be found.

[b] *he.* P.B.V. from Vulg.

38 [c]⌜Keep innocency, and take heed unto the thing that is right⌝ : [1][d]⌜for that shall bring a man peace at the last⌝.

[c] *Mark the perfect man, and behold the upright.* P.B.V. from Vulg.

[d] R.V. *for the latter end of that man is peace.*

39 As for the transgressors, they shall perish together : [e]⌜and the end of the ungodly is, they shall be rooted out at the last⌝.

[e] R.V. *the latter end of the wicked shall be cut off.*

40 But the salvation of the righteous cometh of the LORD : who is also their [f]strength in the time of trouble.

[f] R.V. *stronghold.*

41 And the LORD shall stand by them, and save them : he shall deliver them from the ungodly, and shall save them, because they [g]⌜put their trust⌝ in him.

[g] R.V. *have taken refuge* (as in a stronghold).

[1] R.V. mg. '*for there is a reward* (or *future* or *posterity*) *for the man of peace*' is preferred by many commentators. The meaning is that the posterity of the man of peace shall be continued, while the posterity ('latter end') of the wicked shall be cut off. *v.* 39.

THE EIGHTH DAY

Morning Prayer

PSALM XXXVIII. *Domine, ne in furore.*

The Psalmist is passing through a period of acute suffering in soul and body. His sickness is aggravated by the insults of his enemies and the desertion of his friends. He turns to God as his only Helper.

The third of the Penitential Psalms.

Proper on Ash Wednesday.

PUT me not to rebuke, O LORD, in thine anger : neither chasten me in thy heavy displeasure.

1—3. The Psalmist regards his sickness as God's punishment for his sin. This verse is almost the same as Ps. vi. 1.

2 For thine arrows stick fast in me : and thy hand presseth me sore.

3 There is no health in my flesh, because of thy displeasure : neither is there any rest in my bones, by reason of my sin.

4 For my wickednesses are gone over my head : and are like a sore burden, too heavy for me to bear.

'gone over,' like a flood of water.

5 My wounds stink, and are corrupt : through my foolishness.

'my foolishness,' thus the Psalmist describes his sin which he now sees in its true light.

6 I am [a]⌜brought into so great trouble and misery : that⌝ I go mourning all the day long.

[a] R.V. *pained and bowed down greatly.*

7 For my loins are filled with [b]⌜a sore disease⌝ : and there is no whole part in my body.

[b] R.V. *burning.*

8 I am feeble, and sore smitten : I have roared for the very disquietness of my heart.

9 Lord, thou knowest all my desire : and my groaning is not hid from thee.

'Your Father knoweth what things ye have need of, before ye ask him.' St Matt. vi. 8.

10 My heart panteth, my strength hath failed me : and the [a]sight of mine eyes is gone from me.

[a] *light.*
The eye discloses the state of health. Ps. vi. 7, xxxi. 10.

11 My lovers and my neighbours did stand [b]⌜looking upon my trouble⌝ : and my kinsmen stood afar off.

[b] R.V. *aloof from my plague.*
This verse and Ps. lxxxviii. 7 seem to have suggested St Luke's wording (xxiii. 49), 'All his acquaintance... stood afar off, seeing these things.'

12 They also that sought after my life laid snares for me : and they that went about to do me evil talked of wickedness, and imagined deceit all the day long.

'went about' = endeavoured.

13 As for me, I was like a deaf man, and heard not : and as one that is dumb, who doth not open his mouth.

14 I became even as a man that heareth not : and in whose mouth are no reproofs.

'reproofs' = disproofs : here replies in self-vindication.

15 For in thee, O LORD, have I put my trust : thou shalt answer for me, O Lord my God.

16 [c]⌜I have required that they, even mine enemies, should not triumph over me⌝ : for when my foot slipped, they rejoiced greatly against me.

[c] R.V. *For I said, Lest they rejoice over me.* They would see in the Psalmist's misfortune a proof that God had condemned him.

17 [d]⌜And I, truly, am set in the plague⌝ : and my heaviness is ever in my sight.

[d] *For I am ready to halt.*

18 For I will confess my wickedness : and be sorry for my sin.

19 But mine enemies [e]live, and are mighty : and they that hate me wrongfully are many in number.

[e] *are lively.*

20 They also that reward evil for good are against me : because I follow the thing that good is.

21 Forsake me not, O LORD my God : be not thou far from me.

22 Haste thee to help me : O Lord [1]God of my salvation.

[1] Not in A.R.V., added in P.B.V. from Vulg.

PSALM XXXIX. *Dixi, Custodiam.*

The Psalmist, laid on a bed of sickness and perplexed by the prosperity of the wicked, is confirmed in his trust in God by the consideration of the shortness and uncertainty of life.

Special in Burial Service.

I SAID, I will take heed to my ways : that I offend not in my tongue.

i.e. by complaining about my lot, and so murmuring against God.

2 I will keep my mouth as it were with a bridle : while the ungodly is in my sight.

While I see the ungodly prospering.

3 I held my tongue, and spake nothing : I kept silence, yea, even from good words ; but it was pain and grief to me.

4 My heart was hot within me, and while I was thus musing the fire kindled : and at the last I spake with my tongue ;

Unable any longer to suppress my pent-up feelings.

5 LORD, let me know mine end, and the number of my days : [a]⌜that I may be certified how long I have to live⌝.

5 to end. The words of the Psalmist.

[a] R.V. *let me know how frail I am.* P.B.V. is a paraphrase of Vulg.

6 Behold, thou hast made my days as it were a span long : and mine age is even as nothing in respect of thee ; and verily every man [b]living is altogether [c]vanity.

[b] R.V. *at his best estate.*
[c] R.V. mg. *a breath.*

7 For man walketh in a vain shadow, and disquieteth himself in vain : he heapeth up riches, and cannot tell who shall gather them.

8 And now, Lord, what is my hope : truly my hope is even in thee.

9 Deliver me from all mine offences : and make me not [d]⌜a rebuke unto⌝ the foolish.

[d] *the reproach of.* 'The foolish,' i.e. the ungodly (Ps. xiv. 1), would interpret my sufferings as a proof of God's displeasure.

10 I became dumb, and opened not my mouth : for it was thy doing.

11 Take thy [a]plague away from me : I am even consumed by the means of thy heavy hand.

[a]*stroke*. P.B.V. 'plague,' from Vulg., formerly had this meaning.

12 When thou with rebukes dost chasten man for sin, thou makest his beauty to consume away, like as it were a moth [1]⌜fretting a garment⌝ : every man therefore is but [b]vanity.

[b]R.V. mg. *a breath*.

13 Hear my prayer, O LORD, and with thine ears consider my calling : hold not thy peace at my tears.

14 For I am a stranger with thee : and a sojourner, as all my fathers were.

15 O spare me a little, that I may recover my strength : before I go hence, and be no more [1]seen.

'The land is mine : for ye are strangers and sojourners with me.' Lev. xxv. 23; see 1 Chr. xxix. 15. The words are applied in 1 St Pet. ii. 11 to the condition of the Christian in the world.

PSALM XL. *Expectans expectavi.*

The Psalmist records God's mercy in delivering him from some great trouble in the past, and proceeds to pray for release from present persecution.

Proper on Good Friday and on Circumcision [America].

I WAITED patiently for the LORD : and he inclined unto me, and heard my calling.

2 He brought me also out of the horrible pit, out of the mire and clay : and set my feet upon the rock, and [c]ordered my goings.

A metaphorical description of a position of great danger and difficulty.

[c]*established*, i.e. made firm.

3 And he hath put a new song in my mouth : even a thanksgiving unto our God.

'new,' a fresh expression of gratitude; see Ps. xxxiii. 3.

[1] Not in A.R.V.

4 Many shall see it, and fear : and shall put their trust in the LORD.

5 Blessed is the man that hath set his hope in the LORD : and turned not unto the proud, and to such as [a]⌜go about with lies⌝.

[a]*turn aside to lies*, i.e. to courses opposed to the truth of God.

6 O LORD my God, great are the wondrous works which thou hast done, like as be also thy thoughts which are to us-ward : [b]⌜and yet there is no man that ordereth them unto thee.⌝

[b]R.V. mg. *there is none to be compared unto thee.* P.B.V. means that man has no control over God's works and thoughts; see Is. xl. 14.

7 If I should declare them, and speak of them : they should be more than I am able to express.

8—10. God's goodness and greatness are acknowledged rather by obedience to His will than by sacrifice. Ps. li. 16, 17; 1 Sam. xv. 22. The passage is quoted in Heb. x. 5—9 as finding its complete fulfilment in the obedience of Christ.

8 Sacrifice, and meat-offering, thou [c]⌜wouldest not⌝ : but [1]mine ears hast thou opened.

[c]R.V. *hast no delight in.*

i.e. Thou hast given me the power of hearing Thy commands and obeying them.

9 Burnt-offerings, and sacrifice for sin, hast thou not required : then said I, Lo, I come,

The Psalmist's proffer of service to God.

10 [d]⌜In the volume of the book it is written of me, that I should fulfil thy will, O my God : I am content to do it⌝; yea, thy law is within my heart.

[d]R.V. mg. *In the roll of the book it is prescribed to me: I delight to do thy will, O my God.* The first clause is parenthetical and refers to the Book of the Law in which man's duty is laid down.

An earnest of the days of the New Covenant when God's law would be written in the hearts of all His people. Jer. xxxi. 33; see Ps. xxxvii. 32.

1 'Mine ears hast thou opened.' The quotation of this passage in Heb. x. 5 follows the Sept., 'A body didst thou prepare for me.' The meaning is practically the same, as the body is the instrument through which obedience is put into action. The author of the Epistle sees in the word 'body' a reference to the Incarnation.

11 I have declared thy righteousness in the great congregation : lo, I will not refrain my lips, O LORD, and that thou knowest.

12 I have not hid thy righteousness within my heart : my talk hath been of thy truth, and of thy salvation.

13 I have not kept back thy loving mercy and truth : from the great congregation.

14 Withdraw not thou thy mercy from me, O LORD : let thy lovingkindness and thy truth alway preserve me.

15 For innumerable troubles are come about me ; my sins have [a]⌜taken such hold upon me⌝ that I am not able to look up : yea, they are more in number than the hairs of my head, and my heart hath failed me.

[a] R.V. *overtaken me, so.*

16 O LORD, let it be thy pleasure to deliver me : make haste, O LORD, to help me.

16 to end. These verses appear again, with slight variations, as Ps. lxx.

17 Let them be ashamed, and confounded together, that seek after my soul to destroy it : let them be driven backward, and put to rebuke, that wish me evil.

18 Let them be desolate, and rewarded with shame : that say unto me, [b]⌜Fie upon thee, fie upon thee⌝.

[b] *Aha, Aha.* Thus expressing their delight at my misfortune.

19 Let all those that seek thee be joyful and glad in thee : and let such as love thy salvation say alway, The LORD be praised.

20 As for me, I am poor and needy : but the Lord careth for me.

21 Thou art my helper and [c]redeemer : make no long tarrying, O my God.

[c] *deliverer.*

Evening Prayer

PSALM XLI. *Beatus qui intelligit.*

The Psalmist is lying upon a sick-bed, and is visited by pretended friends who long for his death.

BLESSED is he that considereth the poor [1]⌜and needy⌝ : the LORD shall deliver him in the time of trouble.

1—3. The Psalmist ponders on the blessings which belong to those who shew compassion to the afflicted—compassion which he has not experienced in his own illness. *vv.* 5—9.

2 The LORD preserve him, and keep him alive, that he may be blessed [a]⌜upon earth⌝ : and deliver not thou him into the will of his enemies.

[a] R.V. mg. *in the land* of promise. Ps. xxxvii. 3 &c.

3 The LORD [b]comfort him, when he lieth sick upon his bed : [c]⌜make thou⌝ all his bed in his sickness.

[b] R.V. *will support.* 'Comfort' formerly had this meaning.

[c] R.V. mg. *thou turnest* or *changest* his bed of sickness into one of health. P.B.V., with which A.R.V. agree, refers to the smoothing of the pillow &c. for the refreshment of the patient.

4 I said, LORD, be merciful unto me : heal my soul, for I have sinned against thee.

The Psalmist acknowledges that his sickness is the penalty of his sin.

5 Mine enemies speak evil of me : When shall he die, and his name perish?

6 And if he come to see me, he speaketh vanity : and his heart conceiveth falsehood within himself, and when he cometh forth he telleth it.

'vanity'=falsehood. The person pretends a sympathy which he does not feel. Perhaps some special enemy is referred to; see *v.* 9.

7 All mine enemies whisper together against me : even against me do they imagine this evil.

8 [d]⌜Let the sentence of guiltiness proceed against him⌝ : and now that he lieth, let him rise up no more.

[d] *An evil disease, say they, cleaveth fast unto him.*

[1] Not in A.R.V., added in P.B.V. from Vulg.

9 Yea, even mine own familiar friend, whom I trusted : who did also eat of my bread, hath [a]⌜laid great wait for me⌝.

This verse, with the exception of the words 'mine own familiar friend, whom I trusted,' are applied by our Lord to the treachery of Judas. St John xiii. 18.

[a]*lifted up his heel against me.*

10 But be thou merciful unto me, O LORD : raise thou me up again, and I shall [b]reward them.

[b]*requite.*

11 By this I know thou favourest me : that mine enemy doth not triumph against me.

12 And [c]⌜when I am in my health, thou upholdest me⌝ : and shalt set me before thy face for ever.

[c]*as for me thou upholdest me in mine integrity.*

Words with a Gospel ring. 1 St John iii. 2; Rev. xxii. 4.

13 Blessed be the LORD God of Israel : world without end. Amen.

This doxology marks the close of the First Book of the Psalter.

PSALM XLII. *Quemadmodum.*

A Levite, in exile and surrounded by enemies, expresses his earnest longings for the Temple worship from which he is debarred.

Probably this and the next Psalm, which are similar in subject and language and have a common refrain, originally constituted one poem.

LIKE as the hart desireth the water-brooks : so longeth my soul after thee, O God.

2 My soul is athirst for God, yea, even for the living God : when shall I come to appear before the presence of God?

'the living God,' i.e. the Source of Life, 'the fountain of living waters.' Jer. ii. 13; see Ps. lxxxiv. 2.

The phrase used for going up to the Temple on the Festivals. Ps. lxxxiv. 7; Exod. xxiii. 17; Deut. xvi. 16.

3 My tears have been my meat day and night : while they daily say unto me, Where is now thy God?

'they,' i.e. the Psalmist's heathen neighbours.

4 [a]⌜Now when I think thereupon, I pour out my heart by myself : for⌝ I went with the multitude, and brought them forth into the house of God ;

[a] R.V. *These things I remember, and pour out my soul within me, how.* The Psalmist comforts himself with the recollection of past days when he used to conduct the caravans of pilgrims to Jerusalem.

5 In the voice of praise and thanksgiving : among such as keep holy-day.

Ps. cxx.—cxxxiv. form a collection of sacred songs chanted in these pilgrimages.

6 Why art thou so full of heaviness, O my soul : and why art thou so disquieted within me?

'My soul is exceeding sorrowful' (St Matt. xxvi. 38), our Lord's words at Gethsemane, closely resemble the Sept. here.

7 Put thy trust in God : for I will yet give him thanks [b]⌜for the help of his countenance.

[b] R.V. mg. makes the refrain end here, as in *v.* 15 and Ps. xliii. 6, *who is the health of my countenance and my God.*

8 My God⌝, my soul is vexed within me : therefore [c]⌜will I remember thee concerning the land of Jordan, and the little hill of Hermon⌝.

These words (which also occur in Ps. vi. 3) as they appear in the Sept. were used by our Lord before His Passion, 'Now is my soul troubled.' St John xii. 27.

[c] R.V. *do I remember thee from the land of Jordan, and the Hermons, from the hill Mizar.* The Psalmist's place of exile is the 'land of Jordan,' i.e. the country east of Jordan in the vicinity of the range of Mt Hermon ('the Hermons'), of which 'Mizar' was probably one of the peaks. Mizar = *little* (R.V. mg.) whence P.B.V. rendering.

9 [d]⌜One deep calleth another, because of the noise of the water-pipes⌝ : all thy waves and [e]storms are gone over me.

[d] *Deep calleth unto deep at the noise of thy waterspouts* (R.V. mg. *cataracts*).
[e] *thy billows.*

The mountain torrents of the Jordan supply the Psalmist with images to describe the flood of sorrows which overwhelm him.

10 [1]The LORD hath granted his loving-kindness in the day-time : and in the night-season did I sing of him, and made my prayer unto the God of my life.

The Psalmist's reminiscence of the former time of happiness when day and night the manifestation of Jehovah's loving-kindness ceased not, and the song of praise was uninterrupted.

[1] Note 'the LORD' here contrary to the general usage in Book II.

11 I will say unto [a]⌜the God of my strength⌝, Why hast thou forgotten me : why go I thus heavily, while the enemy oppresseth me?

[a] *God my rock.*

12 My bones are smitten asunder as with a sword : while mine enemies [1]⌜that trouble me⌝ cast me in the teeth;

13 Namely, while they say daily unto me : Where is now thy God?

14 Why art thou so vexed, O my soul : and why art thou so disquieted within me?

15 O put thy trust in God : for I will yet thank him, which is the [b]help of my countenance, and my God.

[b] *health.*

PSALM XLIII. *Judica me, Deus.*

(See Preface to Psalm xlii.)

GIVE sentence with me, O God, and defend my cause against the ungodly people : O deliver me from the deceitful and wicked man.

i.e. the heathen neighbours of the Psalmist in his exile.

2 For thou art the God of my strength, why hast thou put me from thee : and why go I so heavily, while the enemy oppresseth me?

3 O send out thy light and thy truth, that they may lead me : and bring me unto thy holy hill, and to thy dwelling.

'Light' and 'Truth' are described, by a bold figure, as God's messengers despatched to guide the Psalmist to God's House. There may also be an allusion to the Urim and Thummim which in the Sept. are rendered 'Light and Truth.'

4 And that I may go unto the altar of God, even unto the God of my joy and gladness : and upon the harp will I give thanks unto thee, O God, my God.

Equivalent to 'O LORD, my God' in Jehovistic Psalms.

[1] Not in A.R.V., added in P.B.V. from Vulg.

5 Why art thou so heavy, O my soul : and why art thou so disquieted within me?

6 O put thy trust in God : for I will yet give him thanks, which is the [a]help of my countenance, and my God.

[a] *health.*

THE NINTH DAY

Morning Prayer

PSALM XLIV. *Deus, auribus.*

An earnest appeal for Divine succour on behalf of Israel, which though faithful to Jehovah is hard pressed by foes.

WE have heard with our ears, O God, our fathers have told us : what thou hast done in their time of old ;

'O God, we have heard with our ears, and our fathers have declared unto us, the noble works that thou didst in their days, and in the old time before them.' Litany.

2 How thou hast driven out the heathen with thy hand, and planted them in : how thou hast destroyed the nations, and [b]⌜cast them out⌝.

'them,' i.e. our fathers.

[b]R.V. *didst spread them* (i.e. our fathers) *abroad.* Israel's increase is compared to the growth of a tree.

3 For they gat not the land in possession through their own sword : neither was it their own arm that helped them ;

4 But thy right hand, and thine arm, and the light of thy countenance : because thou hadst a favour unto them.

A reminiscence of the priestly benediction. Numb. vi. 25, 26.

5 Thou art my King, O God : [c]⌜send help unto⌝ Jacob.

[c]R.V. *command deliverance for.* As King issue Thy command and it must be obeyed.

6 Through thee will we overthrow our enemies : and in thy Name will we tread them under that rise up against us.

7 For I will not trust in my bow : it is not my sword that shall help me ;

8 But it is thou that savest us from our enemies : and puttest them to confusion that hate us.

Deliverance comes from God alone.

9 We make our boast of God all day long : and will praise thy Name for ever.

10—17. Apparent change in God's attitude towards Israel. *v.* 10 is repeated almost verbally in Ps. lx. 10.

10 But now thou [a]⌜art far⌝ off, and puttest us to confusion : and goest not forth with our armies.

[a] R.V. *hast cast us.*

There may be an allusion here to the practice in earlier times of carrying the ark, the symbol of God's presence, to the field of battle.

11 Thou makest us to turn our backs upon our enemies : so that they which hate us spoil our goods.

12 Thou [b]⌜lettest us be eaten up like sheep⌝ : and hast scattered us among the heathen.

[b] *hast given us like sheep appointed for meat.*

'scattered us,' i.e. by allowing us to be taken captive in war and sold into slavery.

13 Thou sellest thy people for nought : and [c]⌜takest no money for them⌝.

[c] R.V. *hast not increased thy wealth by their price*, i.e. Thou hast gained nothing by abandoning them—a bold expostulation with God !

14 Thou makest us to be rebuked of our neighbours : to be laughed to scorn, and had in derision of them that are round about us.

14, 15. The surrounding nations mock Israel as a people deserted by its God.

This verse occurs again Ps. lxxix. 4.

15 Thou makest us to be a byword among the heathen : and that the [d]people shake their heads at us.

[d] R.V. *peoples.*

16 My confusion is daily before me : and the shame of my face hath covered me ;

17 For the voice of the slanderer and blasphemer : for the enemy and avenger.

'avenger' = revengeful. Ps. viii. 2.

18 And though all this be come upon us, yet [a]⌜do we not forget thee : nor behave ourselves frowardly⌝ in thy covenant.

[a] *have we not forgotten thee, neither have we dealt falsely.*

The Psalmist is not conscious of any national apostasy for which Israel deserves this chastisement.

19 Our heart is not turned back : neither our steps gone out of thy way;

20 [b]⌜No, not when thou hast smitten us into the place of dragons⌝ : and covered us with the shadow of death.

[b] R.V. *That thou hast sore broken us in the place of jackals*, i.e. brought us low, and made our land a wilderness, the haunt of wild beasts; see Jer. ix. 11.

21 If we have forgotten the Name of our God, and holden up our hands to any strange god : shall not God search it out? for he knoweth the very secrets of the heart.

22 For thy sake also are we killed all the day long : and are counted as sheep appointed to be slain.

Applied by St Paul in Rom. viii. 36 to the condition of Christians in his time.

23 Up, Lord, why sleepest thou : [c]⌜awake, and be not absent from us⌝ for ever.

[c] *arise, cast us not off.*

24 Wherefore hidest thou thy face : and forgettest our misery and trouble?

25 For our soul is brought low, even unto the dust : our belly cleaveth unto the ground.

26 Arise, and help us : and deliver us for thy mercy's sake.

PSALM XLV. *Eructavit cor meum.*

A nuptial song composed to celebrate some royal marriage; possibly that of Solomon with the daughter of Pharaoh. It foreshadows the union of the Divine Son of David with His bride the Church.

Proper on Christmas Day.

MY heart [d]⌜is inditing of a good matter : I speak of the things which I have made unto the king⌝.

1, 2. The Psalmist's preface.

[d] R.V. *overfloweth with a goodly matter: I speak the things which I have made touching the king.* 'made,' i.e. composed; so the word 'poet' = maker.

2 My tongue is the pen : of a ready writer.

3 Thou art fairer than the children of men : full of grace are thy lips, [a]because God hath blessed thee for ever.

3—10. The Psalmist addresses the royal bridegroom.

[a] *therefore.*

4 [b]⌜Gird thee with thy sword upon thy thigh, O thou most mighty : according to thy worship and renown⌝.

[b] R.V. *Gird thy sword upon thy thigh, O mighty one, thy glory and thy majesty.* 'Gird' belongs to both clauses.

5 [c]⌜Good luck have thou with thine honour : ride on⌝, because of [d]⌜the word of⌝ truth, of meekness, and righteousness ; and thy right hand shall teach thee terrible things.

[c] R.V. *And in thy majesty ride on prosperously.*

[d] A.R.V. omit 'the word of.' The king is to be the champion of truth, meekness and righteousness.

6 Thy arrows are very sharp, and the [e]people shall be subdued unto thee : [f]⌜even in the midst among⌝ the king's enemies.

[e] R.V. *peoples.*

[f] R.V. *they* (i.e. thy arrows) *are in the heart of.*

7 Thy [g]seat, O God, endureth for ever : the sceptre of thy kingdom is a [h]⌜right sceptre.⌝

[g] *throne.*

The king is here called 'God' as representing and deriving his authority from the Almighty. See Ps. lxxxii. 6; Exod. xxi. 6 for other instances where the title 'God' is assigned to earthly rulers. 'for ever' claims the promise of permanency made to the throne of David which was fulfilled only in Christ, of whom the whole passage must be spiritually interpreted as it is in Heb. i. 8.

[h] R.V. *sceptre of equity.*

8 Thou hast loved righteousness, and hated iniquity : wherefore God, even thy God, hath anointed thee with the oil of gladness above thy fellows.

Reference to the custom of anointing guests on festive occasions; cp. Ps. xxiii. 5.

'thy fellows' = other monarchs.

9 All thy garments smell of myrrh, aloes, and cassia : out of the ivory palaces, [i]⌜whereby they⌝ have made thee glad.

[i] R.V. *stringed instruments.*

10 Kings' daughters [a]were among thy honourable women : upon thy right hand [b]did stand the queen in [c]⌜a vesture of gold, wrought about with divers colours⌝.

[a]R.V. *are.*
[b]R.V. *doth.*
[c]*gold of Ophir.* P.B.V. from Vulg. The 'queen' is the 'king's daughter' of *v.* 14, mentioned here as with the king by anticipation.

11 Hearken, O daughter, and consider, incline thine ear : forget also thine own people, and thy father's house.

11—13. The Psalmist addresses the bride.

12 So shall the king have pleasure in thy beauty : for he is thy Lord [1]God, and worship thou him.

For 'thy lord' (note 'God' should be omitted) cp. Gen. xviii. 12; 1 St Pet. iii. 6, 'Sarah obeyed Abraham, calling him lord.'
'worship,' i.e. pay him homage and respect; cp. St Luke xiv. 10 (A.V.).

13 And the daughter of Tyre shall be there with a gift : like as the rich also among the people shall [d]⌜make their supplication before thee⌝.

i.e. the people of Tyre; cp. the 'daughter of Sion,' Ps. ix. 14.
i.e. Israelites as well as foreigners.
[d]*intreat thy favour.*

14 The king's daughter is all glorious [e]within : her clothing is of wrought gold.

14—16. The bridal procession described.
[e]R.V. *within the palace.*

15 She shall be brought unto the king in raiment of needle-work : the virgins that be her fellows shall bear her company, and shall be brought unto thee.

16 With joy and gladness shall they be brought : and shall enter into the king's palace.

17 Instead of thy fathers thou shalt have children : whom thou [f]mayest make princes in all lands.

17, 18. Address to the bridegroom resumed.
[f]R.V. *shalt.*

18 I will [g]⌜remember thy name⌝ from one generation to another : therefore shall the [h]people give thanks unto thee, world without end.

[g]*make thy name to be remembered.*
[h]R.V. *peoples.*

[1] Not in A.R.V., added in P.B.V. from Vulg.

PSALM XLVI. *Deus noster refugium.*

The safety of those who are under the protection of God. This Psalm and the two following are hymns of triumph and thanksgiving celebrating some great national deliverance, probably the destruction of the army of Sennacherib under the walls of Jerusalem.

Proper on Epiphany [America].

GOD is our hope and strength : a very present help in trouble.

2 Therefore will we not fear, though the earth be moved : and though the hills be carried into the midst of the sea;

3 Though the waters thereof rage and swell : and though the mountains shake at the tempest of the same.

4 [a]⌜The rivers of the flood thereof shall⌝ make glad the city of God : the holy place of the tabernacle of the most Highest.

[a] R.V. *There is a river, the streams whereof.* Amid the turmoil of the world, Sion watered by the river of God's grace, enjoys peace and blessedness.

5 God is in the midst of her, therefore shall she not be [b]removed : God shall help her, [c]⌜and that right early⌝.

[b] *moved.*

[c] R.V. mg. *at the dawn of the morning.* The night of trial will be followed by the morning of deliverance; cp. Ps. xxx. 5. Perhaps there is a special allusion to the morning when the destruction of the Assyrians was discovered. Is. xxxvii. 36.

6 [d]⌜The heathen make much ado, and the kingdoms are moved : but God hath shewed his voice, and the earth shall melt away⌝.

[d] *The nations raged, the kingdoms were moved* (unlike the city of God, *v.* 5)*: he uttered his voice* (i.e. the thunder), *the earth melted.*

7 The LORD of hosts is with us : the God of Jacob is our refuge.

The LORD of the armies of heaven is in our midst. He is none other than the Covenant God of Israel.

8 O come hither, and behold the works of the LORD : what destruction he hath brought upon the earth.

9 He maketh wars to cease in all the world : he breaketh the bow, and knappeth the spear in sunder, and burneth the chariots in the fire.

10 Be still then, and know that I am God : I will be exalted among the heathen, and I will be exalted in the earth.

The LORD speaks.

11 The LORD of hosts is with us : the God of Jacob is our refuge.

Evening Prayer

PSALM XLVII. *Omnes gentes, plaudite.*

An anticipation of the universal acknowledgment of the sovereignty of Jehovah. Composed probably in celebration of the overthrow of Sennacherib.

Proper on Ascension Day and on Epiphany [America].

O CLAP your hands together, all ye [a]people : O sing unto God with the voice of [b]melody.

[a]R.V. *peoples.*
[b]*triumph.*

2 For the LORD is high, and to be feared : he is the great King upon all the earth.

3 He shall subdue the [c]people under us : and the nations under our feet.

[c]R.V. *peoples.*

4 He shall choose out an heritage for us : even [d]⌜the worship of Jacob⌝, whom he loved.

God will confirm His people in the land which He has chosen for them, i.e. the earthly pointing forward to the heavenly Canaan.

[d]*the excellency of Jacob*, i.e. Canaan, the land in which Israel glories, his 'heritage.'

5 God is gone up with a [a]⌜merry noise⌝ : and the LORD with the sound of the trump.

[a] *shout.* God returns in triumph to His heavenly throne after delivering His people from their foes; in Christian eyes a prefiguration of Christ's Ascension after the redemption of the world.

6 O sing praises, sing praises unto our God : O sing praises, sing praises unto our King.

7 For God is the King of all the earth : sing ye praises with understanding.

Cp. 1 Cor. xiv. 15, 'I will sing with the understanding also.'

8 God reigneth over the heathen : God sitteth upon his holy seat.

9 [b]⌜The princes of the people are joined unto the people of the God of Abraham : for God, which is very high exalted, doth defend the earth, as it were with a shield⌝.

[b] R.V. *The princes of the peoples are gathered together to be the people of the God of Abraham: for the shields of the earth belong unto God; he is greatly exalted.* A vision of the world-wide extension of the kingdom of God. 'the shields of the earth' are princes, regarded as the defenders of their people.

PSALM XLVIII. *Magnus Dominus.*

The glorious beauty of Jerusalem, and the discomfiture of its foes by the hand of God. Probably there is a reference to the defeat of Sennacherib.

Proper on Whitsunday—the birthday of the Church, the spiritual Sion—and on Epiphany [America].

GREAT is the LORD, and highly to be praised : in the city of our God, even upon his holy hill.

2 The hill of Sion is a fair place, and the joy of the whole earth : upon the north-side lieth the city of the great King ; God [c]⌜is well known⌝ in her palaces as a sure refuge.

'Is this the city that men called... The joy of the whole earth?' Lam. ii. 15.

'Swear not...by Jerusalem, for it is the city of the great King.' St Matt. v. 34, 35.

[c] R.V. *hath made himself known,* specially by His recent deliverance of the city.

3 For lo, [a]⌜the kings [1]of the earth : are gathered, and gone by together⌝.

[a] R.V. *the kings assembled themselves, they passed by together.* 'the kings' = the petty princes dependent on Sennacherib. 'passed by' = marched along in battle array.

4—6. Description of the panic, flight and ruin of the enemy.

4 [b]⌜They marvelled to see such things : they were astonished, and suddenly cast down⌝.

[b] R.V. *They saw it* (Sion), *then were they amazed; they were dismayed, they hasted away.*

5 Fear came there upon them, and sorrow : as upon a woman in her travail.

6 Thou [c]⌜shalt break the ships of the sea⌝ : through the east-wind.

[c] *breakest the ships of Tarshish*, i.e. ships of largest size such as those that traded with Tartessus in Spain. The same almighty power which wrecks these ships has overthrown the hostile army.

7 Like as we have heard, so have we seen in the city of the LORD of hosts, in the city of our God : God upholdeth the same for ever.

The report of God's marvellous providence in the past has been confirmed by our own experience.

8 We [d]⌜wait for⌝ thy loving-kindness, O God : in the midst of thy temple.

[d] R.V. *have thought on.*

Whither we went to offer our thanksgivings.

9 O God, according to thy Name, so is thy praise unto the world's end : thy right hand is full of righteousness.

10 Let the mount Sion rejoice, and the [e]daughter of Judah be glad : because of thy judgements.

[e] '*daughters* of Judah' = the towns and villages of Judah; see Numb. xxi. 25 mg.; Josh. xv. 45 mg.

11, 12. The siege being raised, the citizens are free to go forth and convince themselves that the walls and buildings of Jerusalem are unscathed.

11 Walk about Sion, and go round about her : and tell the towers thereof.

'tell' = count.

12 Mark well her bulwarks, [f]⌜set up her houses⌝ : that ye may tell them that come after.

[f] *consider her palaces.*

i.e. may bear witness to posterity of the deliverance which God has wrought.

13 For this God is our God for ever and ever : he shall be our guide unto death.

[1] 'of the earth' is not in A.R.V. It is added in P.B.V. from Vulg.

PSALM XLIX. *Audite hæc, omnes.*

The transient prosperity of the wicked and the eternal blessedness of the righteous.

Special in Form of Consecration of a Churchyard [Ireland].

O HEAR ye this, all ye [a]people : ponder it with your ears, all ye that dwell in the world;

[a]R.V. *peoples.*

2 High and low, rich and poor : one with another.

3 My mouth shall speak of wisdom : and my heart shall muse of understanding.

4 I will incline mine ear to [b]⌜the parable⌝ : and [c]⌜shew my dark speech⌝ upon the harp.

[b]*a parable*, i.e. a poem conveying instruction; cp. Ps. lxxviii. 2.

[c]*open my dark saying.*

The Psalmist likens himself to a minstrel bending his ear over the harp until the full tide of inspiration comes to him.

5 Wherefore should I fear in the days of wickedness : and when [d]⌜the wickedness of my heels⌝ compasseth me round about?

[d]R.V. *iniquity at my heels.* Iniquity is compared to a serpent in the path ready to strike.

6 There be some that put their trust in their goods : and boast themselves in the multitude of their riches.

7 But no man may deliver his brother : nor [e]⌜make agreement unto God for him⌝;

Man, however wealthy, is impotent to deliver a fellow-man from death when God demands his life.

[e]*give to God a ransom for him.*

8 [f]⌜For it cost more to redeem their souls : so that he must let that alone for ever⌝;

[f]R.V. (*For the redemption of their soul* [i.e. life] *is costly* [i.e. too costly], *and must be let alone for ever:*)

9 [g]⌜Yea, though he live long : and see not the grave⌝.

[g]R.V. *That he should still live alway, that he should not see corruption.* N.B. *v.* 8 is parenthetical, and *v.* 9 is in close connection with *v.* 7.

10 For he seeth that wise men also die, and perish together : as well as the ignorant and foolish, and leave their riches for other.

However prudently they use their riches.

'other' = others.

11 And yet they think that their houses shall continue for ever : and that their dwelling-places shall endure from one generation to another; and call the lands after their own names.

As if they expected to enjoy them for ever.

12 [a]⌜Nevertheless, man will not abide in honour⌝ : seeing he may be compared unto the beasts that perish ; this is the way of them.

[a] R.V. *But man abideth not in honour*, i.e. his splendour however great terminates in the grave. 'abideth' is the emphatic word.

13 This is their foolishness : and their posterity praise their saying.

Their maxims find favour with subsequent generations.

14 [b]⌜They lie in the hell like sheep, death gnaweth upon them⌝, and the righteous shall have domination over them in the morning : their beauty [c]⌜shall consume in the sepulchre out of their dwelling⌝.

[b] R.V. *They are appointed as a flock for Sheol; Death shall be their shepherd.* The fate which awaits these rich fools. Sheol and Death, personified, will tend and rule them.

'the morning' of deliverance which succeeds the night of suffering ; see Ps. xxx. 5. From the Christian point of view the Resurrection morning.

[c] R.V. *shall be for Sheol to consume, that there be no habitation for it.*

15 But God [d]⌜hath delivered my soul from the place of hell⌝ : for he shall receive me.

[d] R.V. *will redeem my soul from the power of Sheol.* The Psalmist's confident hope of immortal life with God.

'receive' is the same word used in Gen. v. 24 of Enoch, 'he was not; for God *took* him'; see Ps. lxxiii. 23.

16 Be not thou afraid, though one be made rich : or if the glory of his house be increased;

17 For he shall carry nothing away with him when he dieth : neither shall his pomp follow him.

18 [e]For while he lived, he counted himself an happy man : (and so long as thou doest well unto thyself, men will speak good of thee,)

[e] *Though.*

19 He shall follow the generation of his fathers : and shall never see [a]light.

20 Man [b]⌜being in honour hath no understanding : but⌝ is compared unto the beasts that perish.

[a]R.V. *the light.*

[b]*that is in honour, and understandeth not.*

THE TENTH DAY

Morning Prayer

PSALM L. *Deus deorum.*

God sits in judgement upon His people and declares the nature of the service they should render to Him.

Proper on Advent Sunday [America].

THE LORD, even the most mighty God, hath spoken : and called the world, from the rising up of the sun, unto the going down thereof.

'called the world,' to witness His judgement.

2 [c]⌜Out of Sion hath God appeared : in perfect beauty⌝.

[c]R.V. *Out of Zion, the perfection of beauty, God hath shined forth.* 'Is this the city that men called The perfection of beauty.' Lam. ii. 15.

3 Our God shall come, and shall not keep silence : there shall go before him a consuming fire, and a mighty tempest shall be stirred up round about him.

4 He shall call the heaven from above : and the earth, that he may judge his people.

Heaven as well as earth (*v.* 1) is summoned as witness.

5 Gather my saints together unto me : those that have made a covenant with me with sacrifice.

'saints,' i.e. favoured ones (see Ps. iv. 3), here = the whole congregation of Israel, the covenanted nation (as described in next clause).

6 And the heaven shall declare his righteousness : for God is Judge himself.

6. Parenthetical. The heaven, says the Psalmist, as witness, will vouch the justice of God's sentence.

7 Hear, O my people, and I will speak : I myself will testify against thee, O Israel ; for I am God, even thy God.

The judgement opens.

8 I will not reprove thee because of thy sacrifices, [a]⌜or for thy burnt-offerings : because they were not alway before me⌝.

8—15. Condemnation pronounced against formalists.

[a] R.V. *and thy burnt offerings are continually before me.*

9 I will take no bullock out of thine house : nor he-goat out of thy folds.

10 For all the beasts of the forest are mine : and so are the cattle upon a thousand hills.

11 I know all the fowls upon the mountains : and the wild beasts of the field are in my sight.

12 If I be hungry, I will not tell thee : for the whole world is mine, and all that is therein.

13 Thinkest thou that I will eat bulls' flesh : and drink the blood of goats?

14 Offer unto God [b]thanksgiving : and pay thy vows unto the most Highest;

[b] R.V. *the sacrifice of thanksgiving.* Here a spiritual in contrast with a material sacrifice.

15 And call upon me in the time of trouble : so will I [c]hear thee, and thou shalt praise me.

[c] *deliver.*

16 But unto the ungodly said God : Why dost thou preach my laws, and takest my covenant in thy mouth;

16—22. Condemnation pronounced against hypocrites.

17 Whereas thou hatest [d]⌜to be reformed⌝ : and hast cast my words behind thee?

[d] *instruction.*

18 When thou sawest a thief, thou consentedst unto him : and hast been partaker with the adulterers.

19 Thou hast let thy mouth speak wickedness : and with thy tongue thou hast set forth deceit.

20 Thou satest, and spakest against thy brother : yea, and hast slandered thine own mother's son.

'Thou satest' in the company of other slanderers; cp. Ps. i. 1.

21 These things hast thou done, and I held my tongue, and thou thoughtest [1]wickedly, that I am even such a one as thyself : but I will reprove thee, and set before thee the things that thou hast done.

God's non-interference misunderstood as betokening acquiescence in sin.

22 O consider this, ye that forget God : lest I [a]⌜pluck you away⌝, and there be none to deliver you.

[a] *tear you in pieces.*

23 Whoso offereth [b]⌜me thanks and praise, he⌝ honoureth me : and to him that ordereth his conversation right will I shew the salvation of God.

[b] R.V. *the sacrifice of thanksgiving*; see *v.* 14.

Summary of the teaching of *vv.* 8—15.

Summary of the teaching of *vv.* 16—22.

'conversation' = manner of life.

PSALM LI. *Miserere mei, Deus.*

'A Psalm of David' (Title). David's expression of repentance, and prayer for pardon after his great sin.

The fourth of the Penitential Psalms.

Proper on Ash Wednesday (in Commination Service).

[2] HAVE mercy upon me, O God, after thy great goodness : according to the multitude of thy mercies [c]⌜do away⌝ mine [d]offences.

[c] *blot out.*
[d] *transgressions.*

2 Wash me throughly from [e]⌜my wickedness⌝ : and cleanse me from my sin.

[e] *mine iniquity.*

3 For I acknowledge my [f]faults : and my sin is ever before me.

[f] *transgressions.*

[1] Not in A.R.V., added in P.B.V. from Vulg.

[2] 1, 2. In the original three words are here used, as in Ps. xxxii. 1, 2, to express 'misdoing,' meaning: 1. Breaking loose from God (transgressions); 2. Perversion of soul (iniquity); 3. Falling short of the mark (sin). Also the pardon of sin is described under two figures: 1. 'Blot out,' as from a book of remembrance; 2. 'Wash' and 'cleanse' from impurity.

4 Against thee only have I sinned, and done [a]⌜this evil⌝ in thy sight : [b]⌜that thou mightest be justified in thy saying, and clear when thou art judged⌝.

'Against thee only.' The aspect of his deed as a grievous wrong done to his neighbour is superseded in David's mind by the contemplation of it as a sin against God.

[a] R.V. *that which is evil.*

[b] R.V. *that thou mayest be justified when thou speakest* (i.e. givest sentence) *and be clear when thou judgest.* God's righteousness was vindicated by His condemnation of David's sin.

This verse is quoted in Rom. iii. 4 according to the Sept. P.B.V. 'when thou art judged,' is from Vulg.

5 Behold, I was shapen in wickedness : and in sin hath my mother conceived me.

6 But lo, thou requirest truth in the inward parts : and shalt make me to understand wisdom [c]secretly.

[c] *in the hidden part.*

7 Thou shalt purge me with hyssop, and I shall be clean : thou shalt wash me, and I shall be whiter than snow.

Spiritual cleansing is expressed in the terms of the outward purifications required in the case of the leper and the unclean. Lev. xiv. 4 ff.; Numb. xix. 17 ff.

8 Thou shalt make me hear of joy and gladness : that the bones which thou hast broken may rejoice.

9 Turn thy face from my sins : and [d]put out all my misdeeds.

[d] *blot.*

10 [e]Make me a clean heart, O God : and renew a [f]right spirit within me.

[e] *Create in.*

'O God, make clean our hearts within us'; versicle at Matins and Evensong.

[f] R.V. mg. *steadfast.*

11 Cast me not away from thy presence : and take not thy holy Spirit from me.

'And take not thy Holy Spirit from us'; response at Matins and Evensong.

'Holy Spirit,' in O.T. only here and in Is. lxiii. 10, 11.

12 [g]⌜O give me the comfort of thy help again : and stablish me with thy free Spirit⌝.

[g] R.V. *Restore unto me the joy of thy salvation: and uphold me with a free* (mg. *willing*) *spirit*, i.e. a spirit willing to be led by God.

13 Then shall I teach thy ways unto the wicked : and sinners shall be converted unto thee.

See Ps. xxxii. for the carrying out of this resolve.

14 Deliver me from blood-guiltiness, O God, thou that art the God of my [a]health : and my tongue shall sing of thy righteousness.

[a]*salvation.* P.B.V. 'health' = welfare in general.

'thy righteousness' which is displayed as much in pardoning the penitent, as in condemning the wicked. 'If we confess our sins he is *faithful and righteous* to forgive us our sins.' 1 St John i. 9.

15 [b]⌜Thou shalt open my lips, O Lord⌝ : and my mouth shall shew thy praise.

[b]*O Lord, open thou my lips.*

Hence the versicle and response at beginning of Matins and Evensong.

16 For thou desirest no sacrifice, else would I give it thee : but thou delightest not in burnt-offerings.

17 The sacrifice of God is a [c]troubled spirit : a broken and contrite heart, O God, shalt thou not despise.

[c]*broken.* P.B.V. from Vulg.

18 O be favourable and gracious unto Sion : build thou the walls of Jerusalem.

18, 19. Verses probably added to the Psalm during the exile.

19 Then shalt thou be pleased with the [d]sacrifice of righteousness, with the burnt-offerings and oblations : then shall they offer young bullocks upon thine altar.

[d]*sacrifices* of righteousness are those offered in purity of heart. Ps. iv. 5.

PSALM LII. *Quid gloriaris?*

A bold denunciation of some man of wealth and power, who chiefly by unscrupulous slander has become a centre of mischief.

WHY boastest thou thyself, thou tyrant : that thou canst do mischief;

2 Whereas the goodness of God : endureth yet daily?

The tyrant acts in contempt of this great fact.

3 Thy tongue imagineth wickedness : and with lies thou cuttest like a sharp razor.

4 Thou hast loved unrighteousness more than goodness : and [e]⌜to talk of lies more than righteousness⌝.

[e]*lying rather than to speak righteousness.*

5 Thou hast loved to speak all words that may do hurt : O thou false tongue.

6 Therefore shall God destroy thee for ever : he shall take thee, and pluck thee out of thy dwelling, and root thee out of the land of the living.

7 The righteous also shall see this, and fear : and shall laugh him to scorn ;

They shall 'fear,' being awe-struck at the manifestation of the righteous judgement of God.

8 Lo, this is the man that took not God for his strength : but trusted unto the multitude of his riches, and strengthened himself in his wickedness.

The expression of the scorn of the righteous.

9 As for me, I am like a green olive-tree in the house of God : my trust is in the tender mercy of God for ever and ever.

'As for me,' compared with the rich tyrant whose doom is likened to an uprooted tree, *v.* 6.

10 I will always give thanks unto thee for that thou hast done : and I will [a]⌜hope in thy Name, for thy saints like it well⌝.

[a] R.V. *wait on thy name, for it is good, in the presence of thy saints.*

Evening Prayer

PSALM LIII. *Dixit insipiens.*

The depravity of the heathen world and its oppression of Israel. This is another version of Ps. xiv., which has been remodelled so as to refer to some historical event—probably the destruction of the host of Sennacherib.

According to the usage of this Book, 'God' is substituted for 'the LORD' (Jehovah) where that name occurs in Ps. xiv.

THE foolish body hath said in his heart : There is no God.

Folly in Holy Scripture is attributed to those who have forsaken the fear of God ; see Ps. lxxiv. 19, 23 ; 2 Sam. xiii. 12, 13.

2 Corrupt are they, and become abominable in their wickedness : there is none that doeth good.

3 God looked down from heaven upon the children of men : to see if there were any that would understand, and seek after God.

So at Babel, 'The LORD came down to see,' Gen. xi. 5; and before the destruction of Sodom, 'The LORD said...I will go down now and see,' Gen. xviii. 20, 21.

4 But they are all gone out of the way, they are altogether become abominable : there is also none that doeth good, no not one.

5 Are not they without understanding that work wickedness : eating up my people as if they would eat bread? they have not called upon God.

God speaks.
'they' = the foreign oppressors of Israel ('my people').

6 [1]They were afraid where no fear was : for God hath [a]broken the bones of him that besieged thee; thou hast put them to confusion, because God hath despised them.

Where there was no apprehension of danger. Allusion probably to the sudden disaster which befel Sennacherib.
[a]*scattered* round the walls of the city.

7 O that the salvation were given unto Israel out of Sion : [b]⌜O that the Lord would deliver his people out of captivity⌝!

'Sion,' where God dwells among men; see Ps. iii. 4.
[b]*when God bringeth back the captivity of his people.* To 'bring back the captivity' is probably metaphorical for to restore the prosperity, as in Job xlii. 10 and elsewhere.

8 Then [c]should Jacob rejoice : and Israel [c]should be right glad.

[c]*shall.*

PSALM LIV. *Deus, in nomine.*

The Psalmist, exposed to great danger from bitter foes, commends himself to the Divine protection.

The title assigns the Psalm to David when the Ziphites betrayed him to Saul.

Proper on Good Friday.

SAVE me, O God, for thy Name's sake : and [d]avenge me in thy strength.

[d]*judge*, i.e. vindicate.

[1] This verse was altered to suit the later occurrence. The parallel passage in Ps. xiv. (*vv.* 5, 6) reads in R.V., 'There were they in great fear: for God is in the generation of the righteous. Ye put to shame the counsel of the poor, because (mg. but) the LORD is his refuge.'

2 Hear my prayer, O God : and hearken unto the words of my mouth.

3 For strangers are risen up against me : and [a]tyrants, which have not God before their eyes, seek after my soul.

The Ziphites, if they are meant, were of the tribe of Judah, but they behaved to David as though they were foreign enemies.

[a] R.V. *violent men.*

4 Behold, God is my helper : the Lord is [b]⌜with them that uphold my soul⌝.

[b] R.V. *of them that uphold my soul*=my true upholder, according to a Hebrew idiom ; see Ps. cxviii. 7 ; Judg. xi. 35.

5 He shall [c]⌜reward evil⌝ unto mine enemies : destroy thou them in thy truth.

[c] R.V. *requite the evil.*

6 [d]⌜An offering of a free heart will I give thee⌝, and praise thy Name, O LORD : because it is so comfortable.

[d] R.V. *With a freewill offering will I sacrifice unto thee.*

7 For he hath delivered me out of all my trouble : and mine eye hath seen his desire upon mine enemies.

The Psalmist, in the confidence of faith, regards his deliverance as already accomplished.

PSALM LV. *Exaudi, Deus.*

The prayer of an inhabitant of Jerusalem persecuted by active enemies, one of whom was once a trusted friend.

HEAR my prayer, O God : and hide not thyself from my petition.

2 Take heed unto me, and hear me : [e]⌜how I mourn in my prayer, and am vexed⌝.

[e] R.V. *I am restless in my complaint, and moan.*

3 The enemy crieth so, and the ungodly cometh on so fast : for they are minded to do me some mischief; so maliciously are they set against me.

4 My heart is disquieted within me : and the fear of death is fallen upon me.

5 Fearfulness and trembling are come upon me : and an horrible dread hath overwhelmed me.

6 And I said, O that I had wings like a dove : for then would I flee away, and be at rest.

7 Lo, then would I get me away far off : and [a]remain in the wilderness.

[a]R.V. *lodge.*

8 I would make haste to escape : because of the stormy wind and tempest.

9 Destroy their tongues, O Lord, and divide them : for I have spied [b]unrighteousness and strife in the city.

Deal with them as with the builders of Babel. Gen. x. 25, xi. 9.

[b]*violence.*

10 Day and night they go about within the walls thereof : [c]mischief also and [d]sorrow are in the midst of it.

'they' may mean 'the enemy' and 'the ungodly' (*v.* 3); but some suppose 'they' to be 'violence' and 'strife' (*v.* 9) personified; and interpret in the same way 'iniquity,' 'mischief,' 'wickedness,' 'deceit' and 'guile' in this and next verse.

[c]R.V. *iniquity.*

[d]R.V. *mischief.*

11 Wickedness is therein : deceit and guile go not out of [e]their streets.

[e]*her.*

12 For it is not an open enemy, that hath done me this dishonour : for then I could have borne it.

13 Neither was it mine adversary, that did magnify himself against me : for then [1]peradventure I would have hid myself from him.

14 But it was even thou, [f]⌜my companion : my guide⌝, and mine own familiar friend.

[f]R.V. *a man mine equal, my companion.*

15 We took sweet counsel together : and walked in the house of God [g]⌜as friends⌝.

[g]R.V. *with the throng.* P.B.V. follows Vulg.

16 Let death come hastily upon them, and let them go down [h]⌜quick into hell⌝ : for wickedness is in their dwellings, and among them.

[h]R.V. *alive into the pit* (mg. *Sheol*). As Korah and his company perished. Numb. xvi. 33.

'quick' in P.B.V. and A.V. = alive.

[1] Not in A.R.V., added in P.B.V. from Vulg.

17 As for me, I will call upon God : and the LORD shall save me.

18 In the evening, and morning, and at noon-day will I [a]⌜pray, and that instantly⌝ : and he shall hear my voice.

i.e. all day long. The Hebrew day began at sunset, hence evening is mentioned first.

[a]R.V. *complain and moan*; cp. *v.* 2.

P.B.V. 'instantly' = urgently.

19 It is he that hath delivered my soul in peace from the battle that was against me : for there were many [b]⌜with me⌝.

'hath delivered.' The Psalmist, with the assurance of faith, regards his deliverance as already effected.

[b]R.V. *that strove with me.*

20 Yea, even God, that endureth for ever, shall hear me, and bring them down : [c]⌜for they will not turn, nor fear God⌝.

[c]R.V. *the men who have no changes, and who fear not God.* 'no changes,' i.e. of fortune. Their prosperity has always been unruffled, and therefore they think themselves independent of God.

P.B.V. 'turn,' i.e. from sin.

21 He laid his hands upon such as be at peace with him : and he brake his covenant.

21, 22. The perfidious friend (*v.* 14) again singled out.

'his covenant,' of friendship.

22 The words of his mouth were softer than butter, having war in his heart : his words were smoother than oil, and yet be they [d]very swords.

[d]*drawn.*

23 O cast thy burden upon the LORD, and he shall [e]nourish thee : and shall not suffer the righteous to fall for ever.

Quoted 1 St Pet. v. 7 after Sept., 'casting all your anxiety upon him.'

[e]*sustain.* P.B.V. from Vulg.

24 And as for them : thou, O God, shalt bring them into the pit of destruction.

25 The blood-thirsty and deceitful men shall not live out half their days : nevertheless, my trust shall be in thee, [1]⌜O LORD⌝.

[1] Not in A.R.V., added in P.B.V. from Vulg.

THE ELEVENTH DAY

Morning Prayer

PSALM LVI. *Miserere mei, Deus.*

'A Psalm of David: when the Philistines took him in Gath' (Title). The Psalmist hard pressed by foes, is comforted by the assurance that God is with him.

BE merciful unto me, O God, for man goeth about to devour me : he is [a]daily fighting, and troubling me.

'goeth about' = attempts.
[a]R.V. *all the day long.*

2 Mine enemies are [b]daily in hand to swallow me up : for they be many that fight against me, [c]⌜O thou most Highest⌝.

[b]R.V. *all the day long.*
'are in hand,' i.e. are exerting themselves.
[c]R.V. *proudly.*

3 Nevertheless, though I am sometime afraid : yet put I my trust in thee.

4 I will praise God, because of his word : I have put my trust in God, and will not fear [d]⌜what flesh can do unto me⌝.

'his word' of promise.
[d]R.V. *what can flesh do unto me?*

5 [e]⌜They daily mistake⌝ my words : all that they imagine is to do me evil.

[e]R.V. *All the day long they wrest.*

6 [f]⌜They hold all together, and keep themselves close⌝ : and mark my steps, [g]when they lay wait for my soul.

[f]*They gather themselves together, they hide themselves.* P.B.V. has the same meaning.
[g]R.V. *even as.*

7 Shall they escape for their wickedness : [h]⌜thou, O God, in thy displeasure shalt cast them down⌝.

[h]R.V. *in anger cast down the peoples, O God.* The Psalmist looks beyond his enemies, and asks for the extirpation of the world's ungodliness.

8 Thou tellest my flittings ; put my tears into thy bottle : [i]⌜are not these things noted in thy book⌝?

'tellest' = countest. 'flittings' = *wanderings.*
i.e. treasure them as drops of precious wine.
[i]*are they* (my tears) *not in thy book,* i.e. each registered there?

9 Whensoever I call upon thee, then shall mine enemies be put to flight : this I know ; for God is on my side.

10 In God's word will I rejoice : in the LORD's word will I comfort me.

11 Yea, in God have I put my trust : I will not be afraid [a]⌜what man can do unto me⌝.

[a] R.V. *what can man do unto me?* Words repeated Ps. cxviii. 6.

12 Unto thee, O God, will I pay my vows : unto thee will I [b]⌜give thanks⌝.

[b] R.V. *render thank offerings.*

13 For thou hast delivered my soul from death, and my feet from falling : that I may walk before God in the light of the living.

Deliverance is regarded as already effected.

This verse occurs again Ps. cxvi. 8, 9.

PSALM LVII. *Miserere mei, Deus.*

'A Psalm of David: when he fled from Saul, in the cave' (Title). An expression of faith in God in presence of malignant enemies.

Proper on Easter Day, the refrain (vv. 6, 12) being interpreted of Christ's exaltation, and v. 9 of His resurrection.

BE merciful unto me, O God, be merciful unto me, for my soul [c]trusteth in thee : and under the shadow of thy wings shall be my refuge, until this tyranny be over-past.

[c] R.V. *taketh refuge.*

2 I will call unto the most high God : [d]⌜even unto the God that shall perform the cause which I have in hand⌝.

[d] *unto God that performeth all things for me.*

3 He shall send from heaven : and save me [e]⌜from the reproof of him that would eat me up⌝.

[e] R.V. *when he that would swallow me up reproacheth*, taunting me with the absence of succour from God.

4 God shall send forth his mercy and truth : my soul is among lions.

'lions' = my fierce opponents.

5 And I lie even among the children of men, that are set on fire : whose teeth are spears and arrows, and their tongue a sharp sword.

6 Set up thyself, O God, above the heavens : and thy glory above all the earth.

The manifestation of God's glory would involve the downfall of the wicked—the Psalmist's foes among them—and the deliverance of those who trust in Him.

7 They have laid a net for my feet, and pressed down my soul : they have digged a pit before me, and are fallen into the midst of it themselves.

8 My heart is fixed, O God, my heart is fixed : I will sing, and give praise.

'fixed'=steadfast in faith.

9 Awake up, my glory; awake, lute and harp : [a]⌜I myself will awake right early⌝.

'glory,' poetical for 'soul' as being man's noblest part. Ps. vii. 5, xvi. 10, xxx. 13.

[a] R.V. mg. *I will awake the dawn*, i.e. my song shall arouse the morning from its slumber.

10 I will give thanks unto thee, O Lord, among the [b]people : and I will sing unto thee among the nations.

[b] R.V. *peoples*.

11 For the greatness of thy mercy reacheth unto the heavens : and thy truth unto the clouds.

12 Set up thyself, O God, above the heavens : and thy glory above all the earth.

PSALM LVIII. *Si vere utique.*

A denunciation of unrighteous judges.

[c]⌜ARE your minds set upon righteousness, O ye congregation⌝ : and do ye judge the thing that is right, O ye sons of men?

[c] R.V. *Do ye indeed in silence speak righteousness*, i.e. Do you imagine that you give sentence on the side of righteousness when, instead of denouncing wickedness, you keep silence? A sarcastic address to certain judges, called, 'sons of men,' in next clause.

2 [a]⌜Yea, ye imagine mischief in your heart upon the earth : and your hands deal with wickedness⌝.

[a] R.V. *Yea, in heart ye work wickedness; ye weigh out the violence of your hands in the earth.* Ye dispense violence instead of justice.

'The ungodly' = the unjust judges and those whom they favour.

3 The ungodly are [b]froward, even from their mother's womb : as soon as they are born, they go astray, and speak lies.

[b] *estranged.* The word found here in the Sept. is used by St Paul in Eph. iv. 18 'alienated from the life of God,' and in Col. i. 21.

4 They are as venomous as the poison of a serpent : even like the deaf adder that stoppeth her ears;

5 Which refuseth to hear the voice of the charmer : charm he never so wisely.

4, 5. They are obstinate, as well as wicked, for they shut their ears to good advisers.

6 Break their teeth, O God, in their mouths; smite the jaw-bones of the lions, O LORD : let them fall away like water that runneth apace; [c]⌜and when they shoot their arrows let them be rooted out⌝.

[c] R.V. *when he* (one of these wicked men) *aimeth his arrows, let them* (the arrows) *be as though they were cut off,* i.e. broken and rendered harmless.

7 Let them consume away like a snail, and be like the untimely fruit of a woman : [d]⌜and let them not see the sun⌝.

As a snail dries up in time of drought.

[d] R.V. *that hath not seen the sun.*

8 [e]⌜Or ever your pots be made hot with thorns : so let indignation vex him, even as a thing that is raw⌝.

[e] R.V. *Before your pots can feel the thorns, he shall take them away with a whirlwind, the green and the burning alike.*

The illustration is suggested by the preparation by travellers of a meal in the desert. Before the cooking-pot has been heated by the fire just lit, a whirlwind suddenly arising sweeps away the thorns of which the fuel is composed. Thus, almost as soon as they are devised, the schemes of the wicked will be swept away by the wrath of God.

9 The righteous shall rejoice when he seeth the vengeance : he shall wash his footsteps in the blood of the ungodly.

Metaphor founded on the savagery of ancient warfare.

10 So that a man shall say, Verily there is a reward for the righteous : doubtless there is a God that judgeth the earth.

Evening Prayer

PSALM LIX. *Eripe me de inimicis.*

'A Psalm of David: when Saul sent and they watched the house to kill him' (Title).

A prayer that God will frustrate the machinations of hostile men.

DELIVER me from mine enemies, O [a]God : defend me from them that rise up against me.

[a] *my God.*

2 O deliver me from the wicked doers : and save me from the blood-thirsty men.

3 For lo, they lie waiting for my soul : the mighty men are gathered against me, without any offence or fault of me, O LORD.

4 They run and prepare themselves without my fault : arise thou therefore to help me, and behold.

5 Stand up, O LORD God of hosts, thou God of Israel, to visit all the heathen : and be not merciful unto them that offend of malicious wickedness.

'all the heathen.' The Psalmist prays that God's judgement upon evil-doers may not only reach his personal enemies, but be universal in its range.

6 They go to and fro in the evening : they grin like a dog, and run about through the city.

They are like the savage dogs of eastern cities which prowl about in the evening looking for food.

'grin' = snarl.

7 Behold, they [b]speak with their mouth, and swords are in their lips : [c]⌜for who doth hear⌝?

[b] *belch out.*

[c] *for who, say they, doth hear?* They imagine that God pays no heed.

8 But thou, O LORD, shalt have them in derision : and thou shalt laugh all the heathen to scorn.

'all the heathen'; see *v.* 5.

9 [d]⌜My strength will I ascribe unto thee : for thou art the God of my refuge⌝.

[d] R.V. *O my strength, I will wait upon thee: for God is my high tower.*

10 [a]⌜God sheweth me his goodness plenteously⌝: and God shall let me see my desire upon mine enemies.

[a] *The God of my mercy shall prevent me.* 'prevent' = go before. The theological term 'preventing grace' is derived from this passage in the Vulg.

11 Slay them not, lest my people forget it : [b]⌜but scatter them abroad among the people⌝, and put them down, O Lord, our [c]defence.

[b] *scatter them by thy power.*

[c] *shield.*

12 For the sin of their mouth, and for the words of their lips, they shall be taken in their pride : [d]⌜and why? their preaching is of cursing and lies⌝.

[d] *and for cursing and lying which they speak.*

13 Consume them in thy wrath, consume them, that they may perish : and know that it is God that ruleth in Jacob, and unto the ends of the world.

14 And in the evening they will return : grin like a dog, and will go about the city.

'grin' = snarl.

15 They will run here and there for meat : and [e]grudge if they be not satisfied.

The Psalmist is the prey for which they seek.

[e] R.V. *tarry all night.* P.B.V. and A.V. 'grudge' (= murmur) follows Vulg.

16 As for me, I will sing of thy power, and will praise thy mercy betimes in the morning : for thou hast been my defence and refuge in the day of my trouble.

'in the morning.' Although his enemies 'tarry all night' the Psalmist is confident that in the morning he will be able to sing of the power of God which has kept him safe.

17 Unto thee, O my strength, will I sing : for thou, O God, art my [f]refuge, and my merciful God.

[f] R.V. *high tower.*

PSALM LX. *Deus, repulisti nos.*

'[1] Michtam of David: when he strove with Aram-naharaim and with Aram-zobah, and Joab returned, and smote of Edom in the Valley of Salt twelve thousand' (Title); see 2 Sam. viii. 5, 6, 13, 14. The Psalm was probably written after the defeat of the Syrians (Aram), and before the Edomites were crushed by Joab.

God will not forsake His people but will lead them to victory.

1—3. These opening verses allude to some otherwise unrecorded disaster. It was probably inflicted by the Edomites while David was engaged in the Syrian war.

O GOD, thou hast [a]⌜cast us out, and scattered us abroad : thou hast also been displeased; O turn thee unto us again⌝.

[a]R.V. *cast us off, thou hast broken us down; thou hast been angry; O restore us again.*

2 Thou hast [b]⌜moved the land, and divided it : heal the sores thereof⌝, for it shaketh.

[b]R.V. *made the land to tremble; thou hast rent it: heal the breaches thereof.* The metaphor is taken from the effect of an earthquake on land and buildings.

3 Thou hast shewed thy people heavy things : thou hast [c]⌜given us a drink of deadly wine⌝.

[c]R.V. *made us to drink the wine of staggering.*

4 Thou hast given a [d]token for such as fear thee : [e]⌜that they may triumph because of the truth⌝.

[d]*banner.*

[e]*that it may be displayed because* (i.e. on behalf) *of the truth.*

5 [f]⌜Therefore were thy beloved delivered⌝ : [g]⌜help me⌝ with thy right hand, and hear me.

[f]*That thy beloved* (i.e. Israel) *may be delivered.*

[g]*save.*

6 God hath spoken in his holiness; I will rejoice, and divide Sichem : and mete out the valley of Succoth.

6—8. 'I will rejoice &c.' The words of God: as a victorious warrior He claims afresh the whole land of Canaan. The distribution of territory ('divide,' 'mete out,') is the fullest proof of possession. Josh. xviii. 10. Of the localities mentioned, [2]Shechem, Ephraim and Judah represent the country west of Jordan, [2]Succoth and Gilead (inhabited by the half-tribe of Manasseh) the country east of Jordan.

[1] The meaning of 'Michtam' is uncertain. A.V. mg. following the Rabbinical commentators interprets it 'A golden Psalm.'

[2] Shechem and Succoth are probably named because of their association with the history of Jacob, Gen. xxxiii. 17, 18.

7 Gilead is mine, and Manasses is mine : Ephraim also is the [a]strength of my head; Judah is my [b]law-giver;

[a]R.V. *defence.* Ephraim was the most powerful tribe.
[b]R.V. *sceptre.* Judah was the royal tribe.

8 Moab is my wash-pot; over Edom will I cast out my shoe : Philistia, [c]⌜be thou glad of me⌝.

God will extend His conquests to the neighbouring nations.
'wash-pot'; a contemptuous symbol of subjugation.
'cast out &c.'; an eastern sign of taking forcible possession.
[c]R.V. *shout thou because of me*, i.e. acclaim my victory over thee.

9 Who will lead me into the strong city : who will bring me into Edom?

10 Hast not thou cast us [d]out, O God : [e]⌜wilt not thou, O God, go out⌝ with our hosts?

11 [f]⌜O be thou our help in trouble⌝ : for vain is the help of man.

12 Through God will we do great acts : for it is he that shall tread down our enemies.

9—12. The words of David.
'the strong city,' probably Petra, the capital of Edom.
[d]*off.*
[e]R.V. *and thou goest not forth, O God;* see Ps. xliv. 10.
[f]R.V. *Give us help against the adversary.*

PSALM LXI. *Exaudi, Deus.*

'A Psalm of David' (Title). Probably written towards the close of the rebellion of Absalom when David was looking forward with longing to his restoration to Jerusalem.

Proper on Transfiguration [America].

HEAR my crying, O God : give ear unto my prayer.

2 From the ends of the earth will I call upon thee : when my heart is in heaviness.

'the ends of the earth.' So the land beyond Jordan, the place of his exile, appears to David.

3 [g]⌜O set me up upon the rock that is higher than I⌝ : for thou hast been [h]⌜my hope⌝, and a strong tower for me against the enemy.

[g]R.V. mg. *Lead me to a rock that is too high for me*, i.e. too high for me to reach unaided. The Rock is God Himself.
[h]R.V. *a refuge for me.* David bases his prayer on his experience of former deliverances.

4 I will dwell in thy tabernacle for ever : [a]⌜and my trust shall be under the covering of thy wings⌝.

[a] R.V. *I will take refuge in the covert of thy wings.* An allusion to the Cherubim overshadowing the mercy-seat.

5 For thou, O Lord, hast heard my [b] desires : and hast given an heritage unto those that fear thy Name.

[b] *vows.*

'an heritage' = the land of promise. Those faithful to God and His servant David would be confirmed in possession of the heritage which was theirs.

6 Thou shalt grant the king a long life : that his years may endure throughout all generations.

7 He shall dwell before God for ever : O prepare thy loving mercy and faithfulness, that they may preserve him.

6, 7. David claims the Divine promise of permanence to his dynasty, 2 Sam. vii. 13, 16, eventually fulfilled in the everlasting Kingdom of his Divine Son. St Luke i. 32, 33.

8 So will I alway sing praise unto thy Name : that I may daily perform my vows.

THE TWELFTH DAY

Morning Prayer

PSALM LXII. *Nonne Deo?*

'A Psalm of David' (Title). Perhaps written during Absalom's revolt.

The Psalmist persecuted and slandered by enemies is contented to wait patiently for God's deliverance.

MY soul truly waiteth still upon God : for of him cometh my salvation.

'still' = silently.

2 He verily is my strength and my salvation : he is my defence, so that I shall not greatly fall.

3 [c]⌜How long will ye imagine mischief against every man : ye shall be slain all the sort of you; yea, as a tottering wall shall ye be, and like a broken hedge⌝.

[c] R.V. *How long will ye set upon a man, that ye may slay him, all of you, like a bowing wall, like a tottering fence?*

4 [a]⌜Their device is only how to put him out whom God will exalt⌝: their delight is in lies; they give good words with their mouth, but curse with their heart.

[a] *They only consult to thrust him down from his excellency.*

5 Nevertheless, my soul, wait thou still upon God: for my hope is in him.

'still'=silently.

6 He truly is my strength and my salvation: he is my defence, so that I shall not fall.

7 In God is my health, and my glory: the rock of my might, and in God is my [b]trust.

'health'=well-being.

[b] *refuge.*

8 O put your trust in him alway, ye people: pour out your hearts before him, for God is our [c]hope.

'ye people,' here David's adherents especially.

[c] *refuge.*

9 [d]⌜As for the children of men, they are but vanity: the children of men are deceitful upon the weights⌝, they are [e]altogether lighter than vanity itself.

[d] R.V. *Surely men of low degree are vanity* (mg. *a breath*), *and men of high degree are a lie: in the balances they will go up.*

[e] R.V. *together.*

10 O trust not in wrong and robbery, give not yourselves unto vanity: if riches increase, set not your heart upon them.

11, 12. The Divine voice has revealed to the Psalmist the double truth of the power and love of God.

11 God spake once, and twice I have also heard the same: that power belongeth unto God;

'once and twice'=many times, a Hebrew idiom; see Job xxxiii. 14, xl. 5.

12 And that thou, Lord, art merciful: for thou rewardest every man according to his work.

Quoted and commented on by St Paul in Rom. ii. 6 ff.

PSALM LXIII. *Deus, Deus meus.*

'A Psalm of David, when he was in the wilderness of Judah,' (Title), probably in his flight from Absalom. He declares his sense of communion with God, and longing for His Presence.

The morning Psalm (see *v.* 1) of the early Church.

O GOD, thou art my God: early will I seek thee.

2 My soul thirsteth for thee, my flesh also longeth after thee : in a [a]⌜barren and dry⌝ land where no water is.

The wilderness of Judah, where David is, suggests this description of his spiritual thirst.

[a] R.V. *dry and weary.*

3 [b]⌜Thus have I looked for thee in holiness : that I might behold thy power and glory⌝.

[b] R.V. *So have I looked upon thee in the sanctuary, to see thy power and glory.* 'So,' i.e. with fervour like that to which I have now given expression.

4 For thy loving-kindness is better than the life itself : my lips shall praise thee.

5 As long as I live will I magnify thee on this manner : and lift up my hands in thy Name.

'lift up my hands,' the gesture of prayer. Ps. xxviii. 2; 1 Tim. ii. 8.

6 My soul shall be satisfied, even as it were with marrow and fatness : when my mouth praiseth thee with joyful lips.

7 Have I not remembered thee in my bed : and thought upon thee [c]⌜when I was waking⌝?

[c] *in the night watches.*

8 Because thou hast been my helper : therefore under the shadow of thy wings will I rejoice.

9 My soul hangeth upon thee : thy right hand hath upholden me.

10 [d]⌜These also⌝ that seek the hurt of my soul : they shall go [e]⌜under the earth⌝.

[d] *But those.*

[e] *into the lower parts of the earth.* St Paul's expression in Eph. iv. 9, was probably suggested by this passage and Ps. cxxxix. 14.

11 [f]⌜Let them fall upon the edge of the sword⌝ : that they may be a portion for [g]foxes.

[f] R.V. *They shall be given over to the power of the sword.*

[g] R.V. mg. *jackals.*

12 But the king shall rejoice in God : all they also that swear by him shall [h]⌜be commended⌝ : for the mouth of them that speak lies shall be stopped.

'by him,' i.e. by God.

[h] *glory.*

'them that speak lies.' Absalom's revolt was founded upon misrepresentation; see Ps. iv. 2.

PSALM LXIV. *Exaudi, Deus.*

The Psalmist assailed by the plottings of evil men confidently predicts their overthrow.

HEAR my voice, O God, in my prayer : preserve my life from fear of the enemy.

Hence the petitions, 'that we... may not fear the power of any adversaries,' 2nd Collect Matins ; and, 'that we being defended from the fear of our enemies,' &c., 2nd Collect Evensong.

2 Hide me from the [a]⌜gathering together⌝ of the froward : and from the [b]insurrection of wicked doers ;

[a] *secret counsel.*

[b] R.V. *tumult*, i.e. open attacks.

3 Who have whet their tongue like a sword : and shoot out their arrows, even bitter words ;

4 That they may privily shoot at him that is perfect : suddenly do they [c]hit him, and fear not.

[c] *shoot at.*

5 They encourage themselves in mischief : and commune among themselves how they may lay snares, and say that no man shall see them.

6 They imagine wickedness, and practise it : that they keep secret among themselves, every man in the deep of his heart.

7 But God shall suddenly shoot at them with a swift arrow : that they shall be wounded.

See *vv.* 3, 4. The retribution which overtakes them is described in like terms with their offence.

8 Yea, their own tongues shall make them fall : insomuch that whoso seeth them shall laugh them to scorn.

'their own tongues' with which they have plotted. Their subtle schemes turn against themselves.

9 And all men [d]⌜that see it⌝ shall say, This hath God done : for they shall perceive that it is his work.

[d] R.V. *shall fear ; and they.* 'shall fear' God, unlike the ungodly who 'fear not,' *v.* 4.

10 The righteous shall rejoice in the LORD, and put his trust in him : and all they that are true of heart shall be glad.

Evening Prayer

PSALM LXV. *Te decet hymnus.*

A thanksgiving after some signal deliverance, and in prospect of an abundant harvest.

Proper on Circumcision [America]. Special in Harvest Thanksgiving [Ireland].

THOU, O God, art praised in Sion : and unto thee shall the vow be performed [1]⌜in Jerusalem⌝.

2 Thou that hearest [a]⌜the prayer⌝ : unto thee shall all flesh come.

[a]*prayer.* To hear prayer is an essential part of the character of God.

All nations shall some day approach to God.

3 My misdeeds prevail against me : [b]⌜O be thou merciful unto our sins⌝.

The congregation speaks first as one body ('my'), and then resolves itself into individuals ('our').

[b]*as for our transgressions, thou shalt purge them away.*

4 Blessed is the man, whom thou choosest, and receivest unto thee : he shall dwell in thy court, and shall be satisfied with the pleasures of thy house, even of thy holy temple.

The privilege of the Israelite, inherited by the Christian.

5 Thou shalt shew us wonderful things in thy righteousness, O God of our salvation : thou that art the hope of all the ends of the earth, and of them that [c]⌜remain in the broad sea⌝.

'wonderful things,' i.e. great deeds of deliverance like the rescue from Egypt, to which these and similar words are often applied ; see Ps. cvi. 22 ; Deut. x. 21.

[c]*are afar off upon the sea.*

'Far and wide, though all unknowing,
Pants for thee each mortal breast.'

6 Who in his strength setteth fast the mountains : and is girded about with power.

7 Who stilleth the raging of the sea : and the noise of his waves, and the madness of the [d]people.

'his' = its.

[d]R.V. *peoples.*

[1] Not in A.R.V., added in P.B.V. from Vulg.

8 They also that dwell in the uttermost parts of the earth [a]⌜shall be⌝ afraid at thy tokens : thou that makest the outgoings of the morning and evening to praise thee.

[a] *are.*
'thy tokens' = evidences of Thy power; similarly miracles are called 'signs' in N.T.
'the outgoings' &c., i.e. the extreme east and west whence the morning and evening seem to issue.

9 Thou visitest the earth, and blessest it : thou makest it very plenteous.

10 The river of God is full of water : thou preparest their corn, for so thou providest for the earth.

'The river of God' = the rain.

11 Thou waterest her furrows, thou [b]⌜sendest rain into the little valleys⌝ thereof : thou makest it soft with the drops of rain, and blessest the increase of it.

[b] R.V. *settlest the ridges.* The rain presses down the ridges between the furrows.

12 Thou crownest the year with thy goodness : and thy [c]clouds drop fatness.

[c] *paths* drop fatness (as Thou ridest through the heavens). Ps. xviii. 10; Deut. xxxiii. 26.

13 They shall drop upon the [d]dwellings of the wilderness : and the little hills shall rejoice on every side.

13, 14. A.R.V. make all the verbs present, 'They drop' &c. The Psalmist is describing a scene before his eyes.
[d] *pastures.*
'wilderness' = land uncultivated.

14 The folds shall be full of sheep : the valleys also shall stand so thick with corn, that they shall laugh and sing.

PSALM LXVI. *Jubilate Deo.*

Another thanksgiving to God for national mercies recently vouchsafed by Him, perhaps the repulse of Sennacherib. It takes the form of a summons to the whole earth to sing God's praises.

Special in Prayers to be used at Sea (Thanksgiving after a storm).

O BE joyful in God, all ye lands : sing praises unto the honour of his Name, make his praise to be glorious.

2 Say unto God, O how wonderful art thou in thy works : through the greatness of thy power shall thine enemies [a]⌜be found liars⌝ unto thee.

'works' of deliverance such as the rescue from Egypt ; see Ps. lxv. 5.

[a]R.V. mg. *yield feigned obedience.* Heb. *lie*, i.e. pay the insincere allegiance of the vanquished. Ps. xviii. 45, lxxxi. 16.

3 For all the world shall worship thee : sing of thee, and praise thy Name.

An anticipation of the time when the rule of the God of Israel shall be universally accepted.

4 O come hither, and behold the works of God : how wonderful he is in his doing toward the children of men.

4, 5. God's former deliverances are pledges of future ones.

5 He turned the sea into dry land : so that they went through the [b]water on foot ; there did we rejoice [c]thereof.

The passage of the Red Sea.

[b]R.V. *river* = the Jordan.

[c]*in him.*

6 He ruleth with his power for ever; his eyes behold the [d]⌜people⌝ : [e]⌜and such as will not believe shall not be able to exalt themselves⌝.

[d]*nations.*

[e]*let not the rebellious exalt themselves.*

7 O praise our God, ye [f]people : and make the voice of his praise to be heard ;

[f]R.V. *peoples.*

8 Who holdeth our soul in life : and suffereth not our feet to slip.

9 For thou, O God, hast proved us : thou also hast tried us, like as silver is tried.

9—11. By a succession of metaphors the recent danger and deliverance of Israel are described.

10 Thou broughtest us into the snare : and laidest trouble upon our loins.

11 Thou sufferedst men to ride over our heads : we went through fire and water, and thou broughtest us out into a wealthy place.

'a wealthy place' = a position of prosperity.

12 I will go into thine house with burnt-offerings : and will pay thee my vows, which I promised with my lips, and spake with my mouth, when I was in trouble.

'I will go'; note the change to the singular which continues to the end of the Psalm. The representative of the nation, perhaps king Hezekiah, declares his intention of offering sacrifices of thanksgiving for prayer granted.

13 I will offer unto thee fat burnt-sacrifices, with the incense of rams : I will offer bullocks and goats.

'incense' = here the smoke ascending from the sacrifice.

14 O come hither, and hearken, all ye that fear God : and I will tell you what he hath done for my soul.

'my soul' = me. Hezekiah, if he is the speaker, probably refers to his restoration to health which coincided with the deliverance of his people. Is. xxxviii. 5, 6.

15 I called unto him with my mouth : and gave him praises with my tongue.

16 If I incline unto wickedness with mine heart : the Lord will not hear me.

Cp. Hezekiah's protestation of integrity. Is. xxxviii. 3.

17 But God hath heard me : and considered the voice of my prayer.

18 Praised be God who hath not cast out my prayer : nor turned his mercy from me.

PSALM LXVII. *Deus misereatur.*

A harvest thanksgiving hymn, with prayer for the spread of God's Kingdom through the world.

At Evensong, alternative for Nunc Dimittis. Special in Marriage Service and in Harvest Thanksgiving [Ireland].

GOD be merciful unto us, and bless us : and shew us the light of his countenance, [1]⌜and be merciful unto us⌝;

Words borrowed from the priestly blessing (Numb. vi. 24—26) with God (Elohim) substituted for LORD (Jehovah) according to the usage of this Book.

2 That thy way may be known upon earth : thy saving health among all nations.

'thy way' = 'thy saving health,' i.e. God's purpose of blessing. The manifestation of God's goodness to Israel would lead the other nations to His allegiance.

[1] Not in A.R.V., added in P.B.V. from Vulg.

3 Let the [a]people praise thee, O God : yea, let all the [a]people praise thee.

[a] R.V. *peoples.*

4 O let the nations rejoice and be glad : for thou shalt judge the [b]folk righteously, and govern the nations upon earth.

[b] R.V. *peoples.*

5 Let the [c]people praise thee, O God : let all the [c]people praise thee.

[c] R.V. *peoples.*

6 [d]⌜Then shall the earth bring forth⌝ her increase : and God, even our own God, shall give us his blessing.

[d] R.V. *The earth hath yielded.* An abundant harvest had apparently just been reaped.

7 God shall bless us : and all the ends of the world shall fear him.

THE THIRTEENTH DAY

Morning Prayer

PSALM LXVIII. *Exurgat Deus.*

The new triumphal march of the God of Israel, the Conqueror of the world; probably written in Babylon towards the close of the captivity and in view of the restoration to Canaan.

Proper on Whitsunday, as the Festival of the Birthday of the Church, and of the outpouring of the gifts of the Spirit (see *v.* 18). Special in Office of Institution [America].

LET God arise, and let his enemies be scattered : let them also that hate him flee before him.

The words appointed to be used when the ark set forward in the wilderness, with the substitution of God (Elohim) for LORD (Jehovah). Numb. x. 35; cp. Ps. lxvii. 1.

2 Like as the smoke vanisheth, so shalt thou drive them away : and like as wax melteth at the fire, so let the ungodly perish at the presence of God.

'the ungodly' = the heathen as opponents of God and His people.

3 But let the righteous be glad and rejoice before God : let them also be merry and joyful.

'the righteous' = Israel in its ideal character.

4 O sing unto God, and sing praises unto his Name : [a]⌜magnify him that rideth upon the heavens, as it were upon an horse⌝; praise him in his name JAH, and rejoice before him.

[a] R.V. *cast up a highway for him that rideth through the deserts.* The figure is taken from the elaborate preparations made for the journeys of eastern kings; cp. Is. xl. 3, quoted in N.T. of St John the Baptist, 'Prepare ye in the wilderness the way of the LORD' &c.

'JAH,' contracted form of Jehovah. It appears in *Hallelujah*, i.e. 'Praise ye Jah.'

5 He is a Father of the fatherless, and defendeth the cause of the widows : even God in his holy habitation.

'his holy habitation' = heaven.

6 [b]⌜He is the God that maketh men to be of one mind in an house⌝, and bringeth the prisoners out of captivity : but [c]⌜letteth the runagates continue in scarceness⌝.

[b] R.V. mg. *God maketh the solitary to dwell in a house.* As He rescued Israel when lonely outcasts in Egypt, and gave them a fixed habitation, so will He do again.

[c] R.V. *the rebellious dwell in a parched land*, as happened to the murmurers in the wilderness.

P.B.V. 'runagates' = renegades.

7 O God, when thou wentest forth before the people : when thou wentest through the wilderness,

7, 8. God's triumphal march from Egypt to Canaan; the language is borrowed from the song of Deborah. Judg. v. 4, 5.

8 The earth shook, and the heavens dropped at the presence of God : even as Sinai also was moved at the presence of God, who is the God of Israel.

The earthquake and rain that accompanied the giving of the law. Exod. xix. 18; Ps. lxxvii. 17, 18.

'the God of Israel.' At Sinai God entered into covenant-relation with Israel.

9 Thou, O God, sentest a gracious rain upon thine inheritance : and refreshedst it when it was weary.

'a gracious rain' of blessing.

'thine inheritance' = Canaan, allotted to God's people.

10 Thy congregation [d]⌜shall dwell⌝ therein : for thou, O God, [e]hast of thy goodness [f]prepared for the poor.

[d] R.V. *dwelt.*

[e] R.V. *didst.*

[f] R.V. *prepare.*

11—16. The conquest of Canaan. 'He spake and it was done.' Ps. xxxiii. 9.

11 The Lord gave the word : [a]⌜great was the company of the preachers⌝.

[a] R.V. *the women that publish the tidings* (of victory) *are a great host.* Cp. the action of Miriam, Exod. xv. 20, 21, and of Deborah, Judg. v. 1 ff.; see also 1 Sam. xviii. 6, 7.

12 Kings with their armies did flee, and were discomfited : and they of the household divided the spoil.

13 [b]⌜Though ye have lien among the pots, yet shall ye be as the wings of a dove : that is covered with silver wings, and her feathers like gold⌝.

[b] R.V. *Will ye lie among the sheepfolds, as the wings of a dove covered with silver, and her pinions with yellow gold?* An allusion to Deborah's reproach of Reuben for his inactivity. Judg. v. 16. The dove with feathers glistening in the sunshine is an image of prosperity and peace.

In P.B.V. the degradation of Egypt is contrasted with the splendour of Canaan.

14 When [1]the Almighty scattered kings for their sake : [c]⌜then were they as white as snow in Salmon⌝.

[c] R.V. *it was as when it snoweth in Zalmon.* The kings fleeing in confusion are compared to snow flakes falling on Zalmon, the 'dark' mountain as its name imports.

15 [d]⌜As the hill of Basan, so is God's hill : even an high hill, as the hill of Basan⌝.

[d] R.V. *A mountain of God is the mountain of Bashan; an high mountain is the mountain of Bashan.* And yet God did not choose to dwell there!

16 [e]⌜Why hop ye so, ye high hills? this is God's hill, in the which it pleaseth him to dwell⌝ : yea, the LORD will abide in it for ever.

[e] R.V. *Why look ye askance, ye high mountains, at the mountain which God hath desired for his abode?* The lofty range of Bashan looks, as it were, with envy on the lowly hill of Sion which God has honoured with His presence.

17 The chariots of God are twenty thousand, even thousands of angels : and the Lord is among them, [f]⌜as in the holy place of Sinai⌝.

17 ff. God's entrance in triumph into His sanctuary in Sion. Cp. Deut. xxxiii. 2.

[f] R.V. mg. *Sinai is in the sanctuary,* i.e. the glory manifested at Sinai belongs now to the new sanctuary.

[1] 'The Almighty' occurs in the Psalter only here and at xci. 1.

18 Thou art gone up on high, thou hast led [a]captivity captive, and received gifts [b]for men : yea, [c]⌜even for thine enemies⌝, that the LORD God might dwell among them.

'on high,' i.e. to Mount Sion.

[a]R.V. *thy captivity* = thy train of captives.

[b]R.V. *among.*

[c]R.V. *among the rebellious also.* A proof that even those opposed to His rule have yielded to Him.

St Paul (Eph. iv. 8) applies the former part of this verse to our Lord's Ascension, and to the spiritual gifts of Pentecost. He alters 'received gifts among men' into 'gave gifts unto men.' A king receives in order to give.

19 [d]⌜Praised be the Lord daily : even the God who helpeth us, and poureth his benefits upon us⌝.

19. From this verse onward the Psalmist turns to the present and the future; God is still and will be the champion of His people.

[d]R.V. *Blessed be the Lord, who daily beareth our burden, even the God who is our salvation.*

20 [e]⌜He is our God, even the God of whom cometh salvation : GOD is the Lord, by whom we escape death⌝.

[e]R.V. *God is unto us a God of deliverances; and unto JEHOVAH the Lord belong the issues* (i.e. ways of escape) *from death.*

21 [f]⌜God shall wound⌝ the head of his enemies : and the hairy scalp of such a one as goeth on still in his wickedness.

[f]R.V. *But God shall smite through.*

The thick head of hair ('the hairy scalp') is a token of youthful strength and pride.

22 The Lord hath said, [g]⌜I will bring my people again, as I did from Basan : mine own will I bring again, as I did sometime from the deep of the sea⌝.

[g]R.V. *I will bring again from Bashan, I will bring them* (i.e. My enemies, *v.* 21) *again from the depths of the sea.* No matter where they may hide themselves, they will not escape; cp. Amos ix. 2, 3.

23 That thy foot may be dipped in the blood of thine enemies : and that the tongue of thy dogs may be red through the same.

God's future victory is described in imagery drawn from the savage excesses of ancient warfare; see Ps. lviii. 9.

24 It is well seen, O God, how thou goest : how thou, my God and King, goest [h]in the sanctuary.

24, 25, 27. A prophetic vision of the triumphal procession of Israel's God and King when His enemies shall be overthrown.

[h]R.V. *into.*

25 The singers go before, the minstrels follow after : in the midst [i]are the damsels playing with the timbrels.

[i]R.V. *of.* The damsels with their timbrels take part in the procession on either side of the singers and minstrels.

26 [a]⌜Give thanks, O Israel, unto God the Lord in the congregations : from the ground of the heart⌝.

[a] R.V. *Bless ye God in the congregations, even the Lord, ye that are of the fountain of Israel*, i.e. sprung from the patriarch Israel. This verse may be regarded as the refrain of the processional hymn.

27 There is little Benjamin their ruler, and the princes of Judah [b]⌜their counsel⌝ : the princes of Zabulon, and the princes of Nephthali.

Benjamin and Judah represent the southern, [1]Zabulon and Nephthali the northern tribes. Benjamin is called 'little' as being the smallest tribe, and 'their ruler,' because Saul the first king was of Benjamin. The Psalmist looks forward to the reunion of the nation.

[b] *and their council.*

28 Thy God hath sent forth strength for thee : [c]⌜stablish the thing, O God, that thou hast wrought in us⌝.

'thee' = Israel.

[c] R.V. mg. *be strong, O God, thou that hast wrought for us.*

29 [d]⌜For thy temple's sake at Jerusalem : so shall kings⌝ bring presents unto thee.

[d] R.V. *Because of thy temple at Jerusalem kings shall.* The re-establishment of the Temple, the visible sign of God's presence, will attract the homage and tribute of foreign princes; see Ps. lxxvi. 11.

30 [e]⌜When the company of the spear-men, and multitude of the mighty are scattered abroad among the beasts of the people⌝, so that they humbly bring pieces of silver : [f]⌜and when he hath scattered the people⌝ that delight in war ;

[e] R.V. *Rebuke the wild beast of the reeds, the multitude of the bulls with the calves of the peoples.* The 'wild beast of the reeds' = the crocodile, symbolizing Egypt (Ps. lxxiv. 14, 15). The 'bulls' and the 'calves' = the princes and people of the nations.

The Gentiles will offer their riches to God thus declaring their subjection to Him.

[f] R.V. *he hath scattered the peoples.*

31 [g]⌜Then shall the princes come out⌝ of Egypt : [h]⌜the Morians' land⌝ shall soon stretch out her hands unto God.

[g] *Princes shall come out*, i.e. to pay homage and present gifts.

[h] *Ethiopia.* P.B.V. 'Morians' = Moors.

32 Sing unto God, O ye kingdoms of the earth : O sing praises unto the Lord ;

33 Who sitteth in the heavens over all from the beginning : lo, he doth send out his voice, yea, and that a mighty voice.

[1] Zabulon and Nephthali are selected to represent the northern tribes probably because they are specially commended in the Song of Deborah (Judg. v. 18) which was evidently before the author of this Psalm.

34 [a]⌜Ascribe ye the power to God over Israel : his worship, and strength is in the clouds⌝.

35 [b]⌜O God, wonderful art thou in thy holy places⌝ : even the God of Israel; he [c]⌜will give⌝ strength and power unto his people; blessed be God.

[a] R.V. *Ascribe ye strength unto God: his excellency is over Israel, and his strength is in the skies.*

[b] R.V. mg. *Terrible is God out of thy holy places.* Israel is addressed.

[c] *giveth.*

Evening Prayer

PSALM LXIX. *Salvum me fac.*

The prayer of a servant of God deeply and undeservedly afflicted, whose sufferings pre-eminently prefigure those of Christ. Probably written at the commencement of the captivity (see *vv.* 34 ff.), perhaps by Jeremiah. It is quoted in the N.T. more frequently than any part of the O.T. except Psalm xxii.

Proper on Good Friday.

SAVE me, O God : for the waters are come in, even unto my soul.

2 I stick fast in the deep mire, where no ground is : I am come into deep waters, so that the floods run over me.

3 I am weary of crying; my throat is dry : my sight faileth me for waiting so long upon my God.

4 They that hate me without a cause are more than the hairs of my head : they that are mine enemies, and would destroy me guiltless, are mighty.

5 I paid them the things that I never took : God, thou knowest my [d] simpleness, and my faults are not hid from thee.

1, 2. A figurative description of a state of deep calamity; see *vv.* 15, 16.

Words applied by our Lord to His own case. St John xv. 25. They occur also in Ps. xxxv. 19.

Probably a proverbial way of saying, 'I am suffering for sins which I did not commit.'

[d] *foolishness*, i.e. sinfulness; see Ps. xxxviii. 5. The Psalmist, though wrongly accused in the present instance, is conscious of other transgressions.

6 Let not them that trust in thee, O Lord GOD of hosts, be ashamed for my cause : let not those that seek thee be confounded through me, O Lord God of Israel.

6. The Psalmist is suffering for the sake of God (*v.* 7), therefore if he is left unsuccoured, the faithful will be discouraged.

7 And why? for thy sake have I [a]⌜suffered reproof⌝ : shame hath covered my face.

[a] *borne reproach.*

8 I am become a stranger unto my brethren : even an alien unto my mother's children.

Even my nearest relatives are turned against me.

9 For the zeal of thine house hath even eaten me : and the [b]rebukes of them that [b]rebuked thee are fallen upon me.

Words which occurred to the disciples when our Lord cleansed the Temple. St John ii. 17.

[b] *reproaches. reproached.*

Words applied by St Paul to Christ. Rom. xv. 3.

10 I wept, and chastened myself with fasting : and that was turned to my [c]reproof.

10—12. The Psalmist publicly mourned for the dishonour done to God and His House, but he met with only contempt and ridicule.

[c] *reproach.*

11 I put on sackcloth also : and they jested upon me.

12 They that sit in the gate speak against me : and the drunkards make songs upon me.

'the gate' of the city, the general place of concourse.

13 But, LORD, I make my prayer unto thee : in an acceptable time.

Cp. Is. xlix. 8; 2 Cor. vi. 2.

14 Hear me, O God, in the multitude of thy mercy : even in the truth of thy salvation.

15 Take me out of the mire, that I sink not : O let me be delivered from them that hate me, and out of the deep waters.

15, 16. See *vv.* 1, 2.

16 Let not the water-flood drown me, neither let the deep swallow me up : and let not the pit shut her mouth upon me.

17 Hear me, O LORD, for thy loving-kindness is comfortable : turn thee unto me according to the multitude of thy mercies.

18 And hide not thy face from thy servant, for I am in trouble : O haste thee, and hear me.

19 Draw nigh unto my soul, and save it : O deliver me, because of mine enemies.

20 [a]⌜Thou hast known my reproof⌝, my shame, and my dishonour : mine adversaries are all in thy sight.

[a] R.V. *Thou knowest my reproach.*

21 [b]⌜Thy rebuke⌝ hath broken my heart; I am full of heaviness : I looked for some to have pity on me, but there was no man, neither found I any to comfort me.

[b] *Reproach* (omit 'Thy') of man, not of God.

22 They gave me gall to eat : and when I was thirsty they gave me vinegar to drink.

Metaphorical language for the infliction of extreme suffering; cp. Jer. xxiii. 15. St Matthew (xxvii. 34) describes in these words a literal detail in our Lord's passion, and St John (xix. 28) tells us that Christ said, 'I thirst,' 'that the scripture might be accomplished.'

23 Let their table be made a snare to take themselves withal : and let the things that should have been for their wealth be unto them an occasion of falling.

24 Let their eyes be blinded, that they see not : and ever bow thou down their backs.

23, 24. Freely quoted in Rom. xi. 9, 10 of unbelieving Israel.

In return for the table which they spread with gall and vinegar for me, *v.* 22.

'wealth' = well-being, prosperity.

25 Pour out thine indignation upon them : and let thy wrathful displeasure take hold of them.

26 Let their habitation be void : and no man to dwell in their tents.

Quoted in Acts i. 20 as forecasting the fate of Judas.

27 For they persecute him whom thou hast smitten : and they talk how they may vex them whom thou hast wounded.

28 Let them fall from one wickedness to another : and not come into thy righteousness.

29 Let them be wiped out of the book of the living : and not be written among the righteous.

i.e. May they die and thus cease to be enrolled as citizens of Israel, the righteous nation ; cp. Ezek. xiii. 9.

30 As for me, when I am poor and in heaviness : thy help, O God, shall lift me up.

31 I will praise the Name of God with a song : and magnify it with thanksgiving.

32 This also shall please the LORD : better than a bullock that hath horns and hoofs.

i.e. of full age, having 'horns'; and clean, parting the 'hoofs.' Lev. xi. 3.

33 The humble shall consider this, and be glad : [a]⌜seek ye after God, and your soul shall live⌝.

[a] R.V. *ye that seek after God, let your heart live.*

34 For the LORD heareth the poor : and despiseth not his prisoners.

'his prisoners,' i.e. His (the LORD's) people in captivity.

35 Let heaven and earth praise him : the sea, and all that moveth therein.

36 For God will save Sion, and build the cities of Judah : that men may dwell there, and have it in possession.

37 The posterity also of his servants shall inherit it : and they that love his Name shall dwell therein.

PSALM LXX. *Deus, in adjutorium.*

A cry for help against malicious enemies. A repetition, with a few variations, of Psalm xl. 16—21.

HASTE thee, O God, to deliver me : make haste to help me, O LORD.

'O God, make speed to save us.'
'O Lord, make haste to help us.'
Versicle and Response at Matins and Evensong.

2 Let them be ashamed and confounded that seek after my soul : let them be turned backward and put to confusion that wish me evil.

3 Let them for their reward be soon brought to shame : [a]⌜that cry over me, There, there⌝.

[a]*that say, Aha, Aha,* exulting in my misfortune.

4 But let all those that seek thee be joyful and glad in thee : and let all such as delight in thy salvation say alway, The Lord be praised.

5 As for me, I am poor and in misery : haste thee unto me, O God.

'haste thee' &c.; Ps. xl. 20 has 'but the Lord careth for me.'

6 Thou art my helper, and my [b]redeemer : O LORD, make no long tarrying.

[b]*deliverer.*

THE FOURTEENTH DAY

Morning Prayer

PSALM LXXI. *In te, Domine, speravi.*

A prayer for aid in renewed trouble by one who in a long life has known great suffering but has been upheld by faith in God; written perhaps by Jeremiah.

Special in Visitation of the Sick.

IN thee, O LORD, have I put my trust; let me never be put to confusion : but rid me, and deliver me, in thy righteousness; incline thine ear unto me, and save me.

1, 2. Almost identical with Ps. xxxi. 1—4.

'O LORD, in Thee have I trusted: let me never be confounded.' Te Deum.

'in thy righteousness.' The righteous God is pledged to deliver His faithful servant.

2 Be thou my strong hold, whereunto I may alway resort : thou hast promised to help me, for thou art my house of defence, and my castle.

Show Thyself to be that which I know Thou art (see latter clause).

3 Deliver me, O my God, out of the hand of the ungodly : out of the hand of the unrighteous and cruel man.

4 For thou, O Lord GOD, art the thing that I long for : thou art my hope, even from my youth.

'my hope.' 'Christ Jesus our hope.' 1 Tim. i. 1: cp. Col. i. 27.

5 Through thee have I been holden up ever since I was born : thou art he that took me out of my mother's womb; my praise shall be always of thee.

6 I am become as it were [a]⌜a monster⌝ unto many : but my sure trust is in thee.

[a] *a wonder*, as having been signally preserved through so many dangers, 'chastened and not killed.' 2 Cor. vi. 9. P.B.V. 'monster' formerly meant 'portent.'

7 O let my mouth be filled with thy praise : that I may sing of thy glory and honour all the day long.

8 Cast me not away in the time of age : forsake me not when my strength faileth me.

9 For mine enemies speak against me, and they that lay wait for my soul take their counsel together saying : God hath forsaken him; [b]persecute him, and take him, for there is none to deliver him.

[b] R.V. *pursue.*

10 Go not far from me, O God : my God, haste thee to help me.

11 Let them be confounded and perish that are against my soul : let them be covered with shame and dishonour that seek to do me evil.

12 As for me, I will patiently abide alway : and will praise thee more and more.

13 My mouth shall daily speak of thy righteousness and salvation : for I know no end thereof.

14 [c]⌜I will go forth in the strength⌝ of the Lord GOD : and will make mention of thy righteousness only.

[c] R.V. *I will come with the mighty acts*, bringing them as the subject of my praise.

15 Thou, O God, hast taught me from my youth up until now : [a]⌜therefore will I tell of⌝ thy wondrous works.

[a] *and hitherto have I declared.*

16 Forsake me not, O God, in mine old age, when I am gray-headed : until I have shewed thy strength unto [b]this generation, and thy power to all them that are yet for to come.

[b] R.V. *the next.*

17 Thy righteousness, O God, is very high : and great things are they that thou hast done; O God, who is like unto thee?

18 [c]⌜O what great troubles and adversities hast thou shewed me, and yet didst thou turn and refresh me : yea, and broughtest me from the deep of the earth again⌝.

[c] R.V. *Thou, which hast shewed us many and sore troubles, shalt quicken us again, and shalt bring us up again from the depths of the earth.* Note the change to the plural 'us.' The Psalmist enlarges his view to take in the calamities of the nation. 'the depths of the earth' is figurative for a state of extreme peril.

19 [d]⌜Thou hast brought me to great honour : and comforted me on every side.⌝

[d] R.V. *Increase thou my greatness, and turn again and comfort me.*

20 [e]⌜Therefore will I⌝ praise thee and thy faithfulness, O God, playing upon an instrument of musick : unto thee will I sing upon the harp, O thou Holy One of Israel.

[e] *I will also.*

This title of God is found elsewhere in the Psalter only in lxxviii. 42 and lxxxix. 19. It frequently occurs in Isaiah.

21 My lips [f]⌜will be fain⌝ when I sing unto thee : and so will my soul whom thou hast delivered.

[f] *shall greatly rejoice.* P.B.V. 'fain'=glad.

22 My tongue also shall talk of thy righteousness all the day long : for they are confounded and brought unto shame that seek to do me evil.

PSALM LXXII. *Deus, judicium.*

The reign of the ideal King, to be realized only in the Kingdom of Christ. The Title ascribes the Psalm to Solomon, and it may well have been written by him.

Proper on Epiphany [America].

GIVE the king thy judgements, O God : and thy righteousness unto the king's son.

1, 2. 'Give thy servant an understanding heart to judge thy people.' Solomon's prayer, 1 Kings iii. 9.

'the king's son' = the same person as 'the king' above. He is descended from a king.

2 Then shall he judge thy people according unto right : and defend the poor.

3 The mountains also shall bring peace : and the little hills righteousness unto the people.

The 'mountains' and 'hills' as the main features of the scenery of Palestine are put for the whole land.

4 He shall keep the simple folk by their right : defend the children of the poor, and punish the wrong doer.

5 They shall fear thee, as long as the sun and moon endureth : from one generation to another.

'thee,' i.e. God, whom the people ('they') shall fear on account of His righteous rule, *v.* 4.

6 He shall come down like the rain [a]⌜into a fleece of wool⌝ : even as the drops that water the earth.

[a]*upon the mown grass.* In P.B.V. which follows Vulg., an allusion is probably intended to Gideon's fleece. Judg. vi. 37, 38.

7 In his time shall the righteous flourish : yea, and abundance of peace, so long as the moon endureth.

8 His dominion shall be also from the one sea to the other : and from [b]⌜the flood⌝ unto the world's end.

A poetical version of Exod. xxiii. 31, 'I will set thy border from the Red Sea even unto the sea of the Philistines (the Mediterranean) and from the wilderness unto the River (the Euphrates)'; see Zech. ix. 10; Ecclus. xliv. 21.

[b]*the River.*

9 They that dwell in the wilderness shall kneel before him : his enemies shall lick the dust.

10 The kings of [a]Tharsis and of the isles shall give presents : the kings of [b]Arabia and Saba shall bring gifts.

[a] *Tarshish*=Tartessus in Spain.

[b]*Sheba*, in Arabia, which P.B.V. gives, following Vulg.

'Saba'=Meroe in Ethiopia.

11 All kings shall fall down before him : all nations shall do him service.

12 For he shall deliver the poor when he crieth : the needy also, and him that hath no helper.

13 He shall be favourable to the simple and needy : and shall preserve the souls of the poor.

14 He shall deliver their souls from [c]falsehood and wrong : and [d]dear shall their blood be in his sight.

[c]R.V. *oppression*.

[d]*precious*. P.B.V. 'dear'=costly; see Ps. cxvi. 13.

15 [e]He shall live, and unto him shall be given of the gold of [f]Arabia : [g]⌜prayer shall be made ever unto him⌝, and daily shall he be praised.

[e]R.V. *And they*, i.e. 'the poor' of the preceding verses, who being preserved alive, and furthermore made rich by the king's bounty, offer him costly gifts.

[f]*Sheba*. P.B.V. from Vulg.

[g]R.V. *and men shall pray for him continually*.

16 There shall be an heap of corn in the earth, high upon the hills : his fruit shall shake like Libanus, [h]⌜and shall be green in the city like grass upon the earth⌝.

'high upon the hills.' So great shall be the fertility of the country that the cornfields will reach even to the mountain-tops.

'his'=its.

[h]*and they of the city shall flourish like grass of the earth*.

17 His Name shall endure for ever; his Name shall remain under the sun among the posterities : which shall be blessed through him; and all the heathen shall praise him.

18 Blessed be the LORD God, even the God of Israel : which only doeth wondrous things;

18, 19. The doxology which concludes the Second Book of the Psalter.

19 And blessed be the Name of his Majesty for ever : and all the earth shall be filled with his Majesty. Amen, Amen.

A.R.V. add as *v.* 20. 'The prayers of David the son of Jesse are ended.' This was a note placed here probably by the editor of an early collection of Psalms which was afterwards incorporated in the Psalter.

Evening Prayer

PSALM LXXIII. *Quam bonus Israel!*

The difficulties of a righteous soul perplexed by the prosperity of the wicked. The Psalmist amid temptation to despair is upheld by steadfast trust in God and confident hope of future glory with Him.

TRULY God is loving unto Israel : even unto such as are of a clean heart.

'Israel' = Israelites 'indeed' (St John i. 47), as the next clause indicates.

2 Nevertheless, my feet were almost gone : my treadings had well-nigh slipt.

3 And why? I was [a]⌜grieved at the wicked : I do also see⌝ the ungodly in such prosperity.

[a] R.V. *envious at the arrogant, when I saw.*

4 For they are in no peril of death : but are lusty and strong.

'lusty' = vigorous.

5 They come in no misfortune like other folk : neither are they plagued like other men.

6 [b]⌜And this is the cause that they are so holden with pride : and overwhelmed with cruelty⌝.

[b] R.V. *Therefore pride is as a chain about their neck; violence covereth them as a garment.*

7 Their eyes swell with fatness : [c]⌜and they do even what they lust⌝.

[c] R.V. mg. *the imaginations of their heart overflow*, in boastful and arrogant language; see *vv.* following.

P.B.V. 'lust' = desire.

8 [a]⌜They corrupt other, and speak of wicked blasphemy : their talking is against the most High⌝.

[a]R.V. *They scoff, and in wickedness utter oppression : they speak loftily.*

9 [b]⌜For they stretch forth their mouth unto the heaven⌝ : and their tongue goeth through the world.

[b]R.V. *They have set their mouth in the heavens.* They speak from heaven, as it were, with the authority of God.

10 Therefore fall the people unto them : and [c]⌜thereout suck they no small advantage⌝.

[c]R.V. mg. *waters of a full cup are drained out by them.* The 'people' attracted to the company of the wicked drink without stint of the cup full of sinful pleasures. P.B.V. means that the wicked make profit out of the crowds that flock to them.

11 Tush, say they, how should God perceive it : is there knowledge in the most High?

12 Lo, these are the ungodly, these prosper in the world, and these have riches in possession : and I said, Then have I cleansed my heart in vain, and washed mine hands in innocency.

12—14. The reflections of the Psalmist.

Metaphor drawn from the ceremonial purifications of the Jewish Law.

13 All the day long have I been punished : and chastened every morning.

'I,' unlike the wicked.

14 Yea, and I had almost said even as they : but lo, then I should have condemned the generation of thy children.

'thy children' = the true Israel; see *v.* 1.

15 Then thought I to understand this : but it was too hard for me,

16 Until I went into the sanctuary of God : then understood I the end of these men;

17 Namely, how thou dost set them in slippery places : and castest them down, and destroyest them.

18 O how suddenly do they consume : perish, and come to a fearful end!

19 Yea, even like as a dream when one awaketh : [d]⌜so shalt thou make their image to vanish out of the city⌝.

[d]*So, O Lord, when thou awakest, thou shalt despise their image,* i.e. regard their existence as the mere vision of a dream.

20 Thus my heart was grieved : and it went even through my reins.

'the reins' (kidneys) were regarded as the seat of the emotions.

21 So foolish was I, and ignorant : even as it were a beast before thee.

22 Nevertheless, I am alway by thee : for thou hast holden me by my right hand.

23 Thou shalt guide me with thy counsel : and after that receive me [a]⌜with glory⌝.

[a]*to glory*. An anticipation of a glorious hereafter. 'receive' is the same word used in Gen. v. 24 of Enoch, 'he was not; for God *took* him'; see Ps. xlix. 15.

24 Whom have I in heaven but thee : and there is none upon earth that I desire in comparison of thee.

25 My flesh and my heart faileth : but God is the strength of my heart, and my portion for ever.

26 For lo, they that forsake thee shall perish : thou hast destroyed all them that commit fornication against thee.

'commit fornication,' i.e. by unfaithfulness to Jehovah. Israel is the spouse of God ; Is. liv. 5, 6.

27 But it is good for me to hold me fast by God, to put my trust in the Lord GOD : and to speak of all thy works [1]⌜in the gates of the daughter of Sion⌝.

PSALM LXXIV. *Ut quid, Deus?*

A lamentation for the desolation of the land and profanation of the sanctuary, with a cry to God for help.

O GOD, wherefore art thou absent from us so long : why is thy wrath so hot against the sheep of thy pasture?

[1] Not in A.R.V., added in P.B.V. from Vulg.

2 O think upon thy congregation : whom thou hast purchased, and redeemed of old.

'purchased and redeemed' from Egyptian bondage; see Exod. xv. 13, 16.

3 Think upon the tribe of thine inheritance : and mount Sion, wherein thou hast dwelt.

'the tribe.' All Israel, as distinguished from other nations, is reckoned as one tribe.

4 Lift up thy feet, [a]⌜that thou mayest utterly destroy every enemy : which hath done evil in thy sanctuary⌝.

'Lift up thy feet,' i.e. Come with speed.

[a] R.V. *unto the perpetual ruins, all the evil that the enemy hath done in the sanctuary.*

5 Thine adversaries [b]roar in the midst of thy congregations : and set up their banners for tokens.

[b] R.V. *have roared.*

'banners' = military standards or pagan emblems carried into the Temple.

6 [c]⌜He that hewed timber afore out of the thick trees : was known to bring it to an excellent work⌝.

[c] R.V. *They seemed as men that lifted up axes upon a thicket of trees.* In the havoc they wrought in the Temple, they may be compared to woodmen hewing down a plantation of trees.

7 [d]But now they break down all the carved work thereof : with axes and hammers.

[d] R.V. *And.*

8 They have set [e]⌜fire upon thy holy places⌝ : and have defiled the dwelling-place of thy Name, even unto the ground.

[e] R.V. *thy sanctuary on fire.*

9 Yea, they said in their hearts, Let us make havock of them altogether : thus have they burnt up all the [f]houses of God in the land.

[f] *synagogues*, i.e. places for worship other than the Temple.

10 We see not our tokens, there is not one prophet more : no, not one is there among us, that [g]⌜understandeth any more⌝.

'our tokens,' i.e. the outward evidences of our religion, such as sabbath and sacrifice.

[g] *knoweth how long* this persecution will continue.

11 O God, how long shall the adversary do this dishonour : how long shall the enemy blaspheme thy Name, for ever?

12 Why withdrawest thou thy hand : why pluckest thou not thy right hand out of thy bosom to consume the enemy?

13 [a]For God is my King of old : the help that is done upon earth he doeth it himself.

[a]R.V. *Yet*, i.e. notwithstanding His present non-intervention.

14—16. Former instances of God's deliverance of His people.

14 Thou didst divide the sea through thy power : thou brakest the heads of the [b]dragons in the waters.

'the sea'=the Red Sea.

[b]R.V. mg. *sea-monsters*. This word and 'Leviathan' (*v.* 15) signify the crocodile and symbolize Egypt; see Ps. lxviii. 30.

15 Thou smotest the heads of Leviathan in pieces : and gavest him to be meat for the people in the wilderness.

The corpses of the Egyptians, cast up on the shore of the Red Sea, became food for the wild beasts, the denizens ('the people') of the desert.

'meat'=food in general.

16 Thou broughtest out fountains and waters out of the hard rocks : thou driedst up mighty waters.

At Horeb, Exod. xvii. 6, and Kadesh, Numb. xx. 6.

'mighty waters'=the Red Sea and the Jordan.

17 The day is thine, and the night is thine : thou hast prepared the light and the sun.

18 Thou hast set all the borders of the earth : thou hast made summer and winter.

Thou hast fixed the boundaries of the nations.

19 Remember this, O LORD, how the enemy hath [c]rebuked : and how the foolish people hath blasphemed thy Name.

[c]*reproached*.

'foolish people'=the heathen oppressors of Israel, senseless in their antagonism to God; see *v.* 23.

20 O deliver not the soul of thy turtle-dove unto the multitude of the enemies : and forget not the congregation of the poor for ever.

'thy turtle-dove'=Israel.

21 Look upon the covenant : for all the earth is full of darkness, and cruel habitations.

22 O let not the [d]simple go away ashamed : but let the poor and needy give praise unto thy Name.

[d]*oppressed*.

'go away,' after drawing near to Thee in prayer.

23 Arise, O God, maintain thine own cause : remember how the foolish man blasphemeth thee daily.

'the foolish man'=the heathen oppressors, as in *v.* 19.

24 Forget not the voice of thine enemies : the presumption of them that hate thee increaseth ever more and more.

THE FIFTEENTH DAY

Morning Prayer

PSALM LXXV. *Confitebimur tibi.*

God's righteous government of the world. A song of praise called forth by some recent manifestation of God's goodness, probably the overthrow of Sennacherib. 2 Kings xix. 35, 36.

UNTO thee, O God, do we give thanks : yea, unto thee do we give thanks.

2 Thy Name also is so nigh : and that do thy wondrous works declare.

God's Name (Jehovah)=Himself, because it expresses His nature and qualities. Exod. xxxiv. 5—7.

God's nearness to His people had been manifested by His late mercies vouchsafed to them.

3 [a]⌜When I receive the congregation⌝ : I shall judge according unto right.

3—6. God speaks.

[a] R.V. *When I shall find the set time*, i.e. the time ripe for My interposition. P.B.V. means, When I have gathered together the inhabitants of the earth to listen to My judgement; see Ps. vii. 7, l. 5.

4 The earth is weak, and all the inhabiters thereof : I bear up the pillars of it.

Cp. 1 Sam. ii. 8, 'The pillars of the earth are the LORD's.'

5 I said unto the [b]fools, Deal not [b]⌜so madly⌝ : and to the ungodly, [c]Set not up your horn ;

[b] R.V. *arrogant. arrogantly.*

[c] *Lift.*

'horn.' An emblem of power, here with the additional sense of arrogance. The metaphor is taken from animals who use their horns as weapons of offence.

6 [a]Set not up your horn on high : and speak not with a stiff neck.

[a] *Lift.*

7—12. The Psalmist speaks, commenting on God's utterance.

7 For [b]promotion cometh neither from the east, nor from the west : nor yet from the south.

[b] R.V. *lifting up*, i.e. exaltation, deliverance.

If the Psalm celebrates the defeat of the Assyrians, the north is not mentioned because they came from that quarter.

8 And why? God is the Judge : he putteth down one, and [c]setteth up another.

[c] R.V. *lifteth.*

9 For in the hand of the LORD there is a cup, and the wine is red : it is full mixed, and he poureth out of the same.

The cup of God's fury. Is. li. 17. 'mixed' with spices to add to its strength.

10 As for the dregs thereof : all the ungodly of the earth shall drink them, and suck them out.

11 But I will talk of the God of Jacob : and praise him for ever.

12 All the horns of the ungodly also will I break : and the horns of the righteous shall be [d]exalted.

'will I break.' The Psalmist representing Israel the agent of God's judgement, prophesies the ultimate triumph of righteousness.

[d] R.V. *lifted up.*

PSALM LXXVI. *Notus in Judæa.*

No power can withstand the might of God. A hymn of thanksgiving on the occasion of some signal national deliverance, probably the discomfiture of Sennacherib. 2 Kings xix. 35, 36.

IN [e]Jewry is God known : his Name is great in Israel.

[e] *Judah.*

'known' by the manifestation of His power and goodness in His late deliverance of His people.

'Judah' or 'Israel' might be used indifferently to designate the whole nation, after the fall of the northern kingdom.

2 At Salem is his [f]tabernacle : and his [f]dwelling in Sion.

'Salem,' the ancient name of Jerusalem. Gen. xiv. 18.

[f] R.V. mg. *covert. lair*; see *v.* 4.

3 There brake he the arrows of the bow : the shield, the sword, and the battle.

'There' marks out Jerusalem as the place where the victory was gained.

4 [a]⌜Thou art of more honour and might : than the hills of the robbers⌝.

[a] R.V. mg. *Glorious art thou and excellent, from the mountains of prey.* God is compared to a lion going forth to destroy from his lair in Mount Sion, *v.* 2; cp. Is. xiv. 25. P.B.V. means, God's power has prevailed over the Assyrians who were like robbers issuing from mountain strongholds.

5 [b]⌜The proud are robbed⌝, they have slept their sleep : and [c]⌜all the men whose hands were mighty have found nothing⌝.

[b] *The stouthearted are spoiled.*
The 'sleep' of death.
[c] *none of the men of might have found their hands.* The hands which they raised against Jerusalem are paralysed. Is. x. 10—14, 32.

6 At thy rebuke, O God of Jacob : both the chariot and horse are [d]fallen.

[d] *cast into a dead sleep.*

7 Thou, even thou art to be feared : and who may stand in thy sight when thou art angry?

8 Thou didst cause thy judgement to be heard from heaven : the earth trembled, and was still,

9 When God arose to judgement : and to help all the meek upon earth.

10 The [e]fierceness of man shall turn to thy praise : [f]⌜and the fierceness of them shalt thou refrain⌝.

[e] *wrath.*
[f] R.V. *the residue of wrath shalt thou gird upon thee* as an ornament. The thought is that God, far from being injured by man's wrath against Him, will utilize that wrath, to the utmost, for His own honour.

11 Promise unto the LORD your God, and keep it, all ye that are round about him : bring presents unto him that ought to be feared.

'all ye that are round about him,' i.e. not Israel alone, but also the neighbouring nations.

12 He shall refrain the spirit of princes : and is wonderful among the kings of the earth.

PSALM LXXVII. *Voce mea ad Dominum.*

In a time of great national affliction, probably the exile, the Psalmist finds comfort by calling to mind God's dealings with Israel in the past, especially in the deliverance from Egypt.

I WILL cry unto God with my voice : even unto God will I cry with my voice, and he shall hearken unto me.

2 In the time of my trouble I sought the Lord : [a]⌜my sore ran, and ceased not in the night-season; my soul refused comfort⌝.

[a]R.V. *my hand was stretched out* (in prayer) *in the night, and slacked not.*

P.B.V. is figurative for 'my distress found no relief.'

3 [b]⌜When I am in heaviness, I will think upon God : when my heart is vexed, I will complain⌝.

[b]R.V. *I remember God, and am disquieted : I complain, and my spirit is overwhelmed.*

4 Thou holdest mine eyes waking : I am so [c]feeble, that I cannot speak.

i.e. Thou withholdest sleep from mine eyes.

[c]*troubled.*

5 I have considered the days of old : and the years that are past.

6 I call to remembrance my song : and in the night I commune with mine own heart, and search out my spirits.

'my song,' which I sang in former days of happiness.

7 Will the Lord absent himself for ever : and will he be no more intreated?

8 Is his mercy clean gone for ever : and is his promise come utterly to an end for evermore?

9 Hath God forgotten to be gracious : and [d]will he shut up his loving-kindness in displeasure?

[d]*hath.*

10 And I said, It is mine own infirmity : but I will remember the years of the right hand of the most Highest.

It is only my weakness that tempts me to lose faith in God.

'the years of the right hand' &c., i.e. the past ages when God's 'stretched out arm' (Deut. iv. 34) wrought deliverance for His people.

11 I will remember the works of the LORD : and call to mind thy wonders of old time.

12 I will think also of all thy works : and my talking shall be of thy doings.

13 Thy way, O God, is holy : who is so great a God as our God?

14 Thou art the God that doeth wonders : and hast declared thy power among the [a]people.

[a] R.V. *peoples.*

15 Thou hast [b]mightily delivered thy people : even the sons of Jacob and Joseph.

[b] *with thine arm.*

Joseph is specially mentioned as being father of Ephraim and Manasseh from whom the chief tribes of the northern kingdom were descended. The Psalmist may have been connected with that kingdom.

16 The waters saw thee, O God, the waters saw thee, and were afraid : the depths also were troubled.

16—18. A picture, developed from Exod. xiv. 24, 25, of the thunder-storm and earthquake which attended the passage of the Red Sea.

17 The clouds poured out water, the air thundered : and thine arrows went abroad.

18 The voice of thy thunder was heard round about : the lightnings shone upon the ground ; the earth was moved, and shook withal.

19 Thy way [c]is in the sea, and thy paths in the great waters : and thy footsteps [d]are not known.

[c] R.V. *was.*

[d] R.V. *were.* The waters flowed back, and no traces of God's route were left behind.

20 Thou leddest thy people like sheep : by the hand of Moses and Aaron.

Evening Prayer

PSALM LXXVIII. *Attendite, popule.*

The past history of Israel—its record of continual rebellion against God and ingratitude for His mercies—dwelt upon as a warning to the existing generation. The allusions to the sin and rejection of Ephraim, and to the divine selection of David as king, and of Sion as the centre of worship, probably indicate that the Psalmist belonged to the southern kingdom; see *vv.* 10, 61, 68—72.

HEAR my law, O my people : incline your ears unto the words of my mouth.

2 I will open my mouth in a parable : I will [a]⌜declare hard sentences⌝ of old;

3 Which we have heard and known : and such as our fathers have told us;

4 That we should not hide them from the children of the generations to come : but to shew the honour of the LORD, his mighty and wonderful works that he hath done.

5 He made a covenant with Jacob, and gave Israel a law : which he commanded our forefathers to teach their children;

6 That their posterity might know it : and the children which were yet unborn;

7 To the intent that when they came up : they might shew their children the same;

8 That they might put their trust in God : and not to forget the works of God, but to keep his commandments;

'law' here = (R.V. mg.) *teaching* or instruction; cp. use of the word in Proverbs (i. 8 and elsewhere).

[a] *utter dark sayings.*

By 'parable' and 'dark sayings of old' is meant the history of Israel regarded as containing veiled lessons for posterity. What the Psalmist-prophet says here about his mode of teaching is transferred by St Matthew (xiii. 34, 35) to the method of the Great Prophet.

5—8. See Deut. iv. 9, vi. 20 ff.

9 And not to be as their forefathers, a faithless and stubborn generation : a generation that set not their heart aright, and whose spirit [a]⸢cleaveth not stedfastly unto God⸣;

[a] *was not stedfast with God.*

10 [b]⸢Like as the children of Ephraim : who being harnessed⸣, and carrying bows, turned themselves back in the day of battle.

[b] *The children of Ephraim being armed.* Ephraim is singled out, though the reproach belongs to all Israel (*v.* 9), probably to point forward to its future rejection; *v.* 68.

'being armed...turned themselves back.' The language is figurative, Ephraim though well-equipped and pledged to God's service proved faithless and treacherous; see next verse.

11 They kept not the covenant of God : and would not walk in his law;

12 But forgat what he had done : and the wonderful works that he had shewed for them.

13 Marvellous things did he in the sight of [c]our forefathers, in the land of Egypt : even in the field of Zoan.

[c] *their.*

'Zoan,' or Tanis, which is the Sept. reading here, is mentioned in Numb. xiii. 22. This passage seems to identify it with the city of the Pharaoh of the Exodus.

14 He divided the sea, and let them go through : he made the waters to stand on an heap.

15 In the day-time also he led them with a cloud : and all the night through with a light of fire.

Exod. xiii. 21, 22.

16 He clave the hard rocks in the wilderness : and gave them drink thereof, as it had been out of the great depth.

At Horeb; see Exod. xvii. 6, where the same word for rock is found.

17 He brought waters out of the stony rock : so that it gushed out like the rivers.

At Kadesh; see Numb. xx. 8, where the word used here for rock, different from that in *v.* 16, appears.

18 Yet for all this they sinned more against him : and provoked the most Highest in the wilderness.

'sinned more,' i e. in addition to the murmurings at Horeb and Kadesh.

19 They tempted God in their hearts : and required meat for their lust.

'tempted,' i.e. put to the test. They challenged God to prove His power. Deut. vi. 16; see Ps. cvi. 14.
'meat' = food in general.
'lust' = strong desire.

20 They spake against God also, saying : [a]Shall God prepare a table in the wilderness?

Exod. xvi. 2, 3; Numb. xi. 4—6.
[a] *Can.*

21 He smote the stony rock indeed, that the water gushed out, and the streams flowed withal : but can he give bread also, or provide flesh for his people?

22 When the LORD heard this, he was wroth : so the fire was kindled [b]in Jacob, and there came up heavy displeasure against Israel;

At Taberah. Numb. xi. 1—3.
[b] *against.*

23 Because they believed not in God : and put not their trust in his help.

24 [c]So he commanded the clouds above : and opened the doors of heaven.

[c] R.V. *Yet*, i.e. notwithstanding their unbelief.

25 He rained down manna also upon them for to eat : and gave them [d]⌜food from heaven⌝.

[d] *of the corn of heaven.* Exod. xvi. 4; Ps. cv. 39; St John vi. 31.

26 So man did eat angels' food : for he sent them meat enough.

'angels' food,' as being bread from heaven where the angels dwell.
'meat' = food in general.

27 He caused the east-wind to blow under heaven : and through his power he brought in the [e]south-west-wind.

27—29. 'There went forth a wind from the LORD and brought quails from the sea' (i.e. the Red Sea). Numb. xi. 31.
[e] *south wind.*

28 He rained flesh upon them as thick as dust : and feathered fowls like as the sand of the sea.

29 He let it fall among their tents : even round about their habitation.

30 So they did eat, and were well filled; for he gave them their own desire : they were not disappointed of their lust.

'lust' = strong desire.

31 But while the meat was yet in their mouths, the heavy wrath of God came upon them, and slew the wealthiest of them : yea, and smote down the [a]chosen men that were in Israel.

Numb. xi. 33.
God punishes men sometimes by granting their requests.
'the wealthiest' = the most vigorous.
[a] R.V. *young*.

32 But for all this they sinned yet more : and believed not his wondrous works.

33 Therefore their days did he consume in vanity : and their years in trouble.

A reference to the apparently aimless forty-years' wandering in the desert. Numb. xiv. 28—34.

34 When he slew them, they sought him : and turned them early, and inquired after God.

34—40. A picture of human inconstancy and Divine forbearance. Man repents after punishment and then falls again, and yet God's mercy is not exhausted.

35 And they remembered that God was their strength : and that the high God was their redeemer.

36 Nevertheless, they did but flatter him with their mouth : and [b]⌜dissembled with him in⌝ their tongue.

[b] *lied unto him with.*

37 For their heart was not [c]whole with him : neither continued they stedfast in his covenànt.

[c] *right.* 'Thy heart is not right before God,' Acts viii. 21, is a quotation from this verse.

38 But he was so merciful, that he forgave their misdeeds : and destroyed them not.

38, 39. According to Rabbinic tradition, these verses, together with Deut. xxviii. 58, 59, and xxix. 9, were recited while the 'forty stripes save one' (2 Cor. xi. 24) were inflicted on the criminal.

39 Yea, many a time turned he his wrath away : and would not suffer his whole displeasure to arise.

40 For he considered that they were but flesh : and that they were even a wind that passeth away, and cometh not again.

41 Many a time did they provoke him in the wilderness : and grieved him in the desert.

42 They turned back, and tempted God : and moved the Holy One [d]⌜in Israel⌝.

'tempted,' i.e. put to the test, *v.* 19.

[d] *of Israel*; see Ps. lxxi. 20.

43 They thought not of his hand : and of the day when he delivered them from the hand of the enemy;

44 How he had [a]⌜wrought his miracles⌝ in Egypt : and his wonders in the field of Zoan.

[a] R.V. *set his signs*; see Exod. x. 1, 2; Ps. cv. 27.
'Zoan'; see *v.* 13.

45 He turned their waters into blood : so that they might not drink of the rivers.

Exod. vii. 20, 21.
In this enumeration of the plagues, no mention is made of the lice, murrain, boils or darkness.

46 He sent [b]lice among them, and devoured them up : and frogs to destroy them.

[b] R.V. *swarms of flies*. Exod. viii. 24.
Exod. viii. 3—6.

47 He gave their fruit unto the caterpillar : and their labour unto the [c]grasshopper.

Exod. x. 13—15.

[c] *locust*.

48 He destroyed their vines with hail-stones : and their mulberry-trees with the frost.

48, 49. Exod. ix. 23—25.

49 He smote their cattle also with hail-stones : and their flocks with hot thunderbolts.

50 He cast upon them the furiousness of his wrath, anger, displeasure, and trouble : and sent evil angels among them.

'evil angels,' i.e. angels sent on a mission of destruction.

51 He made a [d]⌜way to his indignation⌝, and spared not their soul from death : but gave their life over to the pestilence;

[d] R.V. *path for his anger*.

52 And smote all the first-born in Egypt : [e]⌜the most principal and mightiest⌝ in the dwellings of Ham.

Exod. xii. 29.
[e] *the chief* (R.V. mg. *beginning*) *of their strength*. A phrase used of the first-born, Gen. xlix. 3, Deut. xxi. 17; see Ps. cv. 35.
Ham was father of Mizraim (Egypt). Gen. x. 6.

53 But as for his own people, he led them forth like sheep : and carried them in the wilderness like a flock.

54 He brought them out safely, that they should not fear : and overwhelmed their enemies with the sea.

55 And brought them within the borders of his sanctuary : even to [a]⌜his mountain⌝ which he purchased with his right hand.

'his sanctuary' = Canaan, made holy by God's special Presence.

[a]R.V. mg. *this mountain land*, i.e. Canaan.

56 He cast out the heathen also before them : caused their land to be divided among them for an heritage, and made the tribes of Israel to dwell in their tents.

57 [b]So they tempted, and displeased the most high God : and kept not his testimonies;

[b]*Yet*, i.e. even after their settlement in Canaan.

'tempted,' i.e. put to the test, *vv.* 19, 42.

58 But turned their backs, and fell away like their forefathers : starting aside like a [c]broken bow.

[c]*deceitful*. The same metaphor as at *v.* 10.

59 For they grieved him with their hill-altars : and provoked him to displeasure with their images.

60 When God heard this, he was wroth : and took sore displeasure at Israel.

61 So that he forsook the tabernacle in Silo : even the tent that he had pitched among men.

'he forsook' &c. The ark left Shiloh for ever when it was carried into the battle with the Philistines. 1 Sam. iv. 4; cp. Jer. vii. 12.

62 He delivered [d]⌜their power⌝ into captivity : and [d]⌜their beauty⌝ into the enemy's hand.

[d]*his strength. his glory*. P.B.V. from Vulg. By 'his strength' and 'his glory' (or 'beauty') the ark is designated, as being the visible expression of God's majesty; cp. 1 Sam. iv. 21, 'And she named the child Ichabod, saying, The glory is departed from Israel: because the ark of God was taken'; see Ps. xcvi. 6, cxxxii. 8.

63 He gave his people over also unto the sword : and was wroth with his inheritance.

64 The fire consumed their young men : and their maidens [e]⌜were not given to marriage⌝.

'The fire' of war. Numb. xxi. 28.

[e]R.V. *had no marriage-song*, i.e. remained unmarried. P.B.V. has the same meaning.

65 Their priests were slain with the sword : and [a]⌜there were no widows to make lamentation⌝.

[a] *their widows made no lamentation*, i.e. war prevented the customary ceremonial mourning for the dead. The same words are found in Job xxvii. 15.

66 [b]So the Lord awaked as one out of sleep : and like a giant refreshed with wine.

[b] *Then.*

67 He smote his enemies [c]⌜in the hinder parts⌝ : and put them to a perpetual shame.

[c] R.V. *backward.*

68 He refused the tabernacle of Joseph : and chose not the tribe of Ephraim;

'Joseph,' 'Ephraim.' Shiloh the former habitation of the ark was situated in the tribe of Ephraim, the son of Joseph.

69 But chose the tribe of Judah : even the hill of Sion which he loved.

70 And there he built his temple on high : and laid the foundation of it like the ground which he hath [d]⌜made continually⌝.

[d] *established for ever.*

71 He chose David also his servant : and took him away from the sheep-folds.

72 As he was following the ewes great with young ones he took him : that he might feed Jacob his people, and Israel his inheritance.

The shepherd of the sheep was made the shepherd of the LORD'S flock. 2 Sam. v. 2; cp. Ps. lxxix. 14, lxxx. 1.

73 So he fed them with a faithful and true heart : and ruled them prudently with all his power.

THE SIXTEENTH DAY

Morning Prayer

PSALM LXXIX. *Deus, venerunt.*

A prayer that God may turn away His anger from the land, now crushed under some great calamity.

A companion Psalm to lxxiv., by the same author, or written at the same time.

O GOD, the heathen are come into thine inheritance : thy holy temple have they defiled, and made Jerusalem an heap of stones.

'thine inheritance' = Canaan, which God had chosen for His special abode. Exod. xv. 17.

'an heap of stones'; a fulfilment of Micah's (iii. 12) prophecy.

2 The dead bodies of thy servants have they given to be meat unto the fowls of the air : and the flesh of thy saints unto the beasts of the land.

'the flesh' &c. Quoted with *v.* 3 in 1 Macc. vii. 17.

3 Their blood have they shed like water on every side of Jerusalem : and there was no man to bury them.

4 We are become [a]⌜an open shame⌝ to our [b]enemies : a very scorn and derision unto them that are round about us.

[a] *a reproach.*

[b] *neighbours,* i.e. the surrounding nations, *v.* 13.

This verse is almost an exact repetition of Ps. xliv. 14.

5 LORD, how long wilt thou be angry : shall thy jealousy burn like fire for ever?

6 Pour out thine indignation upon the heathen that [c]⌜have not known thee⌝ : and upon the kingdoms that [d]⌜have not called⌝ upon thy Name.

6, 7, found also in Jer. x. 25.

[c] R.V. *know thee not.*

[d] R.V. *call not.*

7 For they have devoured Jacob : and laid waste his dwelling-place.

8 [a]⌜O remember not our old sins⌝, but have mercy upon us, and that soon : for we are come to great misery.

[a]R.V. *Remember not against us the iniquities of our forefathers.* Cp. Litany, 'Remember not, Lord, our offences, nor the offences of our forefathers.'

9 Help us, O God of our salvation, for the glory of thy Name : O deliver us, and be merciful unto our sins, for thy Name's sake.

'Help us, O God, our Saviour;
And for the glory of thy Name deliver us; be merciful to us sinners, for thy Name's sake.' Commination Service.

Cp. also Litany, 'O Lord, arise, help us, and deliver us for thy Name's sake.'

10 Wherefore [b]do the heathen say : Where is now their God?

[b]*should.* This verse occurs again, Joel ii. 17.

11 O let the [c]vengeance of thy servants' blood that is shed : be openly shewed upon the heathen in our sight.

[c]R.V. *revenging.*

12 O let the sorrowful sighing of the prisoners come before thee : according to the greatness of thy power, preserve thou those that are appointed to die.

'the prisoners,' 'those that are appointed to die,' i.e. Israelites in captivity and in peril of life.

13 And for the [d]blasphemy wherewith our neighbours have [e]blasphemed thee : reward thou them, O Lord, seven-fold into their bosom.

[d]*reproach.*

'our neighbours,' i.e. the surrounding nations who regard God as unable to protect His people, *v.* 4.

[e]*reproached.*

'seven-fold'; cp. Gen. iv. 15, 24 (Cain).

'into their bosom'; metaphor from the use of the folds of the dress as a receptacle. Is. lxv. 6; St Luke vi. 38.

14 So we, that are thy people, and sheep of thy pasture, shall give thee thanks for ever : and will alway be shewing forth thy praise from generation to generation.

PSALM LXXX. *Qui regis Israel.*

May Israel, the vine of God's planting, be restored to its former vigour! Probably written during the exile.

HEAR, O thou Shepherd of Israel, thou that leadest Joseph like a [a]sheep : shew thyself also, thou that sittest upon the cherubim.

'leadest' through the wilderness; cp. Ps. lxxvii. 20.

'Joseph' here includes all Israel, and this suggests that the Psalmist belonged to one of the northern tribes among whom Ephraim and Manasseh, descended from Joseph's sons, were pre-eminent; see *v.* 2.

[a]*flock.*

'the cherubim' which overshadowed the mercy seat of the ark, the throne of God's glory.

2 Before Ephraim, Benjamin, and Manasses : stir up thy strength, and come, and help us.

In the order of the march through the wilderness these tribes came immediately after the ark. Numb. ii. 17—24.

3 Turn us again, O God : [b]⌜shew the light of thy countenance⌝, and we shall be whole.

Restore us to our former state.

[b]*and cause thy face to shine.* Part of the priestly benediction 'The LORD make his face to shine upon thee.' Numb. vi. 25.

4 O LORD God of hosts : how long wilt thou be angry with thy people that prayeth?

5 Thou feedest them with the bread of tears : and givest them plenteousness of tears to drink.

6 Thou hast made us a very strife unto our neighbours : and our enemies laugh us to scorn.

'a very strife.' They vie with one another in attacking us.

7 Turn us again, thou God of hosts : shew the light of thy countenance, and we shall be whole.

See *v.* 3.

8 Thou hast brought a vine out of Egypt : thou hast cast out the heathen, and planted it.

Cp. Is. v. 1, 7; Jer. ii. 21.

9 Thou madest room for it : and when it had taken root it filled the land.

10 The hills were covered with the shadow of it : and the boughs thereof were like the goodly cedar-trees.

11 She stretched out her branches unto the sea : and her boughs unto the river.

10, 11. The ideal boundaries of the Promised Land are here mentioned, viz. the Hill-country on the south, Lebanon with its cedars on the north, the Mediterranean ('the sea') on the west, the Euphrates ('the river') on the east. Deut. xi. 24.

12 Why hast thou then broken down her hedge : that all they that go by pluck off her grapes?

13 The wild boar out of the wood doth root it up : and the wild beasts of the field devour it.

14 Turn thee again, thou God of hosts, look down from heaven : behold, and visit this vine;

15 And the [a]⌜place of the vineyard⌝ that thy right hand hath planted : and the branch that thou madest so strong for thyself.

[a] R.V. *stock*. The 'stock,' and the 'branch' in the parallel clause = Israel.

16 It is burnt with fire, and cut down : and they shall perish at the rebuke of thy countenance.

17 Let thy hand be upon the man of thy right hand : and upon the son of man, whom thou madest so strong for thine own self.

Let Thy protecting hand shield the man (='the stock', *v.* 15) that Thy right hand hath planted. Mystically we may regard 'the man of thy right hand,' 'the son of man,' as Christ the true Vine of Israel.

18 And so will not we go back from thee : [b]⌜O let us live⌝, and we shall call upon thy Name.

[b] R.V. *quicken thou us*, i.e. restore our life as a nation.

19 Turn us again, O LORD God of hosts : shew the light of thy countenance, and we shall be whole.

See *v.* 3.

PSALM LXXXI. *Exultate Deo.*

A song of praise for use on high Festivals.
The traditional New Year's Day Psalm in Jewish worship.

SING we merrily unto God our strength : make a cheerful noise unto the God of Jacob.

2 Take the psalm, bring hither the tabret : the merry harp with the lute.

3 Blow up the trumpet in the new-moon : [a]⌜even in the time appointed, and⌝ upon our solemn feast-day.

'the new-moon.' According to ancient Jewish interpretation the new moon of the seventh month (Tisri) is meant. It was the civil New Year's Day and was called 'the Feast of trumpets.' Numb. xxix. 1.

[a] R.V. *at the full moon.* Another Festival is referred to, viz. the Feast of Tabernacles which began at the full moon on the 15th of Tisri. Trumpets were blown on all Festivals. Numb. x. 10.

4 For [b]⌜this was made⌝ a statute for Israel : and a law of the God of Jacob.

[b] R.V. *it is.* 'it' refers to the celebration of the Feasts mentioned in *v.* 3.

5 This he ordained in Joseph for a testimony : [c]⌜when he came out of⌝ the land of Egypt, [d]⌜and had heard a strange language⌝.

'Joseph' is here put for Israel in general (see *v.* 4). Perhaps the Psalmist belonged to the northern kingdom (see Ps. lxxx. 1); or Joseph, owing to the part he played in Egypt, is regarded as specially representing the nation in connection with that country.

[c] R.V. *when he went out over*, i.e. when God went out for judgement over Egypt. Exod. xi. 4.

[d] R.V. *where I heard a language that I knew not.* The Psalmist speaks in the person of his nation. The language which Israel knew not was the fresh revelation made at the Exodus, poetically embodied in the words of God which follow.

6 I eased his shoulder from the burden : and his hands were delivered from [a]⌜making the pots⌝.

6 to end. God speaks.

[a]R.V. *the basket*, used for carrying bricks.

7 Thou calledst upon me in troubles, and I delivered thee : and heard thee [b]⌜what time as the storm fell upon thee⌝.

[b]*in the secret place of thunder*, i.e. the pillar of fire and of cloud through which God looked forth in the passage of the Red Sea. Exod. xiv. 24.

8 I proved thee also : at the waters of [c]strife.

[c]*Meribah*. Exod. xvii. 7.

9 Hear, O my people, and I will assure thee, O Israel : if thou wilt hearken unto me,

10 There shall no strange god be in thee : neither shalt thou worship any other god.

11 I am the LORD thy God, who brought thee out of the land of Egypt : open thy mouth wide, and I shall fill it.

i.e. God would satisfy their utmost wants.

12 But my people would not hear my voice : and Israel would not obey me.

13 [d]⌜So I gave them up unto their own hearts' lusts : and let them follow their own imaginations⌝.

[d]R.V. *So I let them go after the stubbornness of their heart, that they might walk in their own counsels.*

14 O that my people would have hearkened unto me : for if Israel had walked in my ways,

15 I should soon have put down their enemies : and turned my hand against their adversaries.

16 The haters of the LORD should [e]⌜have been found liars⌝ : but their time should have endured for ever.

[e]R.V. mg. *yield feigned obedience*, Heb. *lie*. i.e. pay the insincere allegiance of the vanquished. Ps. xviii. 45, lxvi. 2.

'their time,' i.e. Israel's time of prosperity.

17 He should have fed them also with the finest wheat-flour : and with honey out of the stony rock should I have satisfied thee.

Evening Prayer

PSALM LXXXII. *Deus stetit.*

God pronounces judgement upon earthly judges.

GOD standeth in the congregation of [a]princes : he is a Judge among gods.

[a] R.V. *God.* 'The congregation of God' = Israel; see Numb. xxvii. 17; Josh. xxii. 16.
'gods' = the judges of Israel, so called as being God's delegates, dispensing justice in His name.

2 How long will ye give wrong judgement : and accept the persons of the ungodly?

2—7. God speaks.

3 Defend the poor and fatherless : see that such as are in need and necessity have right.

4 Deliver the outcast and poor : save them from the hand of the ungodly.

5 They will not be learned nor understand, but walk on still in darkness : all the foundations of the earth are out of course.

'learned,' i.e. taught, instructed.
Owing to the malpractices of the judges, the moral government upon which the well-being of the world is based, is upset.

6 I have said, Ye are gods : and ye are all the children of the most Highest.

'Jesus answered them, Is it not written in your law, I said, Ye are gods? If he called them gods unto whom the word of God came..., say ye of him whom the Father sanctified and sent into the world, Thou blasphemest; because I said, I am the Son of God?' St John x. 34—36[1].

7 But ye shall die like men : and fall like one of the princes.

i.e. you shall not escape the common lot of men and princes notwithstanding your exalted titles and position.

8 Arise, O God, and judge thou the earth : for thou shalt take all heathen to thine inheritance.

The Psalmist prays that God Himself may act as judge, and not of Israel alone, but of all nations.

[1] Our Lord here suited His argument to those whom He addressed, who were not ye capable of accepting His Divine Sonship on higher grounds. Besides, the fact that God under the Old Covenant conferred on men who represented Him the title of gods was a plain foreshadowing of the future union of God and man in the Person of Christ.

PSALM LXXXIII. *Deus, quis similis?*

An earnest appeal to God to succour His people who are threatened by a confederacy of enemies. The occasion is probably the league of hostile nations against Israel in the time of Jehoshaphat. 2 Chron. xx.

HOLD not thy tongue, O God, keep not still silence : refrain not thyself, O God.

2 For lo, thine enemies make a murmuring : and they that hate thee have lift up their head.

'thine enemies.' Israel's foes are the foes of God.

3 They have imagined craftily against thy people : and taken counsel against thy [a]secret ones.

[a]*hidden*. God's 'hidden ones' are those whom He hides in the covert of His presence. Ps. xxxi. 22; see Ps. xvii. 8, xxvii. 5.

4 They have said, Come, and let us root them out, that they be no more a people : and that the name of Israel may be no more in remembrance.

5 For they have cast their heads together with one consent : and are confederate against thee;

6 The [b]tabernacles of the Edomites, and the Ishmaelites : the Moabites, and Hagarenes;

[b]R.V. *tents*.

'Hagarenes.' They are mentioned in 1 Chr. v. 10, 19, 20 (Hagrites) as living east of Gilead, beyond Jordan.

7 Gebal, and Ammon, and Amalek : the Philistines, with them that dwell at Tyre.

'Gebal,' a tribe dwelling south of the Dead Sea.

8 [c]Assur also is joined with them : and have holpen the children of Lot.

[c]R.V. *Assyria*.

'have holpen' (i.e. helped). The subordinate position here assigned to Assyria proves that the Psalm must have been written before it became a world-empire.

'the children of Lot'=Moab and Ammon, the leaders of the allied powers. 2 Chr. xx. 1; see Deut. ii. 9, 19.

9 But do thou to them as unto [a]⌜the Madianites⌝ : unto Sisera, and unto Jabin at the brook of Kison;

[a] R.V. *Midian*, overthrown by Gideon. Judg. vii., viii.; see Is. ix. 4, x. 26.

10 Who perished at Endor : and became as the dung of the earth.

'Endor' was in the neighbourhood of Taanach and Megiddo which are mentioned in Judg. v. 19 as the scene of the rout of Jabin and Sisera; see Josh. xvii. 11.

11 Make them and their princes like Oreb and Zeb : yea, make all their princes like as Zeba and Salmana;

Princes of the Midianites slain after the battle. Judg. vii. 25, viii. 21.

12 Who say, Let us take to ourselves : [b]⌜the houses of God⌝ in possession.

'Who,' i.e. the present foes of Israel.

[b] R.V. mg. *the pastures of God*, i.e. the lands which He has given to Israel.

13 O my God, make them like [c]⌜unto a wheel⌝ : and as the stubble before the wind.

[c] R.V. *the whirling dust.*

14 Like as the fire that burneth up the wood : and as the flame that consumeth the mountains;

15 [d]⌜Persecute them even so⌝ with thy tempest : and make them afraid with thy storm.

[d] R.V. *So pursue them.*

16 Make their faces ashamed, O LORD : that they may seek thy Name.

The defeat of Israel's enemies is prayed for as a means of bringing them to a knowledge of God.

17 Let them be confounded and vexed ever more and more : let them be put to shame, and perish.

18 [e]⌜And they shall⌝ know that thou, whose Name is JEHOVAH : art only the most Highest over all the earth.

[e] R.V. *That they may.*

PSALM LXXXIV. *Quam dilecta!*

The pleasantness of God's House, and the happy lot of those who are privileged to worship in it. A companion Psalm to xlii., xliii.

Proper on Purification of B.V.M. and on Transfiguration [America]. Special in Form of Consecration of a Church [Convocation 1712, Ireland, America] and in Service for the first Sunday on which a minister officiates in a new cure [Ireland].

O HOW amiable are thy dwellings : thou LORD of hosts!

'amiable' = loveable.

2 My soul hath a desire and longing to enter into the courts of the LORD : my heart and my flesh rejoice in the living God.

'soul,' 'heart,' 'flesh' = my whole being.

'the living God,' i.e. the Source of Life, 'the fountain of living waters.' Jer. ii. 13; see Ps. xlii. 2.

3 Yea, the sparrow hath found her an house, and the swallow a nest where she may lay her young : even thy altars, O LORD of hosts, my King and my God.

May I be as privileged as the birds which have entry into the Temple courts!

4 Blessed are they that dwell in thy house : they will be alway praising thee.

5 Blessed is the man whose strength is in thee : in whose heart are [a]⌜thy ways⌝.

[a] R.V. *the highways to Zion*, i.e. whose heart is set on pilgrimage to Jerusalem. P.B.V. means, who meditates on Thy commandments.

6 [b]⌜Who going through the vale of misery use it for a well : and the pools are filled with water⌝.

[b] R.V. *Passing through the valley of Weeping* (mg. *balsam trees*, Heb. *Baca*) *they make it a place of springs; yea, the early rain covereth it with blessings.*

Such is the enthusiasm of the pilgrims that even the arid and barren regions through which they journey seem to them well-watered and fertile. Balsam trees love a dry soil. Some special valley which received its name from these trees is in the Psalmist's mind. 'Weeping' is a less probable interpretation of 'Baca.'

7 They will go from strength to strength : and [a]⌜unto the God of gods⌝ appeareth every one of them in Sion.

'from strength to strength.' Their strength instead of flagging will increase as the journey proceeds.

[a]*before God.* P.B.V. from Vulg.

'To appear before God' is the expression used for going up to the Temple on the Festivals; see Ps. xlii. 2.

8 O LORD God of hosts, hear my prayer : hearken, O God of Jacob.

9 Behold, O God our defender : and look upon the face of thine anointed.

'thine anointed' = the king, in whose well-being that of his people is wrapped up.

10 For one day in thy courts : is better than a thousand.

11 I had rather be a door-keeper in the house of my God : than to dwell in the tents of ungodliness.

12 For the LORD God is [b]⌜a light and defence⌝ : the LORD will give grace and [c]worship, and no good thing shall he withhold from them that live a godly life.

[b]R.V. *a sun and a shield.* Only here in the O.T. is God called a sun.

[c]*glory.* P.B.V. 'worship' has this meaning; see St Luke xiv. 10.

13 O LORD God of hosts : blessed is the man that putteth his trust in thee.

PSALM LXXXV. *Benedixisti, Domine.*

A vision of the glorious indwelling of God in His Church, and of the reign of love and righteousness. Written probably soon after the return from Babylon.

Proper on Christmas Day.

1—3. The Psalmist makes God's mercies to Israel in the past the ground of prayer (*vv.* 4—7) for renewed favours.

LORD, thou [d]⌜art become gracious⌝ unto thy land : thou hast [e]⌜turned away⌝ the captivity of Jacob.

[d]*hast been favourable.*

[e]*brought back.*

The restoration from captivity in Babylon is here probably specially referred to; but 'to bring back the captivity' is a general phrase for 'to restore prosperity'; see Ps. liii. 7.

2 Thou hast forgiven the offence of thy people : and covered all their sins.

3 Thou hast taken away all thy displeasure : and turned thyself from thy wrathful indignation.

4 Turn us then, O God our Saviour : and let thine anger cease from us.

'Turn us,' i.e. Restore us to our former state of Divine favour; see Ps. lxxx. 3.

5 Wilt thou be displeased at us for ever : and wilt thou stretch out thy wrath from one generation to another?

6 Wilt thou not turn again, and quicken us : that thy people may rejoice in thee?

'quicken us,' i.e. revive our national life.

7 Shew us thy mercy, O LORD : and grant us thy salvation.

'O Lord, shew thy mercy upon us.'
'And grant us thy salvation.'
Versicle and Response at Matins and Evensong.

8 I will hearken what the LORD God will say [1]⌜concerning me⌝ : for he shall speak peace unto his people, and to his saints, [a]⌜that they turn not again⌝.

[a]*but let them not turn again to folly.*

9 For his salvation is nigh them that fear him : that glory may dwell in our land.

The glory of God's Presence manifested of old above the mercy-seat. The Psalmist's hope was fulfilled, in a far higher sense, in the Incarnation. 'We beheld his glory, glory as of the only begotten from the Father.' St John i. 14.

10 Mercy and truth are met together : righteousness and peace have kissed each other.

11 Truth shall flourish out of the earth : and righteousness hath looked down from heaven.

12 Yea, the LORD shall [b]⌜shew loving-kindness⌝ : and our land shall give her increase.

[b]*give that which is good.*
Temporal blessings will not be absent in the glorious future.

[1] Not in A.R.V., added in P.B.V. following Vulg.

13 Righteousness shall go before him : and [a]⌜he shall direct his going in the way⌝.

[a] R.V. *shall make his footsteps a way to walk in.* Righteousness shall go before the LORD as His herald (1st clause), and also follow Him to point out His footsteps as the way His people should walk in.

THE SEVENTEENTH DAY

Morning Prayer

PSALM LXXXVI. *Inclina, Domine.*

An expression of unwavering faith in God in time of deep trouble.

Proper on Purification of B.V.M. [America].

BOW down thine ear, O LORD, and hear me : for I am poor, and in misery.

2 Preserve thou my soul, for I am [b]holy : my God, save thy servant that putteth his trust in thee.

[b] A.V. mg. *one whom thou favourest.*
'O Lord, save thy servant;
Which putteth his trust in thee.'
Visitation of the Sick.

3 Be merciful unto me, O Lord : for I [c]will call daily upon thee.

[c] R.V. *do.*

4 Comfort the soul of thy servant : for unto thee, O Lord, do I lift up my soul.

5 For thou, Lord, art good and [d]gracious : and of great mercy unto all them that call upon thee.

[d] *ready to forgive.*

6 Give ear, LORD, unto my prayer : and ponder the voice of my humble desires.

7 In the time of my trouble I will call upon thee : for thou hearest me.

8 Among the gods there is none like unto thee, O Lord : [a]⌜there is not one that can do as thou doest⌝.

[a] *neither are there any works like unto thy works.* 'Great and marvellous are thy works, O Lord God, the Almighty...all the nations shall come and worship before thee.' Rev. xv. 3, 4.

9 All nations whom thou hast made shall come and worship thee, O Lord : and shall glorify thy Name.

10 For thou art great, and doest wondrous things : thou art God alone.

11 Teach me thy way, O LORD, and I will walk in thy truth : [b]⌜O knit my heart unto thee, that I may fear thy Name⌝.

[b] *unite my heart to fear thy name,* i.e. give my heart a single aim; may its affections and powers be directed solely to Thee; see Jer. xxxii. 39.

12 I will thank thee, O Lord my God, with all my heart : and will praise thy Name for evermore.

13 For great is thy mercy toward me : and thou hast delivered my soul from [c]⌜the nethermost hell⌝.

[c] R.V. mg. *Sheol beneath.* The Psalmist has been saved, when in some great peril of death.

14 O God, the proud are risen against me : and the congregations of [d]naughty men have sought after my soul, and have not set thee before their eyes.

[d] *violent.*

15 But thou, O Lord God, art full of compassion and mercy : [e]long-suffering, plenteous in goodness and truth.

[e] R.V. *slow to anger.*

16 O turn thee then unto me, and have mercy upon me : give thy strength unto thy servant, and help the son of thine handmaid.

'the son' &c., i.e. born in the LORD's house—from my earliest years 'of the household of God.' Eph. ii. 19; see Ps. cxvi. 14.

17 Shew some token upon me for good, that they who hate me may see it, and be ashamed : because thou, LORD, hast holpen me, and comforted me.

PSALM LXXXVII. *Fundamenta ejus.*

A vision of the future catholicity of the Church—of the extension of the franchise of the city of God to all nations.

Proper on Purification of B.V.M. [America].

[a]⌜HER foundations are⌝ upon the holy hills : the LORD loveth the gates of Sion more than all the dwellings of Jacob.

[a] *His foundation* (i.e. the city that Jehovah hath built) *is*.

2 [b]⌜Very excellent⌝ things are spoken of thee : thou city of God.

[b] *Glorious*. 'Excellent' formerly meant 'pre-eminent,' 'excelling.'

3 [c]⌜I will think upon Rahab and Babylon : with them that know me⌝.

3, 4. God speaks.

[c] R.V. *I will make mention of Rahab and Babylon as among them that know me*, i.e. acknowledge Me as their God.

'Rahab' = *Egypt* (as in R.V. mg.). The word meant pride or violence, and is used to designate some fierce monster, perhaps the crocodile, which became a symbol of Egypt. Ps. lxxxix. 11; Is. xxx. 7, li. 9.

4 [d]⌜Behold ye the Philistines also : and they of Tyre, with the Morians ; lo, there was he born⌝.

[d] R.V. *Behold Philistia, and Tyre, with Ethiopia; this one was born there.* God points out, as it were, each nation successively as incorporated among the children of Sion, 'born there.' P.B.V. 'Morians' = Moors.

5 [e]⌜And of Sion it shall be reported that he was born in her⌝ : and the most High shall stablish her.

[e] R.V. *Yea, of Zion it shall be said, This one and that one was born in her.* The Psalmist speaks repeating the Divine utterance.

6 [f]⌜The LORD shall rehearse it when he writeth up the people : that he was born there⌝.

[f] R.V. *The LORD shall count, when he writeth up the peoples, This one was born there.* When God registers the nations in His book He will count them as citizens of Sion, equal in privilege to those 'born there.'

7 [a]⌜The singers also and trumpeters shall he rehearse : All my fresh springs shall be in thee⌝.

[a]R.V. *They that sing as well as they that dance shall say, All my fountains* (of salvation) *are in thee* (Sion).

A picture of the rejoicing with which those heretofore aliens will hail their inclusion in the household of God.

PSALM LXXXVIII. *Domine Deus.*

The plaintive supplication of a sufferer in utter desolation and despondency. The gloomiest of all the Psalms.

Proper on Good Friday.

O LORD God of my salvation, I have cried day and night before thee : O let my prayer enter into thy presence, incline thine ear unto my calling.

In the depth of his despondency, the Psalmist has still faith to address Jehovah as 'God of my salvation.'

2 For my soul is full of trouble : and my life draweth nigh unto [b]hell.

[b]R.V. *Sheol.*

3 I am counted as one of them that go down into the pit : and I [c]⌜have been⌝ even as a man that hath no strength ;

[c]*am.*

4 [d]Free among the dead, like [e]⌜unto them that are wounded, and⌝ lie in the grave : [f]⌜who are out of remembrance, and⌝ are cut away from thy hand.

[d]R.V. *Cast off.*

[e]*the slain that.*

[f]*whom thou rememberest no more ; and they.* The Psalmist regards the dead, to whom he compares himself, as separated from God, and forgotten by Him.

5 Thou hast laid me in the lowest pit : in a place of darkness, and in the deep.

6 Thine indignation lieth hard upon me : and thou hast [g]vexed me with all thy storms.

[g]*afflicted.*

7 Thou hast put away mine acquaintance far from me : and made me to be abhorred of them.

This verse and Ps. xxxviii. 11 seem to have suggested the wording of St Luke xxiii. 49, 'All his acquaintance...stood afar off.'

8 I am so fast in prison : that I cannot get forth.

There is a barrier between the Psalmist and his former friends. Some, taking *vv.* 7, 8 literally, suppose the Psalmist to have been a leper under confinement.

9 [a]⌜My sight faileth⌝ for very trouble : LORD, I have called daily upon thee, I have stretched forth my hands unto thee.

[a]R.V. *Mine eye wasteth away.* The dulness of the eye marks suffering. Ps. vi. 7, xxxi. 10, xxxviii. 10.

10 Dost thou shew wonders among the dead : or shall the dead rise up again, and praise thee?

10—12. In the Psalmist's mind the answer to these questions is, No.

11 Shall thy loving-kindness be shewed in the grave : or thy faithfulness in destruction?

12 Shall thy wondrous works be known in the dark : and thy righteousness in the land where all things are forgotten?

13 [b]Unto thee have I cried, O LORD : and early shall my prayer come before thee.

[b]*But unto.* The Psalmist's only resource is prayer.

14 LORD, why [c]⌜abhorrest thou⌝ my soul : and hidest thou thy face from me?

[c]*castest thou off.*

15 I am in misery, and like unto him that is at the point to die : even from my youth up thy terrors have I suffered with a troubled mind.

16 Thy wrathful displeasure goeth over me : [d]⌜and the fear of thee hath undone me⌝.

[d]*thy terrors have cut me off.*

17 They came round about me daily like water : and compassed me together on every side.

'They,' i.e. 'thy terrors,' *v.* 16.

18 My lovers and friends hast thou put away from me : and hid mine acquaintance out of my sight.

Evening Prayer

PSALM LXXXIX. *Misericordias Domini.*

A prayer that the promises made to David but apparently in abeyance, may be fulfilled. Probably written in the early years of the exile.

Proper on Christmas Day and on Annunciation of B.V.M. [America]. The Incarnation was the true answer to the Psalmist's prayer.

MY song shall be alway of the loving-kindness of the LORD : with my mouth will I ever be shewing thy [a]truth from one generation to another.

2 For I have said, Mercy shall be set up for ever : thy [b]truth shalt thou stablish in the heavens.

3 I have made a covenant with my chosen : I have sworn unto David my servant;

4 Thy seed will I stablish for ever : and set up thy throne from one generation to another.

5 O LORD, the very heavens shall praise thy wondrous works : and thy [c]truth in the [d]⌜congregation of the saints⌝.

6 For who is he [e]⌜among the clouds⌝ : that shall be compared unto the LORD?

7 And what is he among the [f]gods : that shall be like unto the LORD?

8 God is very greatly to be feared in the council of the [g]saints : and to be had in reverence of all them that are round about him.

[a] *faithfulness.*

[b] *faithfulness.*

3, 4. God's words. They are a summary of His promises to David and his house given in 2 Sam. vii. 8 ff.

[c] *faithfulness.*

[d] R.V. *assembly of the holy ones*, i.e. the angels.

[e] R.V. *in the skies.*

[f] *sons of the mighty* (R.V. mg. *of God*) = angels; see Ps. xxix. 1.

[g] R.V. *holy ones* = angels.

9 O LORD God of hosts, who is like unto thee : thy [a]truth, most mighty LORD, is on every side.

[a]*faithfulness.*

10 Thou rulest the raging of the sea : thou stillest the waves thereof when they arise.

11 Thou hast subdued [b]Egypt, and destroyed it : thou hast scattered thine enemies abroad with thy mighty arm.

[b]*Rahab*; see Ps. lxxxvii. 3.

12 The heavens are thine, the earth also is thine : thou hast laid the foundation of the [1]round world, and all that therein is.

13 Thou hast made the north and the south : Tabor and Hermon shall rejoice in thy Name.

'Tabor and Hermon,' conspicuous landmarks in the west and east of the Jordan; see Ps. xlii. 8, lxxii. 3.

14 Thou hast a mighty arm : strong is thy hand, and high is thy right hand.

15 Righteousness and equity are the [c]⌜habitation of thy seat⌝ : mercy and truth shall go before thy face.

[c]R.V. *foundation of thy throne.*

16 Blessed is the people, O LORD, that [d]⌜can rejoice in thee⌝ : they shall walk in the light of thy countenance.

[d]*know the joyful* (R.V. mg. *trumpet*) *sound.* An allusion to the blowing of trumpets which ushered in the Festivals. Numb. x. 10.

17 Their delight shall be daily in thy Name : and in thy righteousness [e]⌜shall they make their boast⌝.

[e]R.V. *are they exalted.*

18 For thou art the glory of their strength : and in thy loving-kindness thou shalt lift up our horns.

19 [f]⌜For the LORD is our defence : the Holy One of Israel is our King⌝.

[f]R.V. *For our shield belongeth unto the LORD; and our king to the Holy One of Israel*; see Ps. lxxi. 20. The nation's 'shield' is the king, and he himself is in the LORD's safe-keeping.

[1] Not in A.R.V., P.B.V. suggested by the Vulg. *orbem terrae.*

20—26. A further unfolding of the promise given to the house of David. 2 Sam. vii. 8 ff.

20 Thou spakest sometime in visions unto thy saints, and saidst: I have laid help upon one that is mighty; I have exalted one chosen out of the people.

'sometime' = formerly.

'thy saints' = Israel, for whose benefit the promise was made.

'laid' = bestowed. Ps. xxi. 5.

21 I have found David my servant: with my holy oil have I anointed him.

22 My hand shall hold him fast: and my arm shall strengthen him.

23 The enemy shall not be able to do him violence: the son of wickedness shall not hurt him.

'Let the enemy have no advantage of him;
Nor the wicked approach to hurt him.'
Visitation of the Sick.

'son of wickedness,' Hebraism for 'wicked person.'

24 I will smite down his foes before his face: and plague them that hate him.

25 My [a]truth also and my mercy shall be with him: and in my Name shall his horn be exalted.

[a] *faithfulness.*

26 I will set his dominion also in the sea: and his right hand in [b]⌜the floods⌝.

'the sea' = the Mediterranean.

[b] *the rivers* = Euphrates; the plural is poetic.

27 He shall call me, Thou art my Father: my God, and my strong salvation.

28 And I will make him my first-born: higher than the kings of the earth.

Completely fulfilled only in the Divine Son of David, 'the first-born of the dead, and the ruler of the kings of the earth.' Rev. i. 5.

29 My mercy will I keep for him for evermore: and my covenant shall stand fast with him.

30 His seed also will I make to endure for ever: and his throne as the days of heaven.

31 But if his children forsake my law: and walk not in my judgements;

32 If they break my statutes, and keep not my commandments : I will visit their offences with the rod, and their sin with scourges.

33 Nevertheless, my loving-kindness will I not utterly take from him : nor suffer my [a]truth to fail.

[a]*faithfulness.*

34 My covenant will I not break, nor alter the thing that is gone out of my lips : I have sworn once by my holiness, that I will not fail David.

'once,' i.e. once for all.

35 His seed shall endure for ever : and his [b]seat is like as the sun before me.

[b]*throne.*

36 [c]He shall stand fast for evermore as the moon : [d]⌜and as the faithful witness in heaven⌝.

[c]*It*, i.e. his throne.

[d]R.V. mg. *and the witness in the sky* (i.e. God Himself) *is faithful.*

37—44. The contrast between the calamities of the present, and the divinely promised blessings.

37 But thou hast [e]⌜abhorred and forsaken⌝ thine anointed : and art displeased at him.

[e]R.V. *cast off and rejected.*

'thine anointed'=the kings of David's line. Perhaps Jehoiachin in particular is referred to; see 2 Kings xxiv. 12, 15.

38 Thou hast broken the covenant of thy servant : and cast his crown to the ground.

39 Thou hast overthrown all his hedges : and broken down his strong holds.

'hedges.' The kingdom is likened to a vineyard; see Ps. lxxx. 12 ff.

40 All they that go by spoil him : and he is become a reproach to his neighbours.

41 Thou hast set up the right hand of his enemies : and made all his adversaries to rejoice.

42 Thou [f]⌜hast taken away⌝ the edge of his sword : and givest him not victory in the battle.

[f]R.V. *turnest back.*

43 Thou hast put out his glory : and cast his throne down to the ground.

44 The days of his youth hast thou shortened : and covered him with dishonour.

i.e. the monarchy of David is in a state of premature decay: or the reference is to Jehoiachin who after his accession at 18 reigned only three months. 2 Kings xxiv. 8.

45 LORD, how long wilt thou hide thyself, for ever : and shall thy wrath burn like fire?

The confused question 'How long... for ever?' indicates the perplexity of the Psalmist; cp. Ps. xiii. 1, lxxix. 5.

46 O remember how short my time is : wherefore hast thou made all men for nought?

47 What man is he that liveth, and shall not see death : and shall he deliver his soul from the hand of [a]hell?

46, 47. The Psalmist pleads the shortness of life as a reason that God's anger should speedily give way to mercy. He wishes to survive this time of trouble.

[a]R.V. *Sheol.*

48 Lord, where are thy old loving-kindnesses : which thou swarest unto David in thy [b]truth?

[b]R.V. *faithfulness.*

49 Remember, Lord, the [c]rebuke that thy servants have : and how I do bear in my bosom the [c]rebukes of many [d]people;

[c]*reproach.*

[d]R.V. *peoples.*

50 Wherewith thine enemies have [e]⌜blasphemed thee⌝, and [f]slandered the footsteps of thine anointed: Praised be the LORD for evermore. Amen, and Amen.

[e]*reproached, O LORD.*
[f]*reproached.*

An ancient Jewish comment on this verse is, 'They have scoffed at the slowness of Thy Messiah's footsteps'; and another, 'He delays so long, they say He will never come.'

'Praised be' &c. Doxology added to mark the close of the Third Book of the Psalter.

THE EIGHTEENTH DAY

Morning Prayer

PSALM XC. *Domine, refugium.*

The transitoriness of man's life, and his dependence on the eternal God. The Title is 'A Prayer of Moses the man of God.'

Special in Burial Service. Proper on Circumcision [America].

LORD, thou hast been our [g]refuge : from one generation to another.

[g]*dwelling place.*

2 Before the mountains were brought forth, or ever the earth and the world were made : thou art God from everlasting, and world without end.

'the world' = the fruit-bearing, habitable part of the earth.

3 Thou turnest man to destruction : again thou sayest, Come again, ye children of men.

i.e. God calls a new generation into being to replace the old.

4 For a thousand years in thy sight are but as [a]⌜yesterday : seeing that is past⌝ as a watch in the night.

'One day is with the Lord as a thousand years, and a thousand years as one day.' 2 St Pet. iii. 8.

[a]*yesterday when it is past, and.*

'a watch.' The night was divided by the Israelites into three watches. Judg. vii. 19.

5 [b]⌜As soon as thou scatterest them⌝ they are even as a sleep : and fade away suddenly like the grass.

[b]*Thou carriest them away as with a flood.*

6 In the morning it is green, and groweth up : but in the evening it is cut down, [1]⌜dried up⌝, and withered.

7 For we consume away in thy displeasure : and are afraid at thy wrathful indignation.

'we.' The Psalmist changes to the first person, and records the experience of Israel in general.

8 Thou hast set our misdeeds before thee : and our secret sins in the light of thy countenance.

9 [c]⌜For when thou art angry all our days are gone⌝ : we bring our years to an end, as it were a tale that is told.

[c]*For all our days are passed away in thy wrath.*

10 The days of our age are threescore years and ten ; and though men be so strong that they come to fourscore years : yet is their [d]strength then but labour and sorrow ; so soon passeth it away, and we are gone.

[d]R.V. *pride*, i.e. what men most glory in.

[1] Not in A.R.V., added in P.B.V from Vulg.

11 But who regardeth the power of [a]⌜thy wrath : for even thereafter as a man feareth, so is thy displeasure⌝.

[a]R.V. *thy anger, and thy wrath according to the fear that is due unto thee?* i.e. who considers aright the intensity of God's wrath against sin, so as to fear to offend Him?

12 So teach us to number our days : that we may apply our hearts unto wisdom.

13 Turn thee again, O LORD, at the last : and [b]⌜be gracious unto⌝ thy servants.

Cp. the words of Moses, 'Turn from thy fierce wrath, and repent of this evil against thy people.' Exod. xxxii. 12.

[b]*let it repent thee concerning*, i.e. change from wrath to compassion towards; see Ps. cxxxv. 14.

14 O satisfy us with thy mercy, [c]⌜and that soon⌝ : so shall we rejoice and be glad all the days of our life.

[c]R.V. *in the morning*. When the night of anger is over. Ps. xxx. 5, xlvi. 5.

15 Comfort us again now [d]after the time that thou hast plagued us : and for the years wherein we have suffered adversity.

[d]*according to.* May the chastisement of the past be compensated for by the joy of days spent in God's favour!

16 Shew thy servants thy work : and their children thy glory.

May God's work and glory, i.e. His providential care of Israel, be visibly manifested to His servants and to their posterity!

17 And the [e]⌜glorious Majesty⌝ of the LORD our God be upon us : prosper thou the work of our hands upon us, O prosper thou our handy-work.

[e]*beauty*, or *pleasantness* as the word is rendered in Ps. xxvii. 4 R.V. mg.

May God render effectual man's feeble efforts to carry out His purposes!

PSALM XCI. *Qui habitat.*

The peace and safety of him who commits himself to the care of God.

Proper on St Michael and all Angels [America].

WHOSO dwelleth [f]⌜under the defence⌝ of the most High : shall abide under the shadow of the Almighty.

[f]*in the secret place.*

2 I will say unto the LORD, Thou art my [g]hope, and my strong hold : my God, in him will I trust.

[g]*refuge.*

3 For he shall deliver thee from the snare of the [a]hunter : and from the noisome pestilence.

'thee,' i.e. who dwellest 'in the secret place of the most High,' *v.* 1.
[a]*fowler.*

4 He shall defend thee under his wings, and thou shalt be safe under his feathers : his [1]⌜faithfulness and⌝ truth shall be thy shield and buckler.

i.e. as a bird protects its young.

5 Thou shalt not be afraid for any terror by night : nor for the arrow that flieth by day;

6 For the pestilence that walketh in darkness : nor for the sickness that destroyeth in the noon-day.

7 A thousand shall fall beside thee, and ten thousand at thy right hand : but it shall not come nigh thee.

8 Yea, with thine eyes shalt thou behold : and see the reward of the ungodly.

9 [b]⌜For thou, LORD, art my hope : thou hast set thine house of defence very high⌝.

[b]R.V. mg. *Because thou hast said, The LORD is my refuge;* (and) *thou hast made the Most High thy habitation;*

10 There shall no evil happen unto thee : neither shall any plague come nigh thy dwelling.

11 For he shall give his angels charge over thee : to keep thee in all thy ways.

12 They shall bear thee in their hands : that thou hurt not thy foot against a stone.

11, 12. Quoted by Satan in his temptation of our Lord (St Matt. iv. 6; St Luke iv. 10, 11) with the significant omission of the words 'in all thy ways.' God's providence is pledged to protect those only who continue in the ways of duty.

13 Thou shalt go upon the lion and adder : the young lion and the [c]dragon shalt thou tread under thy feet.

Cp. St Luke x. 19, 'Behold I have given you authority to tread upon serpents and scorpions and over all the power of the enemy'; cp. Rom. xvi. 20 and Litany, 'beat down Satan under our feet.'
[c]R.V. *serpent.*

[1] Not in A.R.V.

14 Because he hath set his love upon me, therefore will I deliver him : I will set him up, because he hath known my Name.

14—16. God speaks, confirming His servant's faith.

15 He shall call upon me, and I will hear him : yea, I am with him in trouble; I will deliver him, and bring him to honour.

16 With long life will I satisfy him : and shew him my salvation.

'God gave unto us eternal life.' 1 St John v. 11.

PSALM XCII. *Bonum est confiteri.*

A Psalm of thanksgiving for God's righteous government of the world. 'For the Sabbath day' (Title). It was appointed for that day after the exile.

At Evensong, *vv.* 1—4 second alternative for Magnificat [America].

IT is a good thing to give thanks unto the LORD : and to sing praises unto thy Name, O most Highest;

2 To tell of thy loving-kindness early in the morning : and of thy [a]truth in the night-season;

[a]*faithfulness.*

3 Upon an instrument of ten strings, and upon the lute : upon a loud instrument, and upon the harp.

4 For thou, LORD, hast made me glad through [b]⌜thy works⌝ : and I will rejoice in giving praise for the [c]operations of thy hands.

[b]*thy work,* wrought by Thee as moral Ruler of the world, see *vv.* 7 to end.

[c]*works.* P.B.V. may have been suggested by Vulg. *operibus.*

5 O LORD, how glorious are thy works : thy thoughts are very deep.

6 [d]⌜An unwise⌝ man doth not well consider this : and a fool doth not understand it.

[d]*A brutish.*

7 When the ungodly are green as the grass, and when all the workers of wickedness do flourish : [a]⌜then shall they⌝ be destroyed for ever; but thou, LORD, art [b]⌜the most Highest⌝ for evermore.

[a] *it is that they shall*; cp. Exod. ix. 16; Rom. ix. 17.
[b] R.V. *on high.* P.B.V. and A.V. from Vulg.

8 For lo, thine enemies, O LORD, lo, thine enemies shall perish : and all the workers of wickedness shall be [c]destroyed.

[c] *scattered.*

9 But mine horn [d]⌜shall be⌝ exalted like the horn of [e]⌜an unicorn⌝ : for I am anointed with fresh oil.

[d] R.V. *hast thou.* The 'horn' is an emblem of vigour; see Ps. lxxv. 5.
[e] R.V. *the wild-ox.* P.B.V. and A.V. from Vulg.
Like a guest at a joyous banquet; see Ps. xxiii. 5.

10 Mine eye also [f]⌜shall see his lust of⌝ mine enemies : and mine [g]⌜ear shall hear his⌝ desire of the wicked that arise up against me.

[f] R.V. *hath seen my desire on.*

[g] R.V. *ears have heard my.*
P.B.V. 'his' = its.

11 The righteous shall flourish like a palm-tree : and shall spread abroad like a cedar in Libanus.

12 Such as are planted in the house of the LORD : shall flourish in the courts [1]⌜of the house⌝ of our God.

The righteous are planted, as it were, in the precincts of God's house, and from its sacred soil draw vitality and fruitfulness.

13 [h]⌜They also shall bring forth more fruit in their age⌝ : and shall be [i]⌜fat and well-liking⌝;

[h] *They shall still bring forth fruit in old age.* A characteristic of the palm-tree.
[i] R.V. *full of sap and green.* P.B.V. 'well-liking' = in good condition.

14 That they may shew how true the LORD my strength is : and that there is no unrighteousness in him.

[1] Not in A.R.V., added in P.B.V. from Vulg.

Evening Prayer

PSALM XCIII. *Dominus regnavit.*

The Throne of God is set above the restless waves of the nations of the earth.

The first of a series of Theocratic Psalms celebrating God's Kingly rule of the world. They continue with one exception (xciv.) to c. They were probably written after the exile for use in the Temple worship.

Proper on Trinity Sunday [America] and on Transfiguration [America].

THE LORD is King, and hath put on glorious apparel : the LORD hath put on his apparel, and girded himself with strength.

2 He hath made the [1]round world so sure : that it cannot be moved.

i.e. God's rule has firmly established the moral and political order of the world.

3 Ever since the world began hath thy [a]seat been prepared : thou art from everlasting.

[a] *throne.*

4 The floods are risen, O LORD, the floods have lift up their voice : the floods lift up their waves.

The floods and the sea symbolize the world-powers that aim at universal conquest; see Jer. xlvi. 8, 'Egypt riseth up like the Nile, and his waters toss themselves like the rivers: and he saith, I will rise up, I will cover the earth.'

5 The waves of the sea are mighty, and rage horribly : but yet the LORD, who dwelleth on high, is mightier.

6 Thy testimonies, O LORD, are very sure : holiness becometh thine house for ever.

[1] Not in A.R.V., P.B.V. suggested by the Vulg. *orbem terrae.*

PSALM XCIV. *Deus ultionum.*

An expression of patient waiting upon God in a time of oppression and perversion of justice.

O LORD God, to whom vengeance belongeth : thou God, to whom vengeance belongeth, shew thyself.

2 Arise, thou Judge of the world : and reward the proud after their deserving.

3 LORD, how long shall the ungodly : how long shall the ungodly triumph?

4 How long shall all wicked doers speak so disdainfully : and make such proud boasting?

5 They smite down thy people, O LORD : and trouble thine heritage.

6 They murder the widow, and the stranger : and put the fatherless to death.

'widow,' 'stranger,' 'fatherless,' types of the helpless. Ps. cxlvi. 9.

7 And yet they say, Tush, the LORD shall not see : neither shall the God of Jacob regard it.

8 Take heed, ye [a]unwise among the people : O ye fools, when will ye understand?

[a] *brutish.*

'the people' of Israel, some of whom, when oppressed, apparently doubted the power of God to protect them.

9 He that planted the ear, shall he not hear : or he that made the eye, shall he not see?

10 Or he that [b]nurtureth the heathen : it is he that teacheth man knowledge, shall not he punish?

[b] R.V. mg. *instructeth.* God's education and discipline reaches beyond Israel to the heathen nations; cp. Rom. ii. 14, 15.

11 The LORD knoweth the thoughts of man : that they are but vain.

Quoted by St Paul in 1 Cor. iii. 20 with the substitution of 'the wise' for 'man' as more suitable to his argument.

12 Blessed is the man whom thou chastenest, O LORD : and teachest him in thy law;

Israel has the special blessing of receiving Divine instruction from direct revelation—'thy law.'

13 That thou mayest give him patience in time of adversity : until the pit be digged up for the ungodly.

14 For the LORD will not fail his people : neither will he forsake his inheritance ;

15 [a]⌜Until righteousness turn again unto judgement⌝ : all such as are true in heart shall follow it.

[a] R.V. *For judgement shall return unto righteousness*, i.e. judgement, so long perverted, shall resume its true character of righteousness.

16 Who will rise up [b]with me against the wicked : or who will take my part against the evil-doers?

[b] *for*. The answer is, No one but God (*v.* 17).

17 If the LORD had not helped me : [c]⌜it had not failed but my soul had been put to silence⌝.

[c] R.V. *my soul had soon dwelt in silence*, i.e. that of the grave.

18 But when I said, My foot hath slipt : thy mercy, O LORD, held me up.

19 In the multitude of [d]⌜the sorrows that I had in my heart⌝ : thy comforts have refreshed my soul.

[d] R.V. mg. *my doubts within me.*

20 [e]⌜Wilt thou have any thing to do with the stool of wickedness : which imagineth mischief as a law?⌝

[e] R.V. *Shall the throne of wickedness have fellowship with thee, which frameth mischief by statute?* i.e. Shall the judgement seat, now become a throne of wickedness which perpetrates wrong under legal forms, claim for its acts the authority of God? P.B.V., in which 'stool' = seat or throne, has the same general meaning.

21 They gather them together against the soul of the righteous : and condemn the innocent blood.

i.e. pass sentence of death against the innocent; cp. St Matt. xxvii. 4, 'I have sinned in that I betrayed innocent blood.'

22 But the LORD is my refuge : and my God is the strength of my confidence.

23 He shall recompense them their wickedness, and destroy them in their own [f]malice : yea, the LORD our God shall destroy them.

[f] R.V. *evil*. P.B.V. from Vulg.

THE NINETEENTH DAY

Morning Prayer

PSALM XCV. *Venite, exultemus.*

A call to worship with a warning against disobedience.

This Psalm has been used from very early times as an introduction to Divine Service.

At Matins, the Invitatory Psalm. In the American Church *vv.* 1—7 are used with the addition of Ps. xcvi. 9, 13.

O COME, let us sing unto the LORD : let us heartily rejoice in the strength of our salvation.

2 Let us come before his presence with thanksgiving : and shew ourselves glad in him with psalms.

3 For the LORD is a great God : and a great King above all gods.

4 In his hand are [a]⌜all the corners⌝ of the earth : and the [b]strength of the hills is his also.

[a] *the deep places.*

[b] R.V. *heights.*

5 The sea is his, and he made it : and his hands prepared the dry land.

6 O come, let us worship, and fall down : and kneel before the LORD our Maker;

'our Maker.' Israel as the LORD's people, were especially His creation; cp. Ps. c. 2; Deut. xxxii. 15; Is. xliv. 2.

7 For he is [1]⌜the Lord⌝ our God : and we are the people of his pasture, and the sheep of his hand.

8 To-day if ye will hear his voice, harden not your hearts : as [c]⌜in the provocation⌝, and as in the day of [d]temptation in the wilderness;

8—11. Quoted in Heb. iii. 7—11 as a warning to Christians.

'harden not' to end of Psalm is the utterance of God's 'voice.'

[c] R.V. *at Meribah.* [d] R.V. *Massah.* Exod. xvii. 7; Numb. xx. 13.

9 When your fathers tempted me : proved me, and saw my works.

'tempted me,' i.e. put me to the test. Deut. vi. 16; see Ps. lxxviii. 19, cvi. 14.

[1] Not in A.R.V., added in P.B.V. from Vulg.

10 Forty years long was I grieved with [a]this generation, and said: It is a people that do err in their hearts, for they have not known my ways;

[a] R.V. *that.*

11 Unto whom I sware in my wrath : that they should not enter into my rest.

'my rest,' i.e. Canaan, Deut. xii. 9; mystically interpreted in Heb. iv. 9, 11, of the rest of heaven.

PSALM XCVI. *Cantate Domino.*

A vision of the universal reign of God. This Psalm is found also in 1 Chron. xvi. 23—33, combined with Ps. cv. 1—15 and cvi. 1, 47, 48.

Proper on Advent Sunday [America].

O SING unto the LORD a new song : sing unto the LORD, all the whole earth.

'new,' i.e. as giving expression to the new aspirations awakened by the return from captivity.

2 Sing unto the LORD, and praise his Name : be telling of his salvation from day to day.

3 Declare his honour unto the heathen : and his [b]wonders unto all [c]people.

[b] R.V. *marvellous works.*

[c] R.V. *the peoples.*

4 For the LORD is great, and cannot worthily be praised : he is more to be feared than all gods.

5 As for all the gods of the heathen, they are but idols : but it is the LORD that made the heavens.

6 Glory and [d]worship are before him : [e]⌜power and honour⌝ are in his sanctuary.

[d] *majesty.*

[e] *strength and beauty.* In Ps. lxxviii. 62, these terms are applied to the ark as the place where God manifested His glory.

7 Ascribe unto the LORD, O ye kindreds of the [f]people : ascribe unto the LORD [g]worship and power.

[f] R.V. *peoples.*

[g] *glory.*

8 Ascribe unto the LORD the honour due unto his Name : bring presents, and come into his courts.

9 O worship the LORD in [a]⌜the beauty of holiness⌝ : let the whole earth stand in awe of him.

[a] R.V. mg. *holy array*; see Ps. xxix. 2. The worshippers of God are to be vested in holiness as the priests in the Temple were arrayed in holy attire.

10 Tell it out among the heathen that [b][1]⌜the LORD is King⌝ : and that it is he who hath made the [2]round world so fast that it cannot be moved; and how that he shall judge the [c]people righteously.

[b] *the LORD reigneth.*

See Ps. xciii. 2.

[c] R.V. *peoples.*

11 Let the heavens rejoice, and let the earth be glad : let the sea make a noise, and all that therein is.

12 Let the field be joyful, and all that is in it : then shall all the trees of the wood rejoice before the LORD;

13 For he cometh, for he cometh to judge the earth : and with righteousness to judge the world, and the [d]people with his truth.

[d] R.V. *peoples.*

PSALM XCVII. *Dominus regnavit.*

The reign of the Divine King and Judge will cover the earth with righteousness and gladness.

Proper on Advent Sunday [America] and on Trinity Sunday [America].

THE LORD is King, the earth may be glad thereof : yea, the multitude of the isles may be glad thereof.

'the isles' of the Mediterranean. The word includes the coast-lands.

2 Clouds and darkness are round about him : righteousness and judgement are the [e]⌜habitation of his seat⌝.

As when he manifested Himself at Sinai. Exod. xix. 16, xx. 21.

[e] R.V. *foundation of his throne.*

[1] This passage appears in the old Latin version as 'The LORD hath reigned from the tree,' and is often so quoted by early Christian writers. As it is not thus found in the Hebrew or in any other version, we must conclude that an addition was made to the text to render the Messianic reference more distinct.

[2] Not in A.R.V., P.B.V. suggested by Vulg. *orbem terrae.*

3 There [a]⸢shall go⸣ a fire before him : and [b]burn up his enemies on every side.

[a] *goeth.*
[b] *burneth.*

4 His lightnings gave shine unto the world : the earth saw it, and was afraid.

5 The hills melted like wax at the presence of the LORD : at the presence of the Lord of the whole earth.

6 The heavens have declared his righteousness : and all the [c]people have seen his glory.

[c] R.V. *peoples.*

7 [d]Confounded be all they that worship carved images, and that delight in vain gods : worship him, all ye gods.

[d] R.V. *Ashamed.* P.B.V. and A.V. from Vulg.

8 Sion heard of it, and rejoiced : and the daughters of Judah were glad, because of thy judgements, O LORD.

This verse occurs also in Ps. xlviii. 10.

'the daughters'=the towns and villages; see Numb. xxi. 25 mg.; Josh. xv. 45 mg.

9 For thou, LORD, art higher than all that are in the earth : thou art exalted far above all gods.

10 O ye that love the LORD, see that ye hate the thing which is evil : [e]⸢the Lord⸣ preserveth the souls of his saints ; he [f]⸢shall deliver⸣ them from the hand of the ungodly.

[e] *He.* P.B.V. from Vulg.
[f] *delivereth.*

11 There is sprung up a light for the righteous : and joyful gladness for such as are true-hearted.

12 Rejoice in the LORD, ye righteous : and give thanks for a remembrance of his holiness.

Evening Prayer

PSALM XCVIII. *Cantate Domino.*

A hymn of praise for restoration from captivity, looking forward to the final victory of righteousness.

At Evensong, alternative for Magnificat.

O SING unto the LORD a new song : for he hath done marvellous things.

'a new song.' The late deliverance demands a fresh expression of thanksgiving.

2 With his own right hand, and with his holy arm : hath he gotten himself the victory.

3 The LORD declared his salvation : his righteousness hath he openly shewed in the sight of the heathen.

4 He hath remembered his mercy and [a] truth toward the house of Israel : and all the ends of the world have seen the salvation of our God.

'remembered.' During the captivity He seemed to have forgotten Israel.

[a] R.V. *faithfulness.*

5 Shew yourselves joyful unto the LORD, all ye lands : sing, rejoice, and give thanks.

6 Praise the LORD upon the harp : sing to the harp with a psalm of thanksgiving.

7 With trumpets also, and shawms : O shew yourselves joyful before the LORD the King.

8 Let the sea make a noise, and all that therein is : the [1] round world, and they that dwell therein.

8—10. The Psalm ends, as it has begun, like Ps. xcvi.

9 Let the floods clap their hands, and let the hills be joyful together before the LORD : for he is come to judge the earth.

10 With righteousness shall he judge the world : and the [b] people with equity.

[b] R.V. *peoples.*

[1] Not in A.R.V., P.B.V. suggested by Vulg. *orbis terrarum.*

PSALM XCIX. *Dominus regnavit.*

Proclamation of the reign of the thrice Holy God (*vv.* 3, 5, 9). Let the whole world worship Him!

Proper on Transfiguration [America].

THE LORD is King, [a]⌜be the people never so impatient⌝: he sitteth between the cherubim, [b]⌜be the earth never so unquiet⌝.

[a] R.V. *let the peoples tremble.*

[b] *let the earth be moved.*

2 The LORD is great in Sion: and high above all [c]people.

[c] R.V. *the peoples.*

3 [d]⌜They shall give thanks unto thy Name: which is great, wonderful, and holy⌝.

[d] R.V. *Let them praise thy great and terrible name: Holy is he.*

4 The King's power loveth judgement; thou [e]⌜hast prepared⌝ equity: thou hast executed judgement and righteousness in Jacob.

'The King' is 'the LORD,' *v.* 1.

[e] *dost establish.*

5 O magnify the LORD our God: and fall down before his footstool, [f]⌜for he is holy⌝.

[f] R.V. *Holy is he.*

6 Moses and Aaron among his priests, and Samuel among such as call upon his Name: these called upon the LORD, and he heard them.

6—8. The example of holy heroes in the past adduced for the encouragement and warning of God's worshippers.

7 He spake unto them out of the cloudy pillar: for they kept his testimonies, and the law that he gave them.

8 Thou heardest them, O LORD our God: thou forgavest them, O God, [g]⌜and punishedst their own inventions⌝.

[g] R.V. *though thou tookest vengeance of their doings*, i.e. even such saints of God were not exempted from God's holy severity against sin. Exod. xxxiv. 7. P.B.V. follows Vulg.

9 O magnify the LORD our God, and worship him upon his holy hill: for the LORD our God is holy.

'his holy hill' = Sion.

PSALM C. *Jubilate Deo.*

An invitation to the whole world to unite in the worship of Jehovah.

At Matins, alternative for Benedictus.

O BE joyful in the LORD, all ye lands : serve the LORD with gladness, and come before his presence with a song.

2 Be ye sure that the LORD he is God : it is he that hath made us, and [a]⌜not we ourselves⌝; we are his people, and the sheep of his pasture.

'made us,' i.e. to be His people; see Ps. xcv. 6. What had been Israel's privilege is regarded as extended to all nations.

[a] R.V. *we are his.*

3 O go your way into his gates with thanksgiving, and into his courts with praise : be thankful unto him, and speak good of his Name.

4 For the LORD is gracious, his mercy is everlasting : and his [b]truth endureth from generation to generation.

[b] R.V. *faithfulness.*

PSALM CI. *Misericordiam et judicium.*

'A Psalm of David' (Title). A king's resolve to make himself, his court and kingdom meet for God's presence. Perhaps written by David just before the removal of the ark to Mount Sion. Cp. the companion Psalms xv. and xxiv.

Proper on King's Accession.

MY song shall be of mercy and judgement : unto thee, O LORD, will I sing.

2 [c]⌜O let me have understanding: in the way of godliness⌝.

[c] *I will behave myself wisely in a perfect way.*

3 [a]⌜When wilt thou come unto me⌝ : I will walk in my house with a perfect heart.

4 I will take no wicked thing in hand; I hate the sins of unfaithfulness : there shall no such cleave unto me.

5 A froward heart shall depart from me : I will not know a wicked person.

6 Whoso privily slandereth his neighbour : him will I destroy.

7 Whoso hath also [b]⌜a proud look and high stomach⌝ : I will not suffer him.

8 Mine eyes look upon such as are faithful in the land : that they may dwell with me.

9 Whoso leadeth a godly life : he shall be my servant.

10 There shall no deceitful person dwell in my house : he that telleth lies shall not tarry in my sight.

11 [c]⌜I shall soon⌝ destroy all the ungodly that are in the land : that I may root out all wicked doers from the city of the LORD.

[a] *O when wilt thou come unto me?* David yearns for the Divine Presence of which the ark was the pledge.

'in my house'; i.e. in my private life, and not only when others witness my conduct.

[b] *an high look and a proud heart.* P.B.V. 'stomach' is figurative for pride.

[c] R.V. *Morning by morning will I.* An allusion to the custom of holding courts of justice in the morning; see 2 Sam. xv. 2; Jer. xxi. 12.

'root out' &c. 'There shall in no wise enter into it (new Jerusalem) anything unclean, or he that maketh an abomination and a lie.' Rev. xxi. 27.

THE TWENTIETH DAY

Morning Prayer

PSALM CII. *Domine, exaudi.*

'A prayer of the afflicted, when he is overwhelmed, and poureth out his complaint before the LORD' (Title). Probably written towards the close of the exile.

The fifth of the Penitential Psalms.

Proper on Ash Wednesday.

HEAR my prayer, O LORD : and let my crying come unto thee.

'Lord, hear our prayers;
And let our cry come unto thee.'
Confirmation, and other Offices.

2 Hide not thy face from me in the time of my trouble : incline thine ear unto me when I call; O hear me, and that right soon.

3 For my days are consumed away like smoke : and my bones are burnt up as it were a fire-brand.

4 My heart is smitten down, and withered like grass : so that I forget to eat my bread.

5 [a] For the voice of my groaning : [b]⌜my bones will scarce cleave to my flesh⌝.

[a] *By reason of.*

[b] R.V. *my bones cleave to my flesh*, i.e. my limbs are stiff and incapable of active motion; cp. Job xix. 20.

6 I am become like a pelican in the wilderness : and like an owl that is in the desert.

7 I have watched, and am even as it were a sparrow : that sitteth alone upon the house-top.

'I have watched,' i.e. spent sleep-less nights.

8 Mine enemies revile me all the day long : and they that are mad upon me [c]⌜are sworn together against me⌝.

[c] R.V. *do curse by me.* Their curses take the form, 'May God do unto thee, as He has done unto this man'; see Jer. xxix. 22; Is. lxv. 15.

9 For I have eaten ashes as it were bread : and mingled my drink with weeping ;

Cp. Ps. xlii. 3, lxxx. 5.

10 And that because of thine indignation and wrath : for thou hast taken me up, and cast me down.

The Psalmist sees in his sufferings God's punishment for his sins.

'taken me up' &c. The metaphor is from a violent storm; see Job xxx. 22.

11 My days are gone like a shadow : and I am withered like grass.

12 But, thou, O LORD, shalt endure for ever : and thy [a]remembrance throughout all generations.

Therefore Thy promises are unfailing!

[a] R.V. *memorial*, i.e. the Name Jehovah, the pledge of God's covenant with Israel. Exod. iii. 14, 15.

13 Thou shalt arise, and have mercy upon Sion : for it is time that thou have mercy upon her, yea, the time is come.

'have mercy upon,' i.e. restore her from her state of ruin.

14 And why? thy servants [b]⌜think upon⌝ her stones : and it pitieth them to see her in the dust.

[b] *take pleasure in.*

If Israelites in exile think piteously of the ruins of Jerusalem, how deep must be the compassion of God!

15 [c]⌜The heathen⌝ shall fear thy Name, O LORD : and all the kings of the earth thy majesty ;

[c] R.V. *So the nations.* The restoration of Jerusalem will bring about the conversion of the world.

16 When the LORD shall build up Sion : and when his glory shall appear ;

17 When he turneth him unto the prayer of the poor destitute : and despiseth not their desire.

'the poor destitute' = exiled Israel.

18 This shall be written for those that come after : and the people which shall be born shall praise the LORD.

The return from captivity will be equivalent to a second birth of the nation.

19 For he hath looked down from his sanctuary : out of the heaven did the LORD behold the earth ;

20 That he might hear the mournings of such as are in captivity : and deliver the children appointed unto death ;

21 That they may declare the Name of the LORD in Sion : and his [a]worship at Jerusalem;

[a] *praise*. P.B.V. 'worship' formerly had this meaning.

22 When the [b]people are gathered together : and the kingdoms also, to serve the LORD.

[b] R.V. *peoples*.

23 He brought down my strength in my journey : and shortened my days.

From the glorious vision of the future the Psalmist returns to his own hapless condition.

24 But I said, O my God, take me not away in the midst of mine age : as for thy years, they endure throughout all generations.

'as for thy years' &c. Whether his prayer for a longer life be granted or not, the Psalmist finds comfort in the thought of the eternity and unchangeableness (*v.* 27) of God, the guarantee of the perpetuity (*v.* 28) of His people.

25 Thou, [1]Lord, in the beginning hast laid the foundation of the earth : and the heavens are the work of thy hands.

25—27. Quoted in Heb. i. 10—12 as addressed to Christ.

26 They shall perish, but thou shalt endure : they all shall wax old as doth a garment;

'wax' = grow.

27 And as a vesture shalt thou change them, and they shall be changed : but thou art the same, and thy years shall not fail.

28 The children of thy servants shall continue : and their seed shall stand fast in thy sight.

PSALM CIII. *Benedic, anima mea.*

The thanksgiving of a full heart to God for spiritual and temporal benefits.

At Evensong, *vv.* 1—4, 21, 22 second alternative for Nunc Dimittis [America]. Proper on Circumcision and St Michael and All Angels [America]. Special in Harvest Thanksgiving [Ireland].

PRAISE the LORD, O my soul : and all that is within me praise his holy Name.

[1] Not in A.R.V., added in P.B.V. from Vulg.

2 Praise the LORD, O my soul : and forget not all his benefits;

3 Who forgiveth all thy sin : and healeth all thine infirmities;

4 Who saveth thy life from destruction : and crowneth thee with mercy and loving-kindness;

5 Who satisfieth thy mouth with good things : making thee young and lusty as an eagle.

An allusion to the long life of the eagle, and its retention of vigour to extreme old age.

'lusty' = vigorous.

6 The LORD executeth righteousness and judgement : for all them that are oppressed with wrong.

7 He shewed his ways unto Moses : his works unto the children of Israel.

Moses' prayer was 'Shew me now thy ways, that I may know thee.' Exod. xxxiii. 13.

8 The LORD is full of compassion and mercy : long-suffering, and of great goodness.

So God revealed Himself to Moses. Exod. xxxiv. 6.

9 He will not alway be chiding : neither keepeth he his anger for ever.

10 He hath not dealt with us after our sins : nor rewarded us according to our wickednesses.

'O Lord, deal not with us after our sins;

Neither reward us after our iniquities.'

Versicle and response in Litany.

11 For look how high the heaven is in comparison of the earth : so great is his mercy also toward them that fear him.

12 Look how wide also the east is from the west : so far hath he set our sins from us.

13 Yea, like as a father pitieth his own children : even so [a]⌈is the LORD merciful⌉ unto them that fear him.

[a] *the LORD pitieth.*

14 For he knoweth whereof we are made : he remembereth that we are but dust

'The LORD God formed man of the dust of the ground.' Gen. ii. 7.

15 The days of man are but as grass : for he flourisheth as a flower of the field.

16 For as soon as the wind goeth over it, it is gone : and the place thereof shall know it no more.

17 But the merciful goodness of the LORD endureth for ever and ever upon them that fear him : and his righteousness upon children's children ;

i.e. 'his righteousness' in observing His covenant ; see *v.* 18.

18 Even upon such as keep his covenant : and think upon his commandments to do them.

'Shewing mercy unto thousands, of them that love me and keep my commandments.' Exod. xx. 6.

19 The LORD hath [a]⌜prepared his seat⌝ in heaven : and his kingdom ruleth over all.

[a] R.V. *established his throne.*

20 O praise the LORD, ye angels of his, ye that excel in strength : ye that fulfil his commandment, and hearken unto the voice of his words.

21 O praise the LORD, all ye his hosts : ye [b]servants of his that do his pleasure.

'Are they (i.e. the angels) not all ministering spirits, sent forth to do service?' Heb. i. 14.

[b] *ministers.*

22 O speak good of the LORD, all ye works of his, in all places of his dominion : praise thou the LORD, O my soul.

Evening Prayer

PSALM CIV. *Benedic, anima mea.*

A hymn of praise to God as the Maker and Sustainer of the Universe. The work of Creation (Gen. i.) regarded as a continuing operation.

Proper on Whitsunday, as being the Festival of the Spirit of Life. Special in Harvest Thanksgiving [Ireland].

PRAISE the LORD, O my soul : O LORD my God, thou art become exceeding glorious ; thou art clothed with majesty and honour.

2 Thou deckest thyself with light as it were with a garment : and spreadest out the heavens like a curtain.

The first day of creation. Gen. i. 3—5. Light is described as the permanent apparel of God.

The second day. Gen. i. 6—8. The heavens or firmament (Gen.) are compared to a canopy extended over the earth.

3 Who layeth the beams of his chambers in the waters : and maketh the clouds his chariot, and walketh upon the wings of the wind.

'the waters' above the firmament. Gen. i. 7. God's chambers are regarded as resting on the reservoir of waters which are conceived as held aloft by the firmament or expanse of heaven.

4 He maketh his angels [a]spirits : and his ministers a flaming fire.

[a]R.V. mg. *winds*. God arrays His messengers with the outward properties of wind and fire. The verse is quoted Heb. i. 7.

5 He laid the foundations of the earth : that it never should move at any time.

Gen. i. 1.

6 Thou coveredst it with the deep like as with a garment : the waters [b]⌜stand in the hills⌝.

'Thou coveredst it,' in the primeval chaos before the separation of the waters from the dry land. Gen. i. 2.

[b]*stood above the mountains*.

7 At thy rebuke they [c]flee : at the voice of thy thunder they [d]⌜are afraid⌝.

7—10. The third day. Gen. i. 9, 10.

[c]*fled*.

[d]*hasted away*.

8 [e]⌜They go up as high as the hills, and down to the valleys beneath⌝ : even unto the place which thou [f]⌜hast appointed⌝ for them.

[e]R.V. *They went up by the mountains, they went down by the valleys.* A description of the rush and commotion of the waters as they fled at the rebuke of God.

[f]R.V. *hadst founded*.

9 Thou hast set them their bounds which they shall not pass : neither turn again to cover the earth.

10 He sendeth the springs into the [g]rivers : [h]which run among the hills.

[g]*valleys*. [h]R.V. *they*, i.e. 'the springs.'

11 All beasts of the field drink thereof : and the wild asses quench their thirst.

The sixth day. Gen. i. 24, 25.

12 Beside them shall the fowls of the air have their habitation : and sing among the branches.

The fifth day. Gen. i. 20.

Omit 'shall' with R.V.

13 He watereth the hills from [a]above : the earth is filled with the fruit of thy works.

14 He bringeth forth grass for the cattle : and green herb for the service of men ;

15 That he may bring food out of the earth, and wine that maketh glad the heart of man : and oil to make him a cheerful countenance, and bread to strengthen man's heart.

16 The trees of the LORD also are [b]⌜full of sap⌝ : even the cedars of Libanus which he hath planted ;

17 Wherein the birds make their nests : and the fir-trees are a dwelling for the stork.

18 The high hills are a refuge for the wild goats : and so are the stony rocks for the conies.

19 He appointed the moon [c]⌜for certain seasons⌝ : and the sun knoweth his going down.

20 Thou makest darkness that it may be night : wherein all the beasts of the forest do [d]move.

21 The lions roaring after their prey : do seek their meat from God.

22 The sun ariseth, and they get them away together : and lay them down in their dens.

[a] *his chambers*, i.e. those mentioned in *v.* 3.

'the fruit' &c. = the vegetable products, such as are mentioned in the following verses, which spring from God's operations.

14—16. The third day. Gen. i. 11—13.

'The trees of the LORD,' i.e. the forest trees as contrasted with crops of human cultivation.

[b] R.V. *satisfied*, i.e. with the rain, *v.* 13.

'conies' or *rock-badgers* ; see Lev. xi. 5 mg.

19—23. The fourth and the sixth days. Gen. i. 14—19, 24—31.

[c] *for seasons*, i.e. to mark divisions of time. Gen. i. 14.

The moon is mentioned before the sun because according to Hebrew reckoning the night preceded the day ; cp. Gen. i. 5, 8 &c.

[d] *creep forth.*

23 Man goeth forth to his work, and to his labour : until the evening.

Man alone of all the animals is called to the dignity of labour. God who made and sustains him has ordained that the support of his life shall depend on his own exertions.

24 O LORD, how manifold are thy works : in wisdom hast thou made them all; the earth is full of thy riches.

25 [a]⌜So is the great and wide sea also⌝ : wherein are things creeping innumerable, both small and great beasts.

25, 26. The fifth day. Gen. i. 21.

[a] R.V. *Yonder is the sea, great and wide.*

26 There go the ships, and there is that leviathan : whom thou hast made to take his pastime therein.

'leviathan,' here used in general for sea-monster.

27 These wait all upon thee : that thou mayest give them meat in due season.

28 When thou givest it them they gather it : and when thou openest thy hand they are filled with good.

29 When thou hidest thy face they are troubled : when thou takest away their breath they die, and are turned again to their dust.

'hidest thy face,' i.e. withdrawest thy sustaining providence.

'Dust thou art, and unto dust shalt thou return.' Gen. iii. 19.

30 [b]⌜When thou lettest thy breath go forth they shall be made⌝ : and thou [c]⌜shalt renew⌝ the face of the earth.

[b] *Thou sendest forth thy spirit, they are created.* Life is ever being renewed by the Spirit of God. The Creation is a continuous process.

[c] *renewest.*

31 The glorious majesty of the LORD shall endure for ever : the LORD shall rejoice in his works.

32 [d]⌜The earth shall tremble at the look of him : if he do but touch the hills, they shall smoke⌝.

[d] R.V. *Who looketh on the earth, and it trembleth; he toucheth the mountains and they smoke.*

33 I will sing unto the LORD as long as I live : I will praise my God while I have my being.

34 And so shall my words please him : my joy shall be in the LORD.

35 As for sinners, they shall be consumed out of the earth, and the ungodly shall come to an end : praise thou the LORD, O my soul, praise the LORD.

And so by the banishment of evil the original harmony of Creation will be restored. 'Every thing' shall again be 'very good' in the sight of God. Gen. i. 31.

'praise the LORD.' R.V. mg. Heb. *Hallelujah.*

THE TWENTY-FIRST DAY

Morning Prayer

PSALM CV. *Confitemini Domino.*

A thanksgiving for God's protecting care of His people in the olden time. Like Ps. lxxviii. and cvi. it narrates the early history of Israel. *vv.* 1—15 are found also in 1 Chron. xvi. 8—22 combined with Ps. xcvi., and cvi. 1, 47, 48,

O GIVE thanks unto the LORD, and call upon his Name : tell the [a]people what things he hath done.

Quoted from Is. xii. 4.

[a] R.V. *peoples.*

2 O let your songs be of him, and praise him : and let your talking be of all his wondrous works.

3 Rejoice in his holy Name : let the heart of them rejoice that seek the LORD.

4 Seek the LORD and his strength: seek his face evermore.

5 Remember the marvellous works that he hath done : his wonders, and the judgements of his mouth,

6 O ye seed of Abraham his servant : ye children of Jacob his [b]chosen.

[b] R.V. *chosen ones.*

7 He is the LORD our God : his judgements are in all the world.

Jehovah is 'our God' by covenant, but His rule extends over all nations.

8 He hath been alway mindful of his covenant and promise : that he made to a thousand generations ;

9 Even the covenant that he made with Abraham : and the oath that he sware unto Isaac;

Gen. xvii. 2 ff.

Gen. xxvi. 3.

10 And [a]appointed the same unto Jacob for a law : and to Israel for an everlasting [b]testament;

[a]*confirmed.* Gen. xxviii. 13 ff., xxxv. 9 ff.

[b]*covenant.*

11 Saying, Unto thee will I give the land of Canaan : the [c]lot of your inheritance;

[c]R.V. mg. *cord* or *line.* A land allotted to Israel by measuring-line; see Ps. xvi. 7, lxxviii. 56.

12 When there were yet but a few of them : and they strangers in the land;

13 What time as they went from one nation to another : from one kingdom to another people;

14 He suffered no man to do them wrong : but reproved even kings for their sakes;

'kings' as Pharaoh, Gen. xii. 17, and Abimelech, Gen. xx. 3.

15 Touch not mine [d]anointed : and do my prophets no harm.

'Touch not.' The expression is taken from Gen. xx. 6, xxvi. 11.

[d]R.V. *anointed ones.* The patriarchs are so designated as consecrated to God's service. Abraham is called a prophet, Gen. xx. 7.

16 Moreover, he called for a dearth upon the land : [e]⌜and destroyed all the provision⌝ of bread.

[e]*he brake the whole staff.* Bread is so called as being the chief support of life. Lev. xxvi. 26.

17 But he had sent a man before them : even Joseph, who was sold to be a bond-servant;

18 Whose feet they hurt [f]⌜in the stocks⌝ : [1]the iron entered into his soul;

[f]*with fetters.*

19 Until the time [g]⌜came that his cause was known⌝ : the word of the LORD tried him.

[g]R.V. *that his word came to pass.* 'word' in both clauses, translating different words in the Hebrew, means God's promise of future exaltation revealed to Joseph in his dreams.

[1] 'the iron entered into his soul.' R.V. *He was laid in chains of iron*, mg. *His soul entered into the iron.* The P.B.V., which follows Vulg., is accepted by many commentators as a fair paraphrase of the original, and as expressing the sense of the passage better than the literal rendering of R.V. mg.

20 The king sent, and delivered him : [a]⌜the prince of the people⌝ let him go free.

[a] R.V. *even the ruler of peoples, and.*

21 He made him lord also of his house : and ruler of all his substance ;

22 [b]⌜That he might inform his princes after his will⌝ : and teach his senators wisdom.

[b] *To bind his princes at his pleasure.* P.B.V. from Vulg.

23 Israel also came into Egypt : and Jacob was a stranger in the land of Ham.

'Israel' = the patriarch Jacob, see next clause.

Ham was father of Mizraim (Egypt), Gen. x. 6.

24 And he increased his people exceedingly : and made them stronger than their enemies ;

'he'=Jehovah.

25 Whose heart turned so that they hated his people : and dealt untruly with his servants.

26 Then sent he Moses his servant : and Aaron whom he had chosen.

27 [c]⌜And these shewed his tokens among them⌝ : and wonders in the land of Ham.

[c] R.V. *They set among them his signs*; see Exod. x. 1, 2 ; Ps. lxxviii. 44.

See *v.* 23.

28 He sent darkness, and it was dark : [d]⌜and they were not obedient unto his word⌝.

Darkness, the ninth plague, is mentioned first, because after it 'the LORD gave the people favour in the sight of the Egyptians.' Exod. xi. 3 ; see next clause.

[d] R.V. *and they* (the Egyptians) *rebelled not against his words.*

29 He turned their waters into blood : and slew their fish.

Exod. vii. 20, 21.

30 Their land [e]⌜brought forth⌝ frogs : yea, even in their kings' chambers.

[e] R.V. *swarmed with.*

Exod. viii. 3—6.

31 He spake the word, and there came all manner of flies : and lice in all their quarters.

Exod. viii. 17, 24.

32 He gave them hail-stones for rain : and flames of fire in their land.

32, 33. Exod. ix. 23—25.

33 He smote their vines also and fig-trees : and destroyed the trees that were in their [a]coasts.

[a]R.V. *borders.*

34 He spake the word, and the [b]grasshoppers came, and caterpillars innumerable : and did eat up all the grass in their land, and devoured the fruit of their ground.

Exod. x. 13—15.
[b]R.V. *locust.*

The plagues of the murrain and of the boils are omitted.

35 He smote all the first-born in their land : even the [c]chief of all their strength.

Exod. xii. 29.
[c]R.V. mg. *beginning.* 'The beginning of his strength' is a phrase used of a man's first-born. Deut. xxi. 17; Gen. xlix. 3; Ps. lxxviii. 52.

36 He brought them forth also with silver and gold : there was not one feeble person among [d]their tribes.

Exod. xii. 35, 36.

[d]R.V. *his,* i.e. Jehovah's.

37 Egypt was glad at their departing : for they were afraid of them.

Exod. xii. 33.

38 He spread out a cloud to be a covering : and fire to give light in the night-season.

The cloud is here apparently regarded as a curtain to screen them from the sun, rather than as (in Exod. xiv. 19) a protection from their enemies.

39 At their desire he brought quails : and he filled them with the bread of heaven.

Numb. xi. 31.

The manna. Exod. xvi. 4; Ps. lxxviii. 25; St John vi. 31.

40 He opened the rock of stone, and the waters flowed out : so that rivers ran in the dry places.

At Horeb. Exod. xvii. 6; see Ps. lxxviii. 16.

41 For why? he remembered his holy promise : and Abraham his servant.

42 And he brought forth his people with joy : and his chosen with [e]gladness;

[e]R.V. *singing.* An allusion to the song of triumph after the passage of the Red Sea. Exod. xv.

43 And gave them the lands of the heathen : and they took the labours of the [f]people in possession;

[f]R.V. *peoples.*

44 That they might keep his statutes : and observe his laws.

A.R.V. add *Praise ye the LORD,* mg. Heb. *Hallelujah.*

Evening Prayer

PSALM CVI. *Confitemini Domino.*

The history of Israel—a record of unfaithfulness. Written towards the end of the captivity (see *v.* 45). A companion Psalm to lxxviii. and cv.

O GIVE thanks unto the LORD, for he is gracious : and his mercy endureth for ever.

A.R.V. prefix, *Praise ye the LORD*, mg. Heb. *Hallelujah*.

This expression of public thanksgiving occurs first in Jer. xxxiii. 11. It is found only in Psalms written during or after the exile.

2 Who can express the noble acts of the LORD : or shew forth all his praise?

3 Blessed are they that alway keep judgement : and do righteousness.

4 Remember me, O LORD, according to the favour that thou bearest unto thy people : O visit me with thy salvation ;

5 That I may see the felicity of thy chosen : and rejoice in the gladness of thy people, and give thanks with thine inheritance.

4, 5. The Psalmist prays that he personally may share in the blessed lot of his people.

6 We have sinned with our fathers : we have done amiss, and dealt wickedly.

The words are taken from Solomon's prayer. 1 Kings viii. 47; cp. Dan. ix. 5; Bar. ii. 12.

7 Our fathers regarded not thy wonders in Egypt, neither kept they thy great goodness in remembrance : but were disobedient at the sea, even at the Red Sea.

8 Nevertheless, he helped them for his Name's sake : that he might make his power to be known.

9 He rebuked the Red Sea also, and it was dried up : so he led them through the deep, as through a [a]wilderness.

[a] R.V. mg. *pasture land.*

10 And he saved them from the adversary's hand : and delivered them from the hand of the enemy.

11 As for those that troubled them, the waters overwhelmed them : there was not one of them left.

12 Then believed they his words : and sang praise unto him.

11, 12. 'Israel saw the great work which the LORD did upon the Egyptians, and the people feared the LORD: and they believed in the LORD, and in his servant Moses. Then sang Moses and the children of Israel this song unto the LORD.' Exod. xiv. 31, xv. 1.

13 But within a while they forgat his works : and [b]⌜would not abide his counsel⌝.

[b] *waited not for his counsel*, i.e. the working out of His plans. P.B.V. has the same meaning.

14 But lust came upon them in the wilderness : and they tempted God in the desert.

Numb. xi. 5.

'tempted,' i.e. tested, by questioning His power to provide them with food. Deut. vi. 16; see Ps. lxxviii. 19—21.

15 And he gave them their desire: and sent leanness withal into their soul.

By sending quails. Numb. xi. 31—34.

16 They [c]angered Moses also in the tents : and Aaron the [d]saint of the LORD.

[c] *envied.*

[d] R.V. mg. *holy one.* The contention of Korah and his company was that all the congregation were holy. Numb. xvi. 3.

17 So the earth opened, and swallowed up Dathan : and covered the congregation of Abiram.

Numb. xvi. 31—33.

18 And the fire was kindled in their company : the flame burnt up the ungodly.

'Fire came forth from the LORD, and devoured the two hundred and fifty men that offered the incense.' Numb. xvi. 35.

19 They made a calf in Horeb : and worshipped the molten image.

Exod. xxxii. 4—6.

20 Thus they turned their glory : into the similitude of a calf that eateth hay.

'their glory,' i.e. Jehovah; see Jer. ii. 11. This passage is referred to in Rom. i. 23.

21 And they forgat God their Saviour : who had done so great things in Egypt;

22 Wondrous works in the land of Ham : and fearful things by the Red Sea.

Ham was father of Mizraim (Egypt). Gen. x. 6.

23 So he said, he would have destroyed them, had not Moses his chosen stood before him in the gap : to turn away his wrathful indignation, lest he should destroy them.

Exod. xxxii. 10 ff.; Deut. ix. 25, 26; cp. Numb. xiv. 11 ff.

Moses' intercession is compared to the action of the brave warrior who fills with his body the breach made in the city wall.

24 Yea, they thought scorn of that pleasant land : and gave no credence unto his word;

The rebellion which followed the report of the spies. Numb. xiv.

25 But murmured in their tents: and hearkened not unto the voice of the LORD.

Deut. i. 27.

26 Then lift he up his hand against them : to overthrow them in the wilderness;

'To lift up the hand' = to swear. Exod. vi. 8; Ezek. xx. 23.

27 To cast out their seed among the nations : and to scatter them in the lands.

28 They joined themselves unto Baal-peor : and ate the offerings of the dead.

Numb. xxv.

'the dead,' i.e. lifeless idols as contrasted with the living God.

29 Thus they provoked him to anger with their [a]⌜own inventions⌝ : and the plague was great among them.

[a] R.V. *doings*. P.B.V. and A.V. from Vulg.

30 Then stood up Phinees and [b]prayed : and so the plague ceased.

[b] *executed judgement*.

31 And that was counted unto him for righteousness : among all posterities for evermore.

Abraham 'believed in the LORD; and he counted it to him for righteousness.' Gen. xv. 6. Phinees was a true heir of Abraham's faith. His reward was 'the covenant of an everlasting priesthood.' Numb. xxv. 13.

32 They angered him also at the waters of [c]strife : so that [d]⌜he punished⌝ Moses for their sakes;

[c] R.V. *Meribah*. Numb. xx. 10—13.

[d] *it went ill with*.

33 Because [e]⌜they provoked his spirit : so that⌝ he spake unadvisedly with his lips.

[e] R.V. *they* (the Israelites) *were rebellious against his* (God's) *Spirit, and*. Is. lxiii. 10.

34 Neither destroyed they the heathen : as the LORD commanded them ;

Judg. i. 21, 27, 29 ff.

35 But were mingled among the heathen : and learned their works.

36 Insomuch that they worshipped their idols, which [a]⌜turned to their own decay⌝ : yea, they offered their sons and their daughters unto devils ;

[a]R.V. *became a snare unto them.* P.B.V. means 'caused their downfall.'

'devils,' R.V. *demons.* The Hebrew word which is found elsewhere only in Deut. xxxii. 17 probably means 'demi-gods.'

37 And shed innocent blood, even the blood of their sons and of their daughters : whom they offered unto the idols of Canaan ; and the land was defiled with blood.

Ezek. xvi. 20, 21, xx. 31.

38 Thus were they stained with their own works : and went a whoring with their [b]⌜own inventions⌝.

Idolatry is spiritual fornication. Exod. xxxiv. 15, 16 ; Judg. ii. 17.

[b]R.V. *doings.* P.B.V. and A.V. from Vulg.

39 Therefore was the wrath of the LORD kindled against his people : insomuch that he abhorred his own inheritance.

The expression is found frequently in Judges (ii. 14, iii. 8 &c.).

40 And he gave them over into the hand of the heathen : and they that hated them were lords over them.

41 Their enemies oppressed them : and had them in subjection.

42 Many a time did he deliver them : but they rebelled against him [c]⌜with their own inventions⌝, and were brought down in their wickedness.

[c]R.V. *in their counsel.*

43 Nevertheless, when he saw their adversity : he heard their complaint.

43, 44. The fulfilment of Solomon's prayer, 1 Kings viii. 49, 50.

44 He thought upon his covenant, and pitied them, according unto the multitude of his mercies : yea, he made all those that led them away captive to pity them.

45 Deliver us, O LORD our God, and gather us from among the heathen : that we may give thanks unto thy holy Name, and make our boast of thy praise.

46 Blessed be the LORD God of Israel from everlasting, and world without end : and let all the people say, Amen.

The doxology which concludes the Fourth Book of the Psalter.

A.R.V. add *Praise ye the LORD*, mg. Heb. *Hallelujah*.

THE TWENTY-SECOND DAY

Morning Prayer

PSALM CVII. *Confitemini Domino.*

A call to the lately returned exiles to thank God for answering their prayers and restoring them to their own land.

Special in Forms of Prayer to be used at Sea.

O GIVE thanks unto the LORD, for he is gracious : and his mercy endureth for ever.

The liturgical doxology as in Ps. cvi. 1.

2 Let them give thanks whom the LORD hath redeemed : and delivered from the hand of the enemy;

'redeemed,' i.e. released from captivity. 'They shall call them,...The redeemed of the LORD.' Is. lxii. 12.

3 And gathered them out of the lands, from the east, and from the west : from the north, and from the south.

Exiles had returned, not only from Babylon, but from all countries where they were scattered.

Four pictures of human peril and Divine deliverance in answer to prayer, each followed by a double refrain varied to suit the occasion.

First picture.

4 They went astray in the wilderness out of the way : and found no city [a]⌜to dwell in⌝;

4—9. Travellers who lose their way in the desert.

[a] R.V. *of habitation*, i.e. which men inhabit.

5 Hungry and thirsty : their soul fainted in them.

6 So they cried unto the LORD in their trouble : and he delivered them from their distress.

6—9. Refrain.

7 He led them forth by the right way : that they might go to [a]⌜the city where they dwelt⌝.

[a] *a city of habitation*, see *v.* 4.

8 O that men would therefore praise the LORD for his goodness : and declare the wonders that he doeth for the children of men !

9 For he satisfieth the [b]empty soul : and filleth the hungry soul with [c]goodness.

[b] *longing*. Quoted in a spiritual sense in the Magnificat (St Luke i. 53), 'He hath filled the hungry with good things'; see St Matt. v. 6.

[c] R.V. *good*.

Second picture.

10—16. Prisoners in a dungeon.

'shadow of death'; see Ps. xxiii. 4.

10 Such as sit in darkness, and in the shadow of death : being fast bound in misery and iron;

11 Because they rebelled against the words of [d]⌜the Lord⌝ : and lightly regarded the counsel of the most Highest;

Their suffering is the Divinely sent punishment of sin.

[d] *God*.

12 He also brought down their heart [e]⌜through heaviness⌝ : they fell down, and there was none to help them.

[e] *with labour*, i.e. the toil imposed upon them as prisoners.

13 So when they cried unto the LORD in their trouble : he delivered them out of their distress.

13—16. Refrain.

14 For he brought them out of darkness, and out of the shadow of death : and brake their bonds in sunder.

See *v.* 10.

15 O that men would therefore praise the LORD for his goodness : and declare the wonders that he doeth for the children of men !

16 For he hath broken the gates of brass : and smitten the bars of iron in sunder.

Fulfilling the promise in Is. xlv. 2.

Third picture.
17—22. Sick persons.

17 Foolish men are plagued for their offence : and because of their wickedness.

'Foolish,' i.e. morally senseless, wicked ; see Ps. xiv. 1.

18 Their soul abhorred all manner of meat : and they were even hard at death's door.

'meat' = food in general.

19 So when they cried unto the LORD in their trouble : he delivered them out of their distress.

19—22. Refrain.

20 He sent his word, and healed them : and they were saved from their destruction.

'his word,' spoken of here almost as God's personal messenger. A forecast of the future revelation of the Incarnate Word.

21 O that men would therefore praise the LORD for his goodness : and declare the wonders that he doeth for the children of men!

22 That they would offer unto him the [a]sacrifice of thanksgiving : and tell out his works with gladness!

[a]*sacrifices*; see Lev. vii. 11 ff.

Fourth picture.
23—32. Seafarers.

23 They that go down to the sea in ships : and [b]⌜occupy their⌝ business in great waters;

[b]*do*. P.B.V. 'occupy' = carry on; cp. Ezek. xxvii. 9 (A.V.); St Luke xix. 13 (A.V.).

24 These men see the works of the LORD : and his wonders in the deep.

25 For at his word the stormy wind ariseth : which lifteth up the waves thereof.

26 They are carried up to the heaven, and down again to the deep : their soul melteth away because of the trouble.

27 They reel to and fro, and stagger like a drunken man : and are at their wits' end.

28 So when they cry unto the LORD in their trouble : he delivereth them out of their distress.

28—32. Refrain.

29 For he maketh the storm to cease : so that the waves thereof are still.

30 Then are they glad, because they are at rest : and so he bringeth them unto the haven where they would be.

31 O that men would therefore praise the LORD for his goodness : and declare the wonders that he doeth for the children of men !

32 That they would exalt him also in the congregation of the people : and praise him in the seat of the elders !

At public worship and in the council of state.

33 Who turneth [a]⌜the floods⌝ into a wilderness : and drieth up the water-springs ;

33 to end. Various illustrations of God's providential government of the world.

[a] *rivers.*

34 A fruitful land maketh he barren : for the wickedness of them that dwell therein.

35 Again, he maketh the wilderness a standing water : and water-springs of a dry ground.

36 And there he setteth the hungry : that they may build them a city [b]⌜to dwell in⌝ ;

[b] R.V. *of habitation* ; see *v.* 4.

37 That they may sow their land, and plant vineyards : to yield them fruits of increase.

38 He blesseth them, so that they multiply exceedingly : and suffereth not their cattle to decrease.

39 And again, when they are minished, and brought low : through oppression, [c]⌜through any plague, or trouble⌝ ;

[c] R.V. *trouble, and sorrow.*

40 [a]⌜Though he suffer them to be evil intreated through tyrants: and let them wander out of the way in the wilderness⌝;

[a] R.V. *He poureth contempt upon princes, and causeth them to wander in the waste, where there is no way.* A quotation from Job xii. 21, 24. The tenor of the passage *vv.* 39—41 is the same as that of St Luke i. 52. 'He hath put down princes from their thrones, and hath exalted them of low degree.'

41 Yet helpeth he the poor out of misery: and maketh him households like a flock of sheep.

Job xxi. 11.

42 The righteous will consider this, and rejoice: and the mouth of all wickedness shall be stopped.

Job xxii. 19.

Job v. 16.

43 Whoso is wise will ponder these things: and they shall understand the loving-kindness of the LORD.

Evening Prayer

PSALM CVIII. *Paratum cor meum.*

A triumphant celebration of God's subjugation of the nations to Himself, coupled with an earnest prayer for help in some time of national danger. It is a combination of Ps. lvii. 8—12 and Ps. lx. 5—12 by a later editor to suit a new crisis.

Proper on Ascension Day, as the day of the inauguration of Christ's triumph.

O GOD, my heart is [b]ready, [1]⌜my heart is ready⌝: I will sing and give praise [c]⌜with the best member that I have⌝.

[b] *fixed*, i.e. steadfast in faith.

[c] *even with my glory.* 'glory' poetical for 'soul' as being man's noblest part. Ps. vii. 5, xvi. 10, xxx. 13; cp. the P.B.V. paraphrase.

2 Awake, thou lute, and harp: [d]⌜I myself will awake right early⌝.

[d] R.V. mg. *I will awake the dawn*, i.e. my song shall arouse the morning from its slumber.

3 I will give thanks unto thee, O LORD, among the [e]people: I will sing praises unto thee among the nations.

[e] R.V. *peoples*.

[1] Not in A.R.V., added in P.B.V. from Vulg., which copies Ps. lvii. 8.

4 For thy mercy is greater than the heavens : and thy truth reacheth unto the clouds.

5 Set up thyself, O God, above the heavens : and thy glory above all the earth.

6 That thy beloved may be delivered : let thy right hand save them, and hear thou me.

'thy beloved'=Israel.

7 God hath spoken in his holiness : [a]⌜I will rejoice therefore⌝, and divide Sichem, and mete out the valley of Succoth.

[a] R.V. *I will exult.*

7—9. 'I will' &c. The words of God: as a victorious warrior He claims afresh the whole land of Canaan. The distribution of territory is the fullest proof of possession. Josh. xviii. 10. Of the localities mentioned, [1] Shechem, Ephraim and Judah represent the country west of Jordan, [1] Succoth and Gilead (inhabited by the half tribe of Manasseh) the country east of Jordan.

8 Gilead is mine, and Manasses is mine : Ephraim also is the [b]strength of my head;

[b] R.V. *defence.* Ephraim was the most powerful tribe.

9 [2] Judah is my [c]law-giver. Moab is my wash-pot : over Edom will I cast out my shoe; upon Philistia will I triumph.

[c] R.V. *sceptre.* Judah was the royal tribe.

'Moab' &c. God will extend His conquests to the neighbouring nations.

'wash-pot'; a contemptuous symbol of subjugation.

'cast out' &c.; an eastern sign of taking forcible possession.

10—13. The words of Israel or of Israel's leader.

10 Who will lead me into the strong city : and who will bring me into Edom?

'the strong city,' probably Petra, the capital of Edom, which nation is now as on the former occasion (Ps. lx.) apparently at war with Israel.

11 Hast not thou forsaken us, O God : and wilt not thou, O God, go forth with our hosts?

12 O help us against the enemy : for vain is the help of man.

13 Through God we shall do great acts : and it is he that shall tread down our enemies.

[1] Shechem and Succoth are probably named because of their association with the history of Jacob. Gen. xxxiii. 17, 18.

[2] 'Judah is my law-giver.' A.R.V. correctly make this sentence part of *v.* 8; see Ps. lx. 7, 8.

PSALM CIX. *Deus, laudem.*

The voice of the persecuted pleading to God for vengeance.

HOLD not thy tongue, O God of my praise : for the mouth of the ungodly, yea, the mouth of the deceitful is opened upon me.

'of my praise,' i.e. the object of my praise.

2 And they have spoken against me with false tongues : they compassed me about also with words of hatred, and fought against me without a cause.

3 For the love that I had unto them, lo, they take now my contrary part : but I give myself unto prayer.

I commit my cause into God's hands.

4 Thus have they rewarded me evil for good : and hatred for my good will.

5 Set thou an ungodly man to be ruler over him : and let [a]Satan stand at his right hand.

'him.' One persecutor is singled out. The Psalmist prays that he may be put on trial before an unrighteous judge, with a prosecutor ready to accuse him.

[a] R.V. *an adversary.*

6 When sentence is given upon him, let him be condemned : and let his prayer be turned into sin.

Cp. Prov. xxviii. 9.

7 Let his days be few : and let another take his office.

Applied in Acts i. 20 to the case of Judas.

8 Let his children be fatherless : and his wife a widow.

9 Let his children be vagabonds, and beg their bread : let them seek it [b]⌜also out of desolate places⌝.

[b] R.V. mg. *far from their desolate places*, i.e. their ruined homes.

10 Let the extortioner consume all that he hath : and let the stranger [c]spoil his labour.

[c] R.V. *make spoil of.*

11 Let there be no man to pity him : nor to have compassion upon his fatherless children.

12 Let his posterity be destroyed : and in the next generation let [a]his name be clean put out.

[a] *their.*

13 Let the wickedness of his fathers be had in remembrance in the sight of the LORD : and let not the sin of his mother be done away.

14 Let them alway be before the LORD : that he may root out the [b]memorial of them from off the earth;

[b] *memory.* P.B.V. 'memorial' had formerly this meaning; cp. Ps. ix. 6.

15 And that, because his mind was not to do good : but persecuted the poor helpless man, that he might slay him that was [c]⌜vexed at the heart⌝.

'poor,' 'helpless,' 'broken in heart,' such as the Psalmist was.

[c] *broken in heart.*

16 His delight was in cursing, and it [d]⌜shall happen⌝ unto him : he loved not blessing, [e]⌜therefore shall it be⌝ far from him.

[d] R.V. *came.*

[e] R.V. *and it was.*

17 He clothed himself with cursing, like as with a raiment : and it [f]⌜shall come⌝ into his bowels like water, and like oil into his bones.

[f] R.V. *came.*

Cursing became a positive refreshment to his nature.

18 Let it be unto him as the cloke that he hath upon him : and as the girdle that he is alway girded withal.

19 [g]⌜Let it thus happen from the LORD unto mine enemies : and to⌝ those that speak evil against my soul.

[g] R.V. *This is the reward of mine adversaries from the LORD and of.*

20 But deal thou with me, O Lord GOD, according unto thy Name : for sweet is thy mercy.

21 O deliver me, for I am helpless and poor : and my heart is wounded within me.

22 I go hence like the shadow that departeth : and am driven away as the [a]grasshopper.

[a] *locust.*

23 My knees are weak through fasting : my flesh is dried up for want of fatness.

24 [b]⌜I became⌝ also a reproach unto them : [c]⌜they that looked upon me shaked⌝ their heads.

[b] R.V. *I am become.*
[c] R.V. *when they see me, they shake.*

25 Help me, O LORD my God : O save me according to thy mercy;

26 And they shall know, how that this is thy hand : and that thou, LORD, hast done it.

27 Though they curse, yet bless thou : [d]⌜and let them be confounded that rise up against me; but let thy servant rejoice⌝.

[d] R.V. *when they arise, they shall be ashamed, but thy servant shall rejoice.*

28 Let mine adversaries be clothed with shame : and let them cover themselves with their own confusion, as with a cloke.

29 As for me, I will give great thanks unto the LORD with my mouth : and praise him among the multitude;

30 For he shall stand at the right hand of the poor : to save his soul from unrighteous judges.

Mark the contrast between this verse and *v.* 5. The LORD stands at the right hand of the persecuted (*v.* 15) poor to protect him; but the adversary stands at the right hand of the persecutor to accuse him (*v.* 5).

THE TWENTY-THIRD DAY

Morning Prayer

PSALM CX. *Dixit Dominus.*

A prophet bears a message from Jehovah to a king, probably David, appointing him His vice-gerent and His priest, and promising him divine aid in war, and victory over his enemies. The message is interpreted in the N.T. as having ultimate reference to the Kingship and Priesthood of Christ.

Proper on Christmas Day.

1 THE LORD [a]said unto my lord : Sit thou on my right hand, until I make thine enemies thy footstool.

1, 2. The Prophet-Psalmist announces the LORD's message to the king ('my lord').

[a] R.V. *saith.*

'Sit thou on my right hand' as sharing my throne and wielding my authority. 1 Chr. xxix. 23. These words are mystically applied in the N.T. to the exaltation of Christ consequent on His death and resurrection. St Matt. xxvi. 64; Acts ii. 34, 35; Eph. i. 20; 1 St Pet. iii. 22 &c.

2 The LORD shall send the rod of thy power out of Sion : be thou ruler, even in the midst among thine enemies.

The 'rod' or sceptre is the symbol of rule.

'saying' is understood before 'be thou' &c. They are the LORD's words.

3 [b]⌜In the day of thy power shall the people offer thee free-will offerings⌝ [c]⌜with an holy worship⌝: [d]⌜the dew of thy birth is of the womb of the morning⌝.

3, 4. The Psalmist's vision of the mustering of the king's army.

[b] R.V. *Thy people offer themselves willingly* (mg. *are freewill offerings*) *in the day of thy power* (mg. *army*).

[c] R.V. mg. *in holy attire*; see Ps. xxix. 2. The warriors of the priest-king (*v.* 4) are themselves priests.

[d] *from the womb of the morning, thou hast the dew of thy youth*, i.e. thy youthful warriors. In their freshness and multitude they are like the dew, the offspring of the morning; cp. 2 Sam. xvii. 11, 12.

1 'How then doth David in the Spirit call him Lord, saying, The Lord said unto my Lord &c.?' St Matt. xxii. 43—45. This question of Christ addressed to the Pharisees shows that they attributed the authorship of this Psalm to David and believed that in this verse he himself is addressing the future Messiah as his Lord. But we are not obliged to conclude that our Lord intended to endorse this opinion and interpretation. It is sufficient to regard Him as taking up the standpoint of His opponents and basing His question upon it. Understanding the passage as they did how could they refuse to see in the Messiah one greater than a mere human son of David? For other questions of our Lord grounded on generally accepted opinions see St Matt. xii. 27; St Mark x. 18.

4 The LORD sware, and will not repent : Thou art a priest for ever after the order of Melchisedech.

The LORD's message continued. The king is solemnly inaugurated as priest, 'after the order (R.V. mg. *manner*) of Melchisedech' who was both king and priest (Gen. xiv. 18) and the office is to be inherited by his successors ('a priest for ever'). The words received their final and adequate fulfilment in Christ the Divine King of David's line. Heb. v., vii.

5—7. The Psalmist's forecast of the king's victory.

5 The Lord upon thy right hand : shall wound even kings in the day of his wrath.

'The Lord' here=Jehovah. He stands at the king's right hand to defend and aid him in the battle.

6 He shall judge among the [a]heathen ; he shall fill the places with the dead bodies : and smite in sunder the heads over divers countries.

'He'=the king. Mystically interpreted this battle-scene represents Christ's conquest of the world. Cp. the imagery of Rev. xix. 11—16.

[a]R.V. *nations*.

7 He shall drink of the brook in the way : therefore shall he lift up his head.

The king in pursuit of his enemies will refresh himself at the stream that crosses his path, and thus renew his energies.

PSALM CXI. *Confitebor tibi.*

The character of God declared by His marvellous acts. The Psalm spiritually understood points forward to Christ as the Bread of Life, the Redeemer and the Mediator of the New Covenant.

This and the following are twin Psalms in form and contents. They are both alphabetical. This Psalm celebrates the glory, the righteousness and the mercy of God ; Ps. cxii. sets forth the blessedness, the righteousness and the beneficence of God's servants.

An alphabetical Psalm.

Proper on Easter Day.

A.R.V. prefix *Praise ye the LORD*, mg. Heb. *Hallelujah*.

I WILL give thanks unto the LORD with my whole heart : [b]⌜secretly among the faithful⌝, and in the congregation.

[b]R.V. *in the council of the upright*, equivalent to 'the congregation' in the parallel clause. The distinction of P.B.V., viz. privately and publicly, is approved by some commentators.

2 The works of the LORD are great : sought out of all them that have pleasure therein.

'The works of the LORD,' specially those wrought by Him for the benefit of Israel, *v.* 6.
'sought out,' i.e. studied and meditated on.
'of' = by.

3 His work is worthy to be praised, and had in honour : and his righteousness endureth for ever.

4 [a]⌜The merciful and gracious LORD hath so done his marvellous works : that they ought to be had in remembrance⌝.

[a] *He hath made his wonderful works to be remembered : the LORD is gracious and full of compassion.* 'to be remembered': the reference is to the Passover, the memorial of God's deliverance of His people from Egypt.

5 He hath given meat unto them that fear him : he shall ever be mindful of his covenant.

'meat' = food, here in particular the Passover meal, the type of the Christian Eucharist.

6 He hath shewed his people the power of his works : [b]⌜that he may give⌝ them the heritage of the heathen.

[b] R.V. *in giving* &c., i.e. by the conquest of Canaan.

7 The works of his hands are verity and judgement : all his commandments are [c]true.

[c] *sure.*

8 They stand fast for ever and ever : and are done in truth and equity.

9 He sent redemption unto his people : he hath commanded his covenant for ever ; holy and reverend is his Name.

'redemption,' i.e. the release from the bondage of Egypt.
'commanded,' i.e. established.

10 The fear of the LORD is the beginning of wisdom : a good understanding have all they that do thereafter ; [d]⌜the praise of it⌝ endureth for ever.

[d] *his praise.*

PSALM CXII. *Beatus vir.*

The character of the servant of God; see introduction to preceding Psalm.

An alphabetical Psalm.

Proper on All Saints' Day [America].

A.R.V. prefix *Praise ye the LORD*, mg. Heb. *Hallelujah.*

BLESSED is the man that feareth the LORD : he hath great delight in his commandments.

2 His seed shall be mighty upon earth : the generation of the faithful shall be blessed.

3 Riches and plenteousness shall be in his house : and his righteousness endureth for ever.

'his righteousness' &c. These words (repeated *v.* 9), which in the preceding Psalm (*v.* 3) are used of God, are here applied to him who fears God. Man's righteousness is a copy of the Divine, and comes to man by God's gift.

4 Unto the godly there ariseth up light in the darkness : he is merciful, loving, and righteous.

5 [a]⌜A good man is merciful, and lendeth : and will guide his words with discretion⌝.

[a] R.V. *Well is it with the man that dealeth graciously and lendeth; he shall maintain his cause in judgement*, i.e. no accusation can overthrow him; see next verse.

6 For he shall never be moved : and the righteous shall be had in everlasting remembrance.

7 He will not be afraid of any evil tidings : for his heart standeth fast, and believeth in the LORD.

8 His heart is established, and will not shrink : until he see his desire upon his enemies.

9 He hath dispersed abroad, and given to the poor : and his righteousness remaineth for ever ; his horn shall be exalted with honour.

Quoted by St Paul, 2 Cor. ix. 9, when exhorting to Christian beneficence.

10 The ungodly shall see it, and it shall grieve him : he shall gnash with his teeth, and consume away ; the desire of the ungodly shall perish.

Note that this Psalm ends, as it begins, like Ps. i.

PSALM CXIII. *Laudate, pueri.*

A hymn of praise to the mighty God who condescends to visit and exalt the lowly.

Ps. cxiii.—cxviii. constitute the Hallel which was sung at all the great Jewish Festivals. At the Passover Ps. cxiii., cxiv. were sung before, and Ps. cxv.—cxviii. after the meal.

Proper on Easter Day and on Purification of B.V.M. [America].

A.R.V. prefix *Praise ye the LORD*, mg. Heb. *Hallelujah*.

PRAISE [a]⌜the LORD, ye servants⌝ : O praise the Name of the LORD.

[a] *O ye servants of the LORD*, i.e. Israel as set apart for the service of Jehovah. P.B.V. follows Vulg.

2 Blessed be the Name of the LORD : from this time forth for evermore.

'Blessed be the Name of the LORD ;
Henceforth, world without end.'
Confirmation Service.

3 The LORD's Name is praised : from the rising up of the sun unto the going down of the same.

'The Lord's Name be praised.' Response at Matins and Evensong.

A foreshadowing of the universal acceptance of God's rule.

4 The LORD is high above all [b]heathen : and his glory above the heavens.

[b]*nations*.

5 Who is like unto the LORD our God, that hath his dwelling so high : and yet humbleth himself to behold the things that are in heaven and earth?

6 He taketh up the simple out of the dust : and lifteth the poor out of the [a]mire;

6, 7. From the song of Hannah, 1 Sam. ii. 8; cp. the Magnificat, St Luke i. 52.

Metaphors for extreme poverty and degradation.

[a]*dunghill.* The allusion is to the refuse-heaps, outside Eastern villages, the haunts of outcasts.

7 That he may set him with the princes : even with the princes of his people.

8 He maketh the barren woman to keep house : and to be a joyful mother of children.

Cp. 1 Sam. ii. 5. Besides the literal meaning, the Psalmist probably has in view the state of Sion before and after her captivity; see Is. liv. 1.

A.R.V. add *Praise ye the LORD*, mg. Heb. *Hallelujah.*

Evening Prayer

PSALM CXIV. *In exitu Israel.*

The awe and commotion of nature as it witnessed God's guidance of His people out of Egypt.

Proper on Easter Day—the Church's celebration of a greater redemption than that of Israel from Egypt.

WHEN Israel came out of Egypt : and the house of Jacob from among the strange people,

2 Judah [b]was his sanctuary : and Israel his dominion.

[b]R.V. *became.* At the Exodus, the nation, designated here by its two historical divisions, was sanctified by God as His abode and kingdom. Exod. xix. 3—6.

'The sea' = the Red Sea.

3 The sea saw that, and fled : Jordan was driven back.

4 The mountains skipped like rams : and the little hills like young sheep.

'The whole mount quaked greatly' (Exod. xix. 18) at the giving of the Law.

5 What aileth thee, O thou sea, that thou fleddest : and thou Jordan, that thou wast driven back?

6 Ye mountains, that ye skipped like rams : and ye little hills, like young sheep?

7 Tremble, thou earth, at the presence of the Lord : at the presence of the God of Jacob;

8 Who turned the hard rock into a standing water : and the flint-stone into a springing well.

At Rephidim and Kadesh. Exod. xvii. 6; Numb. xx. 11.

PSALM CXV. *Non nobis, Domine.*

A prayer to the Living God to vindicate the honour of His Name by succouring those who trust in Him. Probably composed for use in the Second Temple.

Ps. cxv.—cxviii., as forming the part of the Hallel (see Ps. cxiii) which came after the Passover meal, was probably the hymn sung by our Lord and His Apostles before leaving the Supper-room. St Matt. xxvi. 30.

Special in Form of Consecration of a Churchyard [Ireland].

NOT unto us, O LORD, not unto us, but unto thy Name give [a]⌜the praise⌝ : for thy loving mercy, and for thy truth's sake.

[a]*glory.* May God glorify—not us—but His own Name by delivering His people, and thus silencing the taunts of their enemies. It is a prayer, not a thanksgiving.

2 Wherefore shall the heathen say : Where is now their God?

3 As for our God, he is in heaven : he hath done whatsoever pleased him.

3—11 are repeated with some variations in Ps. cxxxv. 6, 15—20.

4 Their idols are silver and gold : even the work of men's hands.

However costly their material, they are merely of human workmanship.

5 They have mouths, and speak not : eyes have they, and see not.

6 They have ears, and hear not : noses have they, and smell not.

7 They have hands, and handle
not ; feet have they, and walk
not : neither speak they through
their throat.

8 They that make them [a]are like
unto them : [b]⌜and so are all such
as put their trust⌝ in them.

[a] R.V. *shall be.*

[b] R.V. *yea, every one that trusteth.*

9—11. The classification 'Israel,' 'house of Aaron,' 'ye that fear the LORD,' appears again in Ps. cxviii. 2—4, also in Ps. cxxxv. 19, 20 with 'house of Levi' added.

9 [c]⌜But thou, house of Israel⌝,
trust thou in the LORD : [d]⌜he is
their succour and defence⌝.

[c] *O Israel.* P.B.V. from Vulg.

[d] *he is their help and their shield.* Probably the response of the choir, hence the change of person 'their.' Note that the response is repeated in *vv.* 10, 11.

10 Ye house of Aaron, put your
trust in the LORD : [e]⌜he is their
helper and defender⌝.

[e] *he is their help and their shield.*

11 Ye that fear the LORD, put
your trust in the LORD : [f]⌜he is
their helper and defender⌝.

[f] *he is their help and their shield.*

12 The LORD hath been mindful
of us, and he shall bless us : even
he shall bless the house of Israel,
he shall bless the house of Aaron.

13 He shall bless them that fear
the LORD : both small and great.

14 The LORD shall increase you
more and more : you and your
children.

15 Ye are the blessed of the
LORD : who made heaven and
earth.

16 [g]⌜All the whole heavens are
the LORD'S⌝ : the earth hath he
given to the children of men.

[g] R.V. *The heavens are the heavens of the LORD.*

17 The dead praise not thee,
O LORD : neither all they that
go down into silence.

18 But we will praise the LORD :
from this time forth for evermore.
Praise the LORD.

'Praise the LORD.' R.V. mg. Heb. *Hallelujah.*

THE TWENTY-FOURTH DAY

Morning Prayer

PSALM CXVI. *Dilexi, quoniam.*

A thanksgiving for recovery from an almost fatal sickness.

Special in the Churching of Women (omitting *vv.* **13—15).**

[a]⌜I AM well pleased : that the LORD hath heard the voice of my prayer⌝;

[a] *I love the* LORD, *because he hath heard my voice and my supplications.*

2 [b]That he hath inclined his ear unto me : therefore will I call upon him as long as I live.

[b] *Because.*

3 The [c]snares of death compassed me round about : and the pains of [d]hell gat hold upon me.

[c] R.V. *cords.* Death is compared to a hunter snaring his prey; see Ps. xviii. 3, 4.

[d] R.V. *Sheol.*

4 [e]⌜I shall find⌝ trouble and heaviness, [f]⌜and I will call⌝ upon the Name of the LORD : O LORD, I beseech thee, deliver my soul.

[e] *I found.*

[f] *then called I.*

5 Gracious is the LORD, and righteous : yea, our God is merciful.

6 The LORD preserveth the simple : I was in misery, and he helped me.

7 Turn again then unto thy rest, O my soul : for the LORD hath [g]rewarded thee.

i.e. Return to thy restful trust in God.

[g] *dealt bountifully with.*

8 And why? thou hast delivered my soul from death : mine eyes from tears, and my feet from falling.

8, 9. Quoted, with slight changes, from Ps. lvi. 13.

9 I will walk before the LORD : in the land of the living.

10 I believed, and therefore will I speak; but I was sore troubled: I said in my haste, All men are liars.

'I believed' &c. In all my tribulation I retained faith in God, and therefore will I speak in the confident tone of *v.* 9. The passage is quoted from the Sept. in 2 Cor. iv. 13.

'All men' &c. My troubles led me to conclude that all human helpers were treacherous; see Rom. iii. 4.

11 What reward shall I give unto the LORD: for all the benefits that he hath done unto me?

12 I will receive the cup of salvation: and call upon the Name of the LORD.

The drink-offering which would accompany the 'sacrifice of thanksgiving' (*v.* 15) is probably meant. The Christian will interpret mystically of the 'cup of blessing.' 1 Cor. x. 16.

13 I will pay [a]⌜my vows⌝ now in the presence of all his people: [b]⌜right dear⌝ in the sight of the LORD is the death of his saints.

[a] *my vows unto the LORD.*

[b] *precious.* P.B.V. 'dear' = costly; see Ps. lxxii. 14. The LORD does not take lightly the death of His saints (i.e. His beloved; see Ps. xvi. 11).

14 Behold, O LORD, how that I am thy servant: I am thy servant, and the son of thine handmaid; thou hast broken my bonds in sunder.

'the son' &c. i.e. born in the LORD's house—from my earliest years 'of the household of God.' Eph. ii. 19; see Ps. lxxxvi. 16.

'bonds' of sickness.

15 I will offer to thee the sacrifice of thanksgiving: and will call upon the Name of the LORD.

For the sacrifice of thanksgiving presented as an acknowledgment of blessings received see Lev. vii. 11 ff.

16 I will pay my vows unto the LORD, in the [c]sight of all his people: in the courts of the LORD'S house, even in the midst of thee, O Jerusalem. Praise the LORD.

[c] *presence.*

'*Praise the LORD*' R.V. mg. Heb. *Hallelujah.*

PSALM CXVII. *Laudate Dominum.*

An invitation to all mankind to praise God for His mercies towards Israel—the pledge of the world's salvation.

Proper on Epiphany [America].

O PRAISE the LORD, all ye heathen: praise him, all ye nations.

Quoted by St Paul, Rom. xv. 11, as predictive of the call of the Gentiles.

2 For his [a]⌜merciful kindness is ever more and more⌝ towards us : and the truth of the LORD endureth for ever. Praise the LORD.

[a] R.V. *mercy is great.* In the passage preceding Rom. xv. 11 St Paul thus comments on this verse. 'For I say that Christ hath been made a minister of the circumcision for the truth of God, that he might confirm the promises given unto the fathers, and that the Gentiles might glorify God for his mercy.'

'*Praise the LORD.*' R.V. mg. Heb. *Hallelujah.*

PSALM CXVIII. *Confitemini Domino.*

A triumphant hymn of thanksgiving to God sung by worshippers in procession to the Temple. It was probably composed for the Feast of Tabernacles recorded in Neh. viii. Subsequently the shout 'Hosannah,' *v.* 25, became specially associated with that Festival.

The last of the Hallel Psalms; see Ps. cxiii.

Proper on Easter Day.

O GIVE thanks unto the LORD, for he is gracious : because his mercy endureth for ever.

1—18. Sung by the procession.

The liturgical doxology as in Ps. cvi. 1, cvii. 1.

2 Let Israel now confess, [1]⌜that he is gracious : and⌝ that his mercy endureth for ever.

2—4. 'Israel,' 'house of Aaron,' 'them that fear the LORD.' This classification occurs also in Ps. cxv. 9—11, and in Ps. cxxxv. 19, 20 with 'house of Levi' added.

3 Let the house of Aaron now confess : that his mercy endureth for ever.

4 Yea, let them now that fear the LORD confess : that his mercy endureth for ever.

5 I called upon the LORD in trouble : and the LORD heard me [b]⌜at large⌝.

'I.' The Psalmist speaks in the name of his nation.

[b] *and set me in a large place,* i.e. freed me from restrictions, and gave me liberty. The reference is to the release from Babylonian captivity.

[1] Not in A.R.V., added in P.B.V. from Vulg.

6 The LORD is on my side : I will not fear [a]⌜what man doeth unto me⌝.

From Ps. lvi. 11, quoted Heb. xiii. 6, according to the Sept.

[a] *what can man do unto me?*

7 The LORD [b]⌜taketh my part with⌝ them that help me : therefore shall I see my desire upon mine enemies.

[b] R.V. *is on my side among*, i.e. is my true upholder, according to a Hebrew idiom; see Ps. liv. 4; Judg. xi. 35.

8 It is better to trust in the LORD : than to put any confidence in man.

9 It is better to trust in the LORD : than to put any confidence in princes.

'princes,' i.e. the Persian kings and governors who frequently hindered the building of the Temple.

10 All nations compassed me round about : but in the Name of the LORD will I destroy them.

'All nations,' i.e. the neighbouring tribes who harassed the restored exiles.

11 They kept me in on every side, they kept me in, I say, on every side : but in the Name of the LORD will I destroy them.

12 They came about me like bees, and are [c]extinct even as the fire among the thorns : for in the Name of the LORD I will destroy them.

[c] *quenched.* P.B.V. 'extinct' = extinguished.

Which blazes up quickly, and as quickly dies out.

13 Thou hast thrust sore at me, that I might fall : but the LORD was my help.

'Thou.' The enemies are addressed as an individual.

14 The LORD is my strength, and my song : and is become my salvation.

From the Song of Moses, Exod. xv. 2. God's care of Israel does not belong only to the past.

15 The voice of joy and [d]health is in the dwellings of the righteous : the right hand of the LORD [e]⌜bringeth mighty things to pass⌝.

[d] *salvation*, i.e. well-being. P.B.V. 'health' has this meaning.

[e] *doeth valiantly*; cp. Exod. xv. 6.

16 The right hand of the LORD hath the pre-eminence : the right hand of the LORD [f]⌜bringeth mighty things to pass⌝.

[f] *doeth valiantly.*

17, 18. Israel, chastened by suffering, will survive to proclaim the doings of the LORD throughout the world.

17 I shall not die, but live : and declare the works of the LORD.

'As dying, and behold we live; as chastened, and not killed. 2 Cor. vi. 9.

18 The LORD hath chastened and corrected me : but he hath not given me over unto death.

19 Open me the gates of righteousness : that I may go into them, and give thanks unto the LORD.

The challenge of the choir as the procession reaches the Temple gates. They are called 'gates of righteousness' because God is righteous, and because He looks for the same character in those who worship in His courts; see next verse.

20 This is the gate of the LORD : the righteous shall enter into it.

The answer of the priests from within the Temple.

21 I will thank thee, for thou hast heard me : and art become my salvation.

21—25. Sung by the procession.

22 The same stone which the builders refused : is become the head-stone in the corner.

23 This is the LORD'S doing : and it is marvellous in our eyes.

22, 23. Israel rejected as of no account by the builders of the world's empires, has been chosen by God as the head-stone of His Spiritual Temple. This vision of the Psalmist was actually fulfilled in Christ, the representative of Israel, and these words are applied by our Lord to Himself. St Matt. xxi. 42; see Acts iv. 11; 1 St Pet. ii. 7.

24 This is the day which the LORD hath made : we will rejoice and be glad in it.

The LORD by His Providence has enabled us to keep this day of gladness.

25 [a]⌜Help me now⌝, O LORD : O LORD, send us now prosperity.

[a] *Save now, we beseech thee.* In Hebrew 'Hosanna,' with which and with the words of *v.* 26 the multitudes welcomed our Lord as the Messiah on Palm Sunday. St Matt. xxi. 9.

26 Blessed be he that cometh in the Name of the LORD : we have [b]⌜wished you good luck, ye that are of the house of the LORD⌝.

The greeting of the priests from within the Temple.

[b] *blessed you out of the house of the LORD.*

27 God is the LORD who hath shewed us light : bind the sacrifice with cords, yea, even unto the horns of the altar.

27—29. Sung by the procession.
'bind the sacrifice...unto the horns of the altar.' As this seems to have formed no part of the sacrificial usage, the meaning probably is, May the victims be so numerous that they will fill the Temple-court up to the very horns of the altar.

28 Thou art my God, and I will thank thee : thou art my God, and I will praise thee.

29 O give thanks unto the LORD, for he is gracious : and his mercy endureth for ever.

Evening Prayer

PSALM CXIX.

The praises of the Law of God sung by one who suffered for his adherence to it. Probably written after the exile.

This is the most elaborate of the alphabetical Psalms. It is divided into twenty-two stanzas corresponding with the number of letters in the Hebrew alphabet. In each stanza all the verses begin with the same letter (indicated in A.V. and R.V.), which follow each other in regular order.

In every verse except two (122 and 132) the Law, which may be taken as meaning the whole of Divine revelation, is referred to either under that name or some equivalent expression.

Beati immaculati. א Aleph.

The blessedness of unreserved obedience to God's Law.

BLESSED are those that are undefiled in the way : and walk in the law of the LORD.

2 Blessed are they that keep his testimonies : and seek him with their whole heart.

3 For they who do no wickedness : walk in his ways.

4 Thou hast charged : that we shall diligently keep thy commandments.

Deut. iv. 2.

5 O that my ways were [a]⌜made so direct : that I might keep⌝ thy statutes!

[a] R.V. *established to observe.*

6 So shall I not be confounded : while I have respect unto all thy commandments.

7 I will thank thee with [b]⌜an unfeigned heart⌝ : when I [c]⌜shall have learned the judgements of thy righteousness⌝.

[b] *uprightness of heart.*

[c] R.V. *learn thy righteous judgements.*

8 I will keep thy [d]ceremonies : O forsake me not utterly.

[d] *statutes.*

In quo corriget? ב Beth.

The young man safeguarded by adherence to God's word.

WHEREWITHAL shall a young man cleanse his way : even by ruling himself after thy word.

i.e. keep his way pure.

10 With my whole heart have I sought thee : O let me not [e]⌜go wrong out of⌝ thy commandments.

[e] *wander from.*

11 [f]⌜Thy words have I hid within⌝ my heart : that I should not sin against thee.

[f] R.V. *Thy word have I laid up in.*

12 Blessed art thou, O LORD : O teach me thy statutes.

13 With my lips have I been telling : of all the judgements of thy mouth.

14 I have had as great delight in the way of thy testimonies : as in all manner of riches.

15 I will [a]⌜talk of⌝ thy commandments : and have respect unto thy ways.

[a] *meditate in.*

16 My delight shall be in thy statutes : and I will not forget thy word.

Retribue servo tuo. ג Gimel.

God's law gives comfort and strength amidst contempt and persecution.

O DO well unto thy servant : that I may live, [b]⌜and keep⌝ thy word.

[b] R.V. *so will I observe.*

18 Open thou mine eyes : that I may see the wondrous things of thy law.

19 I am a stranger upon earth : O hide not thy commandments from me.

Cp. Ps. xxxix. 14; Lev. xxv. 23; 1 St Pet. ii. 11.
'hide not' &c., i.e. reveal to me their inner sense and obligation.

20 My soul [c]⌜breaketh out⌝ for the very fervent desire : that it hath alway unto thy judgements.

[c] *breaketh.*

21 Thou hast rebuked the proud : and cursed are they that do err from thy commandments.

22 O turn from me shame and rebuke : for I have kept thy testimonies.

23 Princes also did sit and speak against me : but thy servant is occupied in thy statutes.

'Princes'=probably, fellow countrymen of high rank and power; cp. *v.* 46.

24 For thy testimonies are my delight : and my counsellors.

Adhæsit pavimento. ד Daleth.

God's word the true consolation in affliction.

MY soul cleaveth to the dust : O quicken thou me, according to thy word.

'quicken me,' i.e. revive my courage and spirits.

26 I have acknowledged my ways, and thou heardest me : O teach me thy statutes.

I have laid open before God all the details of my life.

27 Make me to understand the way of thy commandments : and so shall I [a]talk of thy wondrous works.

[a] R.V. *meditate.*

28 My soul melteth away for very heaviness : [b]comfort thou me according unto thy word.

[b] *strengthen.* P.B.V. 'comfort' formerly had this meaning.

29 Take from me the way of lying : and [c]⌜cause thou me to make much of thy law⌝.

'lying,' i.e. insincerity in serving God, contrasted with 'faithfulness' (*v.* 30).

[c] *grant me* (i.e. make known to me) *thy law graciously.*

30 I have chosen the way of [d]truth : and thy judgements have I laid before me.

[d] R.V. *faithfulness.*

31 I have stuck unto thy testimonies : O LORD, confound me not.

32 I will run the way of thy commandments : when thou [e]⌜hast set my heart at liberty⌝.

[e] *shalt enlarge my heart*, i.e. set it free from care and trouble. Quoted in 2 Cor. vi. 11.

THE TWENTY-FIFTH DAY

Morning Prayer

Legem pone. ה He.

Prayer for fuller knowledge of God's commandments, and for Divine help to keep them.

TEACH me, O LORD, the way of thy statutes : and I shall keep it unto the end.

34 Give me understanding, and I shall keep thy law : yea, I shall keep it with my whole heart.

35 Make me to go in the path of thy commandments : for therein is my desire.

36 Incline my heart unto thy testimonies : and not to covetousness.

37 O turn away mine eyes, lest they behold vanity : and quicken thou me in thy way.

'vanity' = falsehood, here that which is unreal and worthless, as opposed to God.

38 O stablish thy word in thy servant : that I may fear thee.

39 Take away the [a]rebuke that I am afraid of : for thy judgements are good.

[a] *reproach* of those who scorn me because of my faithfulness to God's law; see *vv.* 22, 23, 42.

40 Behold, my delight is in thy commandments : O quicken me in thy righteousness.

Et veniat super me. ו Vau.

Trust in God's word gives courage to confess Him before men.

LET thy loving mercy come also unto me, O LORD : even thy salvation, according unto thy word.

42 So shall I make answer unto [b]⌜my blasphemers⌝ : for my trust is in thy word.

'So,' i.e. by being able to appeal to manifest proofs of God's loving mercy, *v.* 41.

[b] *him that reproacheth me* for my loyalty to God's law.

43 O take not the word of thy truth utterly out of my mouth : for my hope is in thy judgements.

44 So shall I alway keep thy law : yea, for ever and ever.

45 And I will walk at liberty : for I seek thy commandments.

True 'liberty' is gained only by conformity to the law of God, 'whose service is perfect freedom.' 2nd Collect at Matins.

46 I will speak of thy testimonies also, even before kings : and will not be ashamed.

'kings,' i.e. the godless rulers who persecuted the faithful, *v.* 23.

47 And my delight shall be in thy commandments : which I have loved.

48 My hands also will I lift up unto thy commandments, which I have loved : and my study shall be in thy statutes.

'lift up,' making vow of obedience; see Gen. xiv. 22.

Memor esto servi tui. ז Zain.

God's word is the source of comfort in trouble, and of joy in life's pilgrimage.

[a]⌜O THINK upon thy servant, as concerning thy word⌝ : wherein thou hast caused me to put my trust.

[a] *Remember the word unto thy servant.*

50 The same is my comfort in my trouble : for thy word hath quickened me.

51 The proud have had me exceedingly in derision : yet have I not shrinked from thy law.

52 For I remembered [b]⌜thine everlasting judgements⌝, O LORD : and received comfort.

[b] *thy judgements of old.*

53 [c]⌜I am horribly afraid : for⌝ the ungodly that forsake thy law.

[c] R.V. *Hot indignation hath taken hold upon me, because of.*

54 Thy statutes have been my songs : in the house of my pilgrimage.

'I am a stranger upon earth,' *v.* 19.

55 I have thought upon thy Name, O LORD, in the night-season : and have kept thy law.

56 This I had : because I kept thy commandments.

'This,' i.e. all the blessings enumerated in this stanza—comfort, courage, zeal, cheerfulness, recollection of God.

Portio mea, Domine. ח Cheth.

A declaration of earnestness and constancy in keeping God's Law.

THOU art my portion, O LORD: I have promised to keep thy Law.

58 I made my humble petition in thy presence with my whole heart : O be merciful unto me, according to thy word.

59 I called mine own ways to remembrance : and turned my feet unto thy testimonies.

60 I made haste, and [a]⌜prolonged not the time⌝ : to keep thy commandments.

61 [b]⌜The congregations of the ungodly have robbed me⌝ : but I have not forgotten thy law.

62 At midnight I will rise to give thanks unto thee : because of thy righteous judgements.

63 I am a companion of all them that fear thee : and keep thy commandments.

64 The earth, O LORD, is full of thy mercy : O teach me thy statutes.

[a] *delayed not.* P.B.V. has the same meaning.

[b] R.V. *The cords of the wicked have wrapped me round,* as a hunter ensnares his prey.

Bonitatem fecisti. ט Teth.

Devotion to God's law is taught in the school of adversity.

O LORD, thou hast dealt graciously with thy servant : according unto thy word.

66 O learn me true understanding and knowledge : for I have believed thy commandments.

'learn' = teach.

67 Before I was troubled, I went wrong : but now have I kept thy word.

Cp. *v.* 75.

68 Thou art good and [a]gracious : O teach me thy statutes.

[a] *doest good.*

69 The proud have [b]imagined a lie against me : but I will keep thy commandments with my whole heart.

[b] *forged.*

70 Their heart is as fat as [c]brawn: but my delight hath been in thy law.

[c] *grease.* A figure for obduracy and insensibility.

71 It is good for me that I have been in trouble : that I may learn thy statutes.

72 The law of thy mouth is dearer unto me : than thousands of gold and silver.

Evening Prayer

Manus tuæ fecerunt me. Jod.

God's word is pledged to revive and comfort those whom He afflicts.

THY hands have made me and fashioned me : O give me understanding, that I may learn thy commandments.

74 They that fear thee will be glad when they see me : because I have put my trust in thy word.

75 I know, O LORD, that thy judgements are right : and that thou of very faithfulness hast caused me to be troubled.

Cp. *v.* 67.

76 O let thy merciful kindness be my comfort : according to thy word unto thy servant.

Though God's chastisement is just and beneficial (*v.* 75), yet may its bitterness be tempered by His mercy!

77 O let thy loving mercies come unto me, that I may live : for thy law is my delight.

78 Let the proud be confounded, for they [a]⌜go wickedly about to destroy me⌝ : but I will [b]⌜be occupied⌝ in thy commandments.

[a] R.V. mg. *have overthrown me with falsehood.*
'go about'=endeavour.
[b] *meditate.* P.B.V. has this meaning.

79 Let such as fear thee, [c]⌜and have known thy testimonies : be turned unto me⌝.

[c] R.V. *turn unto me, and they shall know thy testimonies,* from what they see is my experience.

80 O let my heart be sound in thy statutes : that I be not ashamed.

Defecit anima mea. כ Caph.

God's word gives hope in days of gloom and persecution.

MY soul [d]⌜hath longed⌝ for thy salvation : [e]and I have a good hope because of thy word.

[d] *fainteth.*
[e] *but.*

82 Mine eyes [f]⌜long sore⌝ for thy word : saying, O when wilt thou comfort me?

[f] *fail* ; cp. *v.* 123 ; Ps. lxix. 3.

83 For I am become like a bottle in the smoke : yet do I not forget thy statutes.

i.e. like a wine-skin suspended from the rafters, blackened and shrivelled by the smoke.

84 How many are the days of thy servant : when wilt thou [g]⌜be avenged of⌝ them that persecute me?

The sense of the shortness of life prompts the prayer for the speedy manifestation of God's righteous judgement.
[g] *execute judgement on.*

85 The proud have digged pits for me : [h]which are not after thy law.

[h] R.V. *who*, i.e. the proud.

86 All thy commandments are [i]true : they persecute me falsely ; O be thou my help.

[i] *faithful.*

87 They had almost made an end of me upon earth : but I forsook not thy commandments.

88 O quicken me after thy loving-kindness : and so shall I keep the testimonies of thy mouth.

In æternum, Domine. ל Lamed.

God's word is eternal, unchangeable and unlimited in range.

O LORD, thy word : endureth for ever in heaven.

90 Thy [a] truth also remaineth from one generation to another : thou hast laid the foundation of the earth, and it abideth.

[a] *faithfulness.*

91 They continue this day according to thine ordinance : for all things serve thee.

'They,' i.e. 'heaven' (*v.* 89) and 'earth' (*v.* 90).

92 If my delight had not been in thy law : I should have perished in my trouble.

The comfort of God's Law has sustained the Psalmist in his affliction.

93 I will never forget thy commandments : for with them thou hast quickened me.

94 I am thine, O save me : for I have sought thy commandments.

95 The ungodly laid wait for me to destroy me : but I will consider thy testimonies.

96 I see that all things come to an end : but thy commandment is exceeding broad.

All earthly things are limited and imperfect, but God's commandment—that which His word reveals—has an infinite range.

Quomodo dilexi! מ Mem.

God's Law imparts a higher than worldly wisdom.

[1] LORD, what love have I unto thy law : all the day long is my study in it.

98 Thou through thy commandments hast made me wiser than mine enemies : for they are ever with me.

'wiser,' i.e. the possessor of a better wisdom.

'they' = 'thy commandments.'

[1] Not in A.R.V., added in P.B.V. from Vulg.

99 I have more understanding than [a]my teachers : for thy testimonies are my study.

[a] *all my.*

100 I am wiser than the aged : because I keep thy commandments.

101 I have refrained my feet from every evil way : that I may keep thy word.

102 I have not [b]shrunk from thy judgements : for thou teachest me.

[b] R.V. *turned aside.*

103 O how sweet are thy words unto my throat : yea, sweeter than honey unto my mouth.

104 Through thy commandments I get understanding : therefore I hate [c]⌜all evil ways⌝.

[c] *every false way*, i.e. all insincerity in serving God, *vv.* 29, 128, 163.

THE TWENTY-SIXTH DAY

Morning Prayer

Lucerna pedibus meis. נ Nun.

God's word gives light and joy and strength in times of danger and sorrow.

THY word is a lantern unto my feet : and a light unto my paths.

106 I have sworn, and am stedfastly purposed : to keep thy righteous judgements.

107 I am troubled above measure: quicken me, O LORD, according to thy word.

108 Let the free-will offerings of my mouth please thee, O LORD : and teach me thy judgements.

i.e. my prayers and vows of obedience; see Ps. xix. 14, l. 14.

109 My soul is alway in my hand : yet do I not forget thy law.

i.e. My life is in constant jeopardy owing to the plots of enemies (*v.* 110); see Judg. xii. 3; 1 Sam. xix. 5.

110 The ungodly have laid a snare for me : but yet I swerved not from thy commandments.

Cp. *v.* 157.

111 Thy testimonies have I claimed as mine heritage for ever : and why? they are the very joy of my heart.

God's Law was the faithful Israelite's true inheritance, more permanent than the land of promise. Exod. xxxii. 13.

112 I have applied my heart to fulfil thy statutes alway : even unto the end.

Iniquos odio habui. ס Samech.

The safety of those who keep God's commandments contrasted with the downfall of those who depart from them.

I HATE them that [a]⌜imagine evil things⌝ : but thy law do I love.

[a] R.V. *are of a double mind*, i.e. waver in their allegiance to God. 1 Kings xviii. 21; St James i. 8.

114 Thou art my [b]defence and shield : and my trust is in thy word.

[b] *hiding place.*

115 Away from me, ye wicked : [c]⌜I will⌝ keep the commandments of my God.

[c] R.V. *that I may.*

116 O stablish me according to thy word, that I may live : and let me not be disappointed of my hope.

116, 117. Yet to keep God's commandments (*v.* 115) I need His assistance.

117 Hold thou me up, and I shall be safe : yea, my delight shall be ever in thy statutes.

118 Thou hast [d]⌜trodden down⌝ all them that depart from thy statutes : for they imagine but deceit.

[d] R.V. *set at nought.*

119 Thou puttest away all the ungodly of the earth like dross : therefore I love thy testimonies.

'dross' which the refiner separates from the pure ore.

120 My flesh trembleth for fear of thee : and I am afraid of thy judgements.

Feci judicium. ע Ain.

God's word, when despised by the world, becomes more precious to the righteous.

[a]⌜I DEAL with the thing that is lawful and right⌝ : O give me not over unto mine oppressors.

[a] *I have done judgement and justice.*

122 [b]⌜Make thou thy servant to delight in that which is good⌝ : that the proud do me no wrong.

[b] *Be surety for thy servant for good,* i.e. Guarantee his welfare.

This and *v.* 132 are the only verses in this Psalm which do not refer to God's Law.

123 Mine eyes [c]⌜are wasted away with looking for thy health⌝ : and for the word of thy righteousness.

[c] *fail for thy salvation*; cp. *v.* 82. P.V.B. 'health' = well-being in general.

124 O deal with thy servant according unto thy loving mercy : and teach me thy statutes.

125 I am thy servant, O grant me understanding : that I may know thy testimonies.

126 It is time for thee, LORD, to [d]⌜lay to thine hand⌝ : for they have destroyed thy law.

[d] *work.* P.B.V. has this meaning.

127 [e]For I love thy commandments : above gold [f]⌜and precious stone⌝.

[e] *Therefore.* Because evil men have abrogated God's Law (*v.* 126), it becomes all the more precious to me.

[f] *yea, above fine gold.* P.B.V. follows Vulg.

128 Therefore hold I straight all thy commandments : and all false ways I utterly abhor.

'hold straight,' i.e. regard as right, approve.

'false ways,' i.e. insincerity in the service of God, *vv.* 29, 104, 163.

Mirabilia. פ Pe.

God's word enlightens the mind and preserves from evil those who keep it.

THY testimonies are wonderful : therefore doth my soul keep them.

130 [a]⌜When thy word goeth forth : it giveth light and⌝ understanding unto the simple.

[a] R.V. *The opening* (i.e. unveiling) *of thy words giveth light; it giveth.*

131 I opened my mouth, and [b]⌜drew in my breath⌝ : for [c]⌜my delight was in⌝ thy commandments.

[b] *panted.* An expression implying eager desire.
[c] *I longed for.*

132 O look thou upon me, and be merciful unto me : as thou usest to do unto those that love thy Name.

This and *v.* 122 are the only verses in this Psalm which do not refer to God's Law.

133 Order my steps in thy word : and [d]⌜so shall no⌝ wickedness have dominion over me.

[d] *let not any.*

134 O deliver me from the wrongful dealings of men : and so shall I keep thy commandments.

135 [e]⌜Shew the light of thy countenance⌝ upon thy servant : and teach me thy statutes.

[e] *Make thy face to shine.* A part of the priestly blessing. Numb. vi. 25; see Ps. xxxi. 18.

136 Mine eyes gush out with water : because men keep not thy law.

Cp. *v.* 158.

Justus es, Domine. צ Tzade.

The righteousness, purity and truth of God's Law.

RIGHTEOUS art thou, O LORD : and [f]⌜true is thy judgement⌝.

[f] *upright are thy judgements.*

138 The testimonies that thou hast commanded : are exceeding righteous and true.

139 My zeal hath even consumed me : because mine enemies have forgotten thy words.

See Ps. lxix. 9.

140 Thy word is [a]⌜tried to the uttermost⌝ : and thy servant loveth it.

[a] *very pure.* P.B.V. 'tried' = refined, as metals are in a furnace.

141 I am small, and of no reputation : yet do I not forget thy commandments.

142 Thy righteousness is an everlasting righteousness : and thy law is the truth.

143 Trouble and heaviness have taken hold upon me : yet is my delight in thy commandments.

144 The righteousness of thy testimonies is everlasting : O grant me understanding, and I shall live.

Evening Prayer

Clamavi in toto corde meo. ק Koph.

Earnest and constant prayer needful for the due observance of God's statutes.

I CALL with my whole heart : hear me, O LORD, I will keep thy statutes.

146 Yea, even unto thee do I call : help me, and I shall keep thy testimonies.

147 [b]⌜Early in the morning do I cry unto thee⌝ : for in thy word is my trust.

[b] *I prevented* (i.e. anticipated) *the dawning of the morning, and cried.*

148 Mine eyes [c]prevent the night-watches : that I might be occupied in thy words.

[c] R.V. *prevented.*
The Israelites divided the night into three watches. Judg. vii. 19; 1 Sam. xi. 11; Lam. ii. 19.

149 Hear my voice, O LORD, according unto thy loving-kindness : quicken me, according [d]⌜as thou art wont⌝.

[d] R.V. *to thy judgements*; cp. *v.* 156.

150 They draw nigh that of malice persecute me : and are far from thy law.

151 Be thou nigh at hand, O LORD : for all thy commandments are true.

When my enemies are 'nigh' (*v.* 150) to assail me, be Thou 'nigh' to succour me.

152 As concerning thy testimonies, I have known long since : that thou hast [a]grounded them for ever.

[a]*founded.*

Vide humilitatem. ר Resh.

Prayer for grace to keep God's commandments.

O CONSIDER mine adversity, and deliver me : for I do not forget thy law.

154 [b]Avenge thou my cause, and deliver me : quicken me, according to thy word.

[b]*Plead.*

155 [c]Health is far from the ungodly : for they regard not thy statutes.

[c]*Salvation.* P.B.V. 'Health' = well-being in general.

156 Great is thy mercy, O LORD : quicken me, [d]⌜as thou art wont⌝.

[d]*according to thy judgements* ; cp. *v.* 149.

157 Many there are that trouble me, and persecute me : yet do I not swerve from thy testimonies.

Cp. *v.* 110.

158 It grieveth me when I see the transgressors : because they keep not thy law.

Cp. *v.* 136.

159 Consider, O LORD, how I love thy commandments : O quicken me, according to thy loving-kindness.

160 [e]⌜Thy word is true from everlasting⌝ : all the judgements of thy righteousness endure for evermore.

[e]R.V. *The sum of thy word is truth.* So the Incarnate Word said 'I am the Truth.' St John xiv. 6.

Principes persecuti sunt. ש Shin.

The joy, peace and hope of those who love God's commandments.

PRINCES have persecuted me without a cause : but my heart standeth in awe of thy word.

'Princes,' probably Israelites of high rank and power; see *v.* 23.

162 I am as glad of thy word : as one that findeth great spoils.

163 As for lies, I hate and abhor them : but thy law do I love.

'lies' = insincerity in the service of God, *vv.* 29, 104, 128.

164 Seven times a day do I praise thee : because of thy righteous judgements.

'Seven times,' i.e. constantly; cp. Prov. xxiv. 16.

165 Great is the peace that they have who love thy law : and they [a]⌜are not offended at it⌝.

[a] R.V. *have none occasion of stumbling.* The N.T. paraphrase of the passage is, 'He that loveth his brother abideth in the light, and there is none occasion of stumbling in him.' 1 St John ii. 10.

166 LORD, I have looked for thy [b]⌜saving health⌝ : and done after thy commandments.

Cp. Jacob's words, 'I have waited for thy salvation, O LORD.' Gen. xlix. 18.

[b] *salvation.*

167 My soul hath kept thy testimonies : and loved them exceedingly.

168 I have kept thy commandments and testimonies : for all my ways are before thee.

Supported by an approving conscience the Psalmist fearlessly appeals to the all-seeing God in witness of his integrity.

Appropinquet deprecatio. ת Tau.

The knowledge of God's commandments reveals to man his helplessness, and need of succour.

LET my [a]complaint come before thee, O LORD : give me understanding, according to thy word.

[a] *cry.*

170 Let my supplication come before thee : deliver me, according to thy word.

171 My lips shall speak of thy praise : [b]⌜when thou hast taught⌝ me thy statutes.

[b] R.V. *for thou teachest.*

172 Yea, my tongue shall sing of thy word : for all thy commandments are righteous.

173 Let thine hand help me : for I have chosen thy commandments.

174 I have longed for thy [c]⌜saving health⌝, O LORD : and in thy law is my delight.

[c] *salvation.*

175 O let my soul live, and it shall praise thee : and thy judgements shall help me.

176 I have gone astray like a sheep that is lost : O seek thy servant, for I do not forget thy commandments.

'We have erred, and strayed from thy ways like lost sheep.' General Confession.

The Psalmist concludes with a confession of failure and shortcoming, which must be read into his former protestations of obedience to God's law; see *vv.* 110, 168 &c. He was not devoid of the spiritual dissatisfaction which compels us Christians to acknowledge that 'if we say that we have no sin, we deceive ourselves, and the truth is not in us.' 1 St John i. 8.

THE TWENTY-SEVENTH DAY

Morning Prayer

PSALM CXX. *Ad Dominum.*

A prayer for deliverance from the intrigues of treacherous neighbours.

This and the next fourteen Psalms are entitled 'Songs of Ascents' ('of degrees' A.V.). They were probably so called as forming a collection arranged for the use of pilgrims 'going up' to keep the great Festivals at Jerusalem. Exod. xxxiv. 24; 1 Kings xii. 27, 28; Is. xxx. 29.

WHEN I was in trouble I called upon the LORD : and he heard me.

As the LORD answered me when I prayed to Him in a former time of distress,

2 Deliver my soul, O LORD, from lying lips : and from a deceitful tongue.

so now, too, will I pray to Him to save me from my present enemies.

3 [a]⌜What reward shall be given or done⌝ unto thee, thou [b]false tongue : [c]⌜even mighty and sharp arrows, with hot burning coals⌝.

[a]R.V. *What shall be given unto thee, and what shall be done more.* Cp. the formula, 'God do so to thee, and more also,' 1 Sam. iii. 17.

[b]R.V. *deceitful.*

[c]*sharp arrows of the mighty* (i.e. God) *with coals of juniper.* A metaphorical description of God's punishment of the deceitful tongue. 'Juniper,' R.V. mg. *broom,* was used for fuel and was remarkable for retaining heat a long time.

4 Woe is me, that I am constrained to dwell with Mesech : and to have my habitation among the tents of Kedar.

'Mesech,' a barbarous tribe living between the Black and the Caspian Seas, and 'Kedar,' a predatory horde of Arabians, are put for the rough and quarrelsome neighbours who troubled the Psalmist. The allusion may be to the Samaritans and other foreigners who hindered the rebuilding of the Temple and of the city walls after the return from the exile. Ezra iv.; Neh. ii.—iv.

5 My soul hath long dwelt among them : that are enemies unto peace.

6 I labour for peace, but when I speak unto them thereof : they make them ready to battle.

PSALM CXXI. *Levavi oculos.*

God the Keeper of His people.

'A Song of Ascents' (Title). Perhaps sung by the pilgrims when they first came in sight of the hills on which Jerusalem stands.

Proper on King's Accession and on All Saints' Day [America].

I WILL lift up mine eyes unto the hills : [a]⌜from whence cometh my help⌝.

The 'holy hills' (Ps. lxxxvii. 1) on which the Temple stood.

[a] R.V. *from whence shall my help come?* The answer is given in *v.* 2.

2 My help cometh even from the LORD : who hath made heaven and earth.

3 He will not suffer thy foot to be moved : and he that keepeth thee will not sleep.

'thy,' the Psalmist addresses himself.

4 Behold, he that keepeth Israel : shall neither slumber nor sleep.

5 The LORD himself is thy keeper : the LORD is thy [b] defence upon thy right hand ;

[b] *shade.*

'upon thy right hand,' the position of a protector. Ps. xvi. 9, cix. 30. The metaphor in *vv.* 5—8 varies between 'shade' and championship.

6 So that the sun shall not burn thee by day : neither the moon by night.

7 The LORD shall preserve thee from all evil : yea, it is even he that shall keep thy soul.

8 The LORD shall preserve thy going out, and thy coming in : from this time forth for evermore.

'thy going out and thy coming in' = all the occupations and interests of life. Deut. xxviii. 6.

PSALM CXXII. *Lætatus sum.*

The meditation and prayer of a pilgrim who has reached Jerusalem, inspired by the sight of the city.

'A Song of Ascents' (Title).

Special in Form of Consecration of a Church [Convocation, 1712, Ireland, America], in Service for the first Sunday on which a minister officiates in a new cure [Ireland] and in Office of Institution [America].

I WAS glad when they said unto me : We will go into the house of the LORD.

2 Our feet [a]⌈shall stand in⌉ thy gates : O Jerusalem.

[a] R.V. *are standing within.*

3 Jerusalem [b]⌈is built as a city : that is at unity in itself⌉.

[b] R.V. *that art builded as a city that is compact together*, i.e. restored from its ruins so that the buildings are joined closely one to another with no gaps between.

4 [c]⌈For thither⌉ the tribes go up, even the tribes of the LORD : to testify unto Israel, to give thanks unto the Name of the LORD.

[c] *Whither.*

'to testify,' i.e. to be a testimony of the unity of the nation and of its relation to Jehovah.

5 For there [d]⌈is the seat of judgement : even the seat⌉ of the house of David.

[d] R.V. *are set thrones for judgement, the thrones.* Jerusalem was the location of the supreme court of justice, ideally administered by the king of David's line and those whom he should associate with himself. Deut. xvii. 8, 9; 2 Sam. xv. 2. Cp. our Lord's words to His Apostles, 'Ye shall sit on thrones judging the twelve tribes of Israel.' St Luke xxii. 30.

6 O pray for the peace of Jerusalem : they shall prosper that love thee.

Our Lord's words when He wept over Jerusalem have probably a reference to this verse 'If thou hadst known in this day...the things which belong unto peace.' St Luke xix. 42.

7 Peace be within thy walls : and [e]plenteousness within thy palaces.

[e] *prosperity.* The Hebrew words for 'peace' (shalom) and 'prosperity' (shālvah) correspond in sound with the final syllables of 'Jerusalem.'

8 For my brethren and companions' sakes : I will [a]⌜wish thee prosperity⌝.

[a] *now say, Peace be within thee.*

9 Yea, because of the house of the LORD our God : I will seek to do thee good.

PSALM CXXIII. *Ad te levavi oculos meos.*

The eye of hope fixed patiently upon God in a time of desolation and contempt.

'A Song of Ascents' (Title). Perhaps written when the returned exiles were exposed to the ridicule and persecution of Samaritans and others.

UNTO thee lift I up mine eyes : O thou that dwellest in the heavens.

2 Behold, even as the eyes of servants look unto the hand of their masters, and as the eyes of a maiden unto the hand of her mistress : even so our eyes wait upon the LORD our God, until he have mercy upon us.

The slave of the East, in utter dependence on his master, watches anxiously for the faintest expression of his will.

3 Have mercy upon us, O LORD, have mercy upon us : for we are utterly despised.

4 Our soul is filled with the [b]⌜scornful reproof of the wealthy⌝ : and with the despitefulness of the proud.

[b] *scorning of those that are at ease.* P.B.V. 'wealthy'=prosperous.

PSALM CXXIV. *Nisi quia Dominus.*

'There is none other that fighteth for us, but only Thou, O God.'

'A Song of Ascents' (Title). Perhaps a thanksgiving after the deliverance from the attack of Sanballat and his confederates on the rising walls of Jerusalem related in Neh. iv. 7 sq.

IF the LORD himself had not been on our side, now may Israel say : if the LORD himself had not been on our side, when men rose up against us ;

2 They had swallowed us up quick : when they were so wrathfully displeased at us.

'quick' = (R.V.) *alive.*

3 Yea, the waters had drowned us : and the stream had gone over our soul.

4 The deep waters of the proud : had gone even over our soul.

A metaphorical description of the enemies' insolence.

5 But praised be the LORD : who hath not given us over for a prey unto their teeth.

6 Our soul is escaped even as a bird out of the snare of the fowler : the snare is broken, and we are delivered.

7 Our help standeth in the Name of the LORD : who hath made heaven and earth.

Hence Versicle and Response in Confirmation Service.

PSALM CXXV. *Qui confidunt.*

Trust in Jehovah, the sure remedy against temptation to apostasy. Theme suggested probably by the perils which beset the returned exiles.

'A Song of Ascents' (Title).

THEY that put their trust in the LORD shall be even as the mount Sion : which may not be removed, but standeth fast for ever.

2 The hills stand about Jerusalem : even so standeth the LORD round about his people, from this time forth for evermore.

The higher hills which encompass Jerusalem are a symbol of Jehovah's guardianship of His people.

3 For [a]⌜the rod of the ungodly cometh not into⌝ the lot of the righteous : lest the righteous put their hand unto wickedness.

[a] R.V. *the sceptre of wickedness* (i.e. the rule of heathen tyranny) *shall not rest upon.*

'the lot of the righteous' = Canaan, the land allotted to Israel.

'lest the righteous' &c., i.e. lest Israel by the continuance of oppression, in despair of Divine succour, join in the wickedness of the heathen.

4 Do well, O LORD : unto those that are good and true of heart.

5 As for such as turn [a]⌜back unto their own wickedness⌝ : the LORD shall lead them forth with the evil-doers ; [b]⌜but peace shall be upon Israel⌝.

[a] *aside unto their crooked ways.*

[b] R.V. *Peace be upon Israel.*

Evening Prayer

PSALM CXXVI. *In convertendo.*

May the shallow streams of returned exiles become abundant rivers fertilizing the land!

'A Song of Ascents' (Title).

WHEN the LORD turned again the captivity of Sion : then were we like unto them that dream.

'that dream.' So strange was our change of lot, that we could hardly believe it real.

2 Then was our mouth filled with laughter : and our tongue with joy.

3 Then said they among the heathen : The LORD hath done great things for them.

4 Yea, the LORD hath done great things for us [1]already : whereof we rejoice.

5 Turn our captivity, O LORD : as the rivers in the south.

Bring back our exiles in such crowds that they may be compared to the water channels of South Palestine when the dry season has passed and they are filled by the autumn rains. The word (Negeb) translated 'the south' literally means 'the dry country'; see Gen. xii. 9 mg.; Judg. i. 15.

6 They that sow in tears : shall reap in joy.

'Blessed are they that mourn : for they shall be comforted.' St Matt. v. 4.

7 He that now goeth on his way weeping, and beareth forth good seed, shall doubtless come again with joy, and bring his sheaves with him.

[1] Not in A.R.V.

PSALM CXXVII. *Nisi Dominus.*

'Every good gift and every perfect boon is from above.'
'A Song of Ascents' (Title).

Special in Churching of Women.

EXCEPT the LORD build the house : their labour is but lost that build it.

2 Except the LORD keep the city : the watchman waketh but in vain.

3 It is but lost labour that ye haste to rise up early, and so late take rest, and eat the bread of [a]carefulness : for so he giveth his beloved sleep.

[a] R.V. *toil.*

'so,' i.e. without anxiety on their part. 'Sleep' is here put for all necessary things. 'The blessing of the LORD, it maketh rich, and toil addeth nothing thereto.' Prov. x. 22 mg.; see St Matt. vi. 25—34.

4 Lo, children and the fruit of the womb : are an heritage and gift that cometh of the LORD.

5 Like as the arrows in the hand of [b]⌜the giant⌝ : even so are the [c]⌜young children⌝.

[b] *a mighty man.*

[c] R.V. *children of youth* (i.e. of those that marry young), specially mentioned as likely to be vigorous in health, and to grow up to be the support and protection of their father's old age.

6 Happy is the man that hath his quiver full of them : they shall not be ashamed when they speak with their enemies in the gate.

'they,' i.e. the fathers of such families.

'the gate,' the place of judgement and public concourse. Deut. xxi. 19; Ps. lxix. 12. The father of stalwart sons has a guarantee that in suits with opponents, and in business transactions, he will be treated fairly.

PSALM CXXVIII. *Beati omnes.*

The family happiness of the God-fearing man.
'A Song of Ascents' (Title).

Special in Marriage Service.

BLESSED are all they that fear the LORD : and walk in his ways.

2 For thou shalt eat the labours of thine hands : O well is thee, and happy shalt thou be.

'thou shalt eat' &c., not robbed of the fruits of thy toil by blight or the raids of enemies.

3 Thy wife shall be as the fruitful vine : [a]⌜upon the walls⌝ of thine house.

[a] R.V. *in the innermost parts,* i.e. in the women's apartments.

4 Thy children like the olive-[b]branches : round about thy table.

[b] *plants.*

5 Lo, thus shall the man be blessed : that feareth the LORD.

6 The LORD from out of Sion shall so bless thee : that thou shalt see Jerusalem in prosperity all thy life long ;

7 Yea, that thou shalt see thy children's children : [c]⌜and peace upon Israel⌝.

[c] R.V. *Peace be upon Israel.*

PSALM CXXIX. *Sæpe expugnaverunt.*

Israel's history, a record of suffering and deliverance.
'A Song of Ascents' (Title).

MANY a time have they [d]⌜fought against⌝ me from my youth up : may Israel now say ;

[d] *afflicted.*
Israel's 'youth' was spent in Egyptian bondage.

2 Yea, many a time have they [e]vexed me from my youth up : but they have not prevailed against me.

[e] *afflicted.*
'We are pressed on every side, yet not straitened ;...smitten down, yet not destroyed.' 2 Cor. iv. 8, 9.

3 The plowers plowed upon my back : and made long furrows.

Metaphorical for savage maltreatment. The words have been understood mystically of our Lord's scourging.

4 But the righteous LORD : hath [a]⸢hewn the snares of the ungodly in pieces⸣.

[a]*cut asunder the cords of the wicked,* 'the cords' with which Israel was bound.

5 Let them be confounded and turned backward : as many as have evil will at Sion.

6 Let them be even as the grass growing upon the house-tops : which withereth afore it [b]⸢be plucked⸣ up;

[b]*groweth.* P.B.V. from Vulg.

7 Whereof the mower filleth not his hand : neither he that bindeth up the sheaves his bosom.

'bosom.' The fold of the robe was used as a receptacle. St Luke vi. 38.

8 [c]⸢So that they who go by say not so much as, The LORD prosper you : we wish you good luck in the Name of the LORD⸣.

[c]*Neither do they which go by say, The blessing of the LORD be upon you; We bless you in the name of the LORD.* The latter clause is the answer of the reapers to the salutation of the passers-by. Cp. Ruth ii. 4, 'Boaz came from Bethlehem, and said unto the reapers, The LORD be with you. And they answered him, The LORD bless thee.'

PSALM CXXX. *De profundis.*

A cry from the deep waters of distress for pardon to a forgiving God.

'A Song of Ascents' (Title).

The sixth of the Penitential Psalms.

Proper on Ash Wednesday. Special in Visitation of the Sick [America].

OUT of the deep have I called unto thee, O LORD : Lord, hear my voice.

'the deep.' A figure for overwhelming trouble. Ps. lxix. 1, 2.

2 O let thine ears consider well : the voice of my [d]complaint.

[d]*supplications.*

3 If thou, LORD, wilt be extreme
to mark what is done amiss : O
Lord, who may abide it?

4 [a]⌜For there is mercy⌝ with thee :
[b]⌜therefore shalt thou⌝ be feared.

[a] *But there is forgiveness.*
[b] *that thou mayest.* The knowledge that God is forgiving calls forth, as no other motive can, the filial and reverential fear of the forgiven.

5 I look for the LORD ; my soul
doth wait for him : in his word is
my trust.

6 My soul [c]⌜fleeth unto⌝ the
Lord : [d]⌜before the morning watch,
I say, before the morning watch⌝.

[c] R.V. *looketh for.*
[d] R.V. *more than watchmen look for the morning; yea, more than watchmen for the morning.*

7 O Israel, trust in the LORD,
for with the LORD there is mercy :
and with him is plenteous redemption.

8 And he shall redeem Israel :
from all his sins.

PSALM CXXXI. *Domine, non est.*

The tranquillity of soul and contentment that come from self-discipline.

'A Song of Ascents' (Title).

Proper on Annunciation of B.V.M. [America].

LORD, I am not high-minded :
I have no proud looks.

2 I do not exercise myself in
great matters : which are too high
for me.

3 [e]⌜But I refrain my soul, and
keep it low, like as a child that is
weaned from his mother : yea, my
soul is even as a weaned child⌝.

[e] R.V. *Surely I have stilled and quieted my soul; like a weaned child with his mother, my soul is with me like a weaned child,* who having ceased to long fretfully for the breast rests peacefully and contentedly in its mother's arms.

4 O Israel, trust in the LORD :
from this time forth for evermore.

THE TWENTY-EIGHTH DAY

Morning Prayer

PSALM CXXXII. *Memento, Domine.*

Israel restored from captivity prays that God will fulfil His promise to David.

'A Song of Ascents' (Title).

Proper on Christmas Day and on Annunciation of B.V.M. [America]. Special in Service for the first Sunday on which a minister officiates in a new cure [Ireland], in Office of Institution [America], and in Consecration of a Church [Convocation, 1712; Ireland; America].

LORD, remember [a]⌜David : and⌝ all his [b]trouble;

2 How he sware unto the LORD : and vowed a vow unto the [c]⌜Almighty God⌝ of Jacob;

3 I will not come within the tabernacle of mine house : nor climb up into my bed;

4 I will not suffer mine eyes to sleep, nor mine eye-lids to slumber : [1]⌜neither the temples of my head to take any rest⌝,

5 Until I find out a place for [2]⌜the temple of⌝ the LORD : an habitation for the [d]⌜mighty God⌝ of Jacob.

6 Lo, [e]⌜we heard of the same⌝ at [3]Ephrata : and found it in the [f]wood.

[a] R.V. *for* (i.e. with respect to) *David.*

[b] R.V. *affliction*; cp. 1 Chron. xxii. 14.

[c] R.V. *Mighty One.* Gen. xlix. 24. Vulg. has 'God of Jacob.'

3—5. David's vow.

[d] R.V. *Mighty One.* Vulg. has 'God of Jacob' as in *v.* 2.

[e] *we heard of it.* The people of David's time are introduced as the speakers. 'it' = the ark, which is implied in *v.* 5, though not expressly mentioned until *v.* 8.

[f] R.V. *field of the wood*, mg. *Jaar.* Jaar is probably a contracted form of Kiriath-jearim, 'the city of the woods,' where the ark lay many years before its removal to Sion. 1 Sam. vii. 1, 2.

[1] Not in A.R.V., added in P.B.V. from Vulg.

[2] Not in A.R.V.

[3] 'Ephrata' also probably = Kiriath-jearim, which from 1 Chron. ii. 19, 50, iv. 4, appears to have stood in the relation of daughter-city to Bethlehem, and may therefore have shared in its second name of Ephrathah. Gen. xxxv. 19, Ruth iv. 11, Mic. v. 2. The Chronicler's statement is that Hur the son of Caleb and Ephrath, or Ephrathah, was the father of Bethlehem, and that Hur's son Shobal was the father of Kiriath-jearim.

7 We will go into his tabernacle : and fall low on our knees before his footstool.

8 Arise, O LORD, into thy resting-place : thou, and the ark of thy strength.

Suggested by the prayer appointed to be used on behalf of Israel in the wilderness when the ark set forward 'to seek out a resting place for them.' Numb. x. 33, 35 ; see Ps. lxviii. 1.

For 'ark of thy strength,' see Ps. lxxviii. 62.

9 Let thy priests be clothed with righteousness : and let thy saints sing with joyfulness.

'Endue thy ministers with righteousness ;
And make thy chosen people joyful.'
Versicle and Response at Matins and Evensong.

10 For thy servant David's sake : [a]⌜turn not away the presence⌝ of thine anointed.

[a] *turn not away the face*, i.e. reject not the prayer.

'thine anointed' = the reigning king of David's line.

11 The LORD hath made a faithful oath unto David : and he shall not shrink from it ;

11 to end. Jehovah's answer to the prayer of *v.* 1.

12 Of the fruit of thy body : shall I set upon thy [b]seat.

12, 13. A summary of the Divine promise recorded in 2 Sam. vii. 12 ff.; see Ps. lxxxix. 20 ff.

[b] *throne*.

13 If thy children will keep my covenant, and my testimonies that I shall learn them : their children also shall sit upon thy [c]seat for evermore.

'learn' = teach.

[c] *throne*.

14 For the LORD hath chosen Sion to be an habitation for himself : he hath longed for her.

15 This shall be my [d]rest for ever : here will I dwell, for I have a delight therein.

[d] R.V. *resting place*, as in *v.* 8.

16 I will bless her victuals with increase : and will satisfy her poor with bread.

17 I will [e]deck her priests with [f]health : and her saints shall rejoice and sing.

See *v.* 9.

[e] *clothe*.

[f] *salvation*. P.B.V. 'health' = well-being in general.

18 There shall I make the horn of David to [a]flourish : I have ordained a lantern for mine anointed.

Interpreted of Christ in St Luke i. 68, 69, 'The Lord...hath raised up a horn of salvation for us in the house of his servant David.'

[a]*bud.*

'a lantern.' The lighted lamp in a house is a symbol of the continued life and prosperity of the family; see Ps. xviii. 28; 1 Kings xi. 36; Job xviii. 6.

19 As for his enemies, I shall clothe them with shame : but upon himself shall his crown flourish.

'crown.' The Hebrew word denotes not only the kingly crown but also the high-priestly mitre. The king Messiah of David's line should also be high priest.

PSALM CXXXIII. *Ecce, quam bonum!*

An exhortation to brotherly fellowship among the people of God.

'A Song of Ascents' (Title).

Proper on Transfiguration [America]. Special in Office of Institution [America].

BEHOLD, how good and joyful a thing it is : [b]brethren, to dwell together in unity!

[b]*for brethren.*

2 It is like the precious [c]ointment upon the head, that ran down unto the beard : even unto Aaron's beard, and went down to the skirts of his clothing;

[c]R.V. *oil.*

Aaron represented Israel, the priestly nation; and the consecrating oil which spread from his head to his beard and clothing symbolized the unity of the race. For the Christian analogy see 1 Cor. xii. 12 ff.

3 Like as the dew of Hermon : [d]⌜which fell⌝ upon the hill of Sion.

[d]R.V. *that cometh down.*

'Hermon' in the north, abundant in dew, fertilizes, in the thought of the Psalmist, arid 'Sion' in the south—another symbol of the unity and mutual interdependence of Israelites.

4 For there the LORD promised his blessing : and life for evermore.

'there,' in Sion, the religious centre and meeting place of the nation.

PSALM CXXXIV. *Ecce nunc.*

The congregation greet the priests and levites who are conducting the night services in the Temple, and receive their blessing.

'A Song of Ascents' (Title). It has been placed at the end of these 'Songs,' that they may conclude with a benediction.

Proper on Purification of B.V.M. [America].

BEHOLD now, [a]praise the LORD : all ye servants of the LORD;

1—3. The greeting to the Temple ministrants 'ye servants of the LORD.'
[a]*bless ye.*

2 Ye that by night stand in the house of the LORD : [1]⌜even in the courts of the house of our God⌝.

To 'stand before the LORD' is the usual expression for the service of the priests and levites. Deut. x. 8.

3 Lift up your hands in the sanctuary : and [b]praise the LORD.

The attitude of prayer. Ps. xxviii. 2, lxiii. 5; 1 Tim. ii. 8.
[b]R.V. *bless ye.*

4 The LORD that made heaven and earth : give thee blessing out of Sion.

4. The counter-greeting of the night-watch.
'thee.' The singular is used because the words are taken from the priestly blessing. Numb. vi. 24.

PSALM CXXXV. *Laudate Nomen.*

Thanksgiving to the God of Israel, the God of gods, for His preservation of His people.

Probably composed for liturgical use in the Second Temple.

Proper on Epiphany [America].

O PRAISE the LORD, laud ye the Name of the LORD : praise it, O ye servants of the LORD;

1, 2. See Ps. cxxxiv. 1, 2.
'O praise the LORD.' R.V. mg. Heb. *Hallelujah.*
'servants' &c. = the priests and levites engaged in the Temple worship.

2 Ye that stand in the house of the LORD : in the courts of the house of our God.

'stand' the word used for the service of the Temple ministers; see Ps. cxxxiv. 2.

3 O praise the LORD, for the LORD is gracious : O sing praises unto his Name, for it is [c]lovely.

[c]*pleasant*; see Ps. xxvii. 4, xc. 17.

[1] Not in A.R.V., added in P.B.V. from Vulg. which copies Ps. cxxxv. 2.

4 For why? the LORD hath chosen Jacob unto himself : and Israel for his [a]⌜own possession⌝.

[a]*peculiar treasure*; see Exod. xix. 5; Deut. vii. 6; 1 St Pet. ii. 9.

5 For I know that the LORD is great : and that our Lord is above all gods.

6 Whatsoever the LORD pleased, that did he in heaven, and in earth : and in the sea, and in all deep places.

6. From Ps. cxv. 3.

7 He [b]⌜bringeth forth the clouds⌝ from the ends of the world : and sendeth forth lightnings with the rain, bringing the winds out of his [c]treasures.

7. A quotation from Jer. x. 13.
[b]*causeth the vapours to ascend.*
'from the ends' &c., i.e. from the horizon where they seem to gather.
[c]*treasuries.*

8 He smote the first-born of Egypt : both of man and beast.

Exod. xii. 29.

9 He hath sent tokens and wonders into the midst of thee, O [1]⌜thou land of⌝ Egypt : upon Pharaoh, and all his servants.

10 He smote divers nations : and slew mighty kings;

11 Sehon king of the Amorites, and Og the king of Basan : and all the kingdoms of Canaan;

Numb. xxi. 21 ff.

12 And gave their land to be an heritage : even an heritage unto Israel his people.

13 Thy Name, O LORD, endureth for ever : [d]⌜so doth⌝ thy memorial, O LORD, from one generation to another.

[d]Omit with A.R.V. 'so doth.' The LORD'S Name is His memorial because it brings to mind His nature and operations. Exod. iii. 15.

14 For the LORD will [e]avenge his people : and [f]⌜be gracious unto⌝ his servants.

14. A quotation from Deut. xxxii. 36.
'For.' Thus does He prove that the memorial of His Name endures for ever.
[e]*judge*, i.e. vindicate. Ps. liv. 1.
[f]*repent himself concerning*, i.e. change from wrath to compassion towards; see Ps. xc. 13.

[1] Not in A.R.V.

15 As for the images of the heathen, they are but silver and gold : the work of men's hands.

15—20. Taken from Ps. cxv. 4—11. However costly their material, they are merely of human workmanship.

16 They have mouths, and speak not : eyes have they, but they see not.

17 They have ears, and yet they hear not : neither is there any breath in their mouths.

18 They that make them [a]are like unto them : [b]⌜and so are all they that put their trust⌝ in them.

[a]R.V. *shall be.*

[b]R.V. *yea, everyone that trusteth.*

19 Praise the LORD, ye house of Israel : praise the LORD, ye house of Aaron.

20 Praise the LORD, ye house of Levi : ye that fear the LORD, praise the LORD.

19, 20. The classification '(house of) Israel,' 'house of Aaron,' 'ye that fear the Lord' found before in Ps. cxv. 9—11, and cxviii. 2—4, appears here again with 'house of Levi' added.

21 Praised be the LORD out of Sion : who dwelleth at Jerusalem.

A.R.V. add *Praise ye the LORD,* R.V. mg. Heb. *Hallelujah.*

Evening Prayer

PSALM CXXXVI. *Confitemini.*

A hymn of praise for the mercy of the LORD manifested in nature, and in the past history of His people.

Probably composed for liturgical use in the Second Temple.

O GIVE thanks unto the LORD, for he is gracious : and his mercy endureth for ever.

2 O give thanks unto the God of all gods : for his mercy endureth for ever.

3 O thank the Lord of all lords : for his mercy endureth for ever.

4 Who only doeth great wonders : for his mercy endureth for ever.

'Who alone workest great marvels.' Prayer for the Clergy and People.

5 Who by his excellent wisdom made the heavens : for his mercy endureth for ever.

'excellent' formerly meant 'pre-eminent,' 'excelling.'

6 Who laid out the earth above the waters : for his mercy endureth for ever.

See Ps. xxiv. 2.

7 Who hath made great lights : for his mercy endureth for ever;

7—9. Gen. i. 14—18.

8 The sun to rule the day : for his mercy endureth for ever;

9 The moon and the stars to govern the night : for his mercy endureth for ever.

10 Who smote Egypt with their first-born : for his mercy endureth for ever;

10—22. A repetition, with additions, of Ps. cxxxv. 8—12.

11 And brought out Israel from among them : for his mercy endureth for ever;

12 With a mighty hand, and stretched out arm : for his mercy endureth for ever.

13 Who divided the Red Sea [a]⌜in two parts⌝ : for his mercy endureth for ever;

[a] R.V. *in sunder.* P.B.V. is a printer's error for 'into parts' as in A.V.

14 And made Israel to go through the midst of it : for his mercy endureth for ever.

15 But as for Pharaoh and his host, he overthrew them in the Red Sea : for his mercy endureth for ever.

16 Who led his people through the wilderness : for his mercy endureth for ever.

17 Who smote great kings : for his mercy endureth for ever;

18 Yea, and slew mighty kings : for his mercy endureth for ever;

19 Sehon king of the Amorites : for his mercy endureth for ever;

20 And Og the king of Basan : for his mercy endureth for ever;

21 And gave away their land for an heritage : for his mercy endureth for ever;

22 Even for an heritage unto Israel his servant : for his mercy endureth for ever.

23 Who remembered us [a]⌜when we were in trouble⌝ : for his mercy endureth for ever.

[a] *in our low estate,* i.e. in our exile.

24 And hath delivered us from our enemies : for his mercy endureth for ever.

25 Who giveth food to all flesh : for his mercy endureth for ever.

Cp. Ps. civ. 27, cxlv. 15.

26 O give thanks unto the God of heaven : for his mercy endureth for ever.

'the God of heaven.' This title occurs here only in the Psalter; cp. Ezra i. 2; Dan. ii. 18; Rev. xi. 13.

27 [1]⌜O give thanks unto the Lord of lords : for his mercy endureth for ever⌝.

PSALM CXXXVII. *Super flumina.*

A picture of Israel's despondency in the land of exile. Probably written shortly after the return.

BY the waters of Babylon we sat down and wept : when we remembered thee, O Sion.

2 As for our harps, we hanged them up : upon the [b]trees that are therein.

[b] *willows.*

3 For they that led us away captive required of us then a song,
[c]⌜and melody, in our heaviness⌝ :
Sing us one of the songs of Sion.

[c] *and they that wasted us required of us mirth, saying.*

[1] Not in A.R.V., added in P.B.V. from Vulg. which repeats *v.* 3.

4 How shall we sing the LORD'S song : in a strange land?

5 If I forget thee, O Jerusalem : let my right hand forget her cunning.

'cunning' = skill.

6 If I do not remember thee, let my tongue cleave to the roof of my mouth : yea, if I prefer not Jerusalem [a]⌜in my mirth⌝.

'cleave' &c., i.e. lose the power of speech and song.

[a]*above my chief joy.*

7 [b]⌜Remember the children of Edom, O LORD, in the day of Jerusalem⌝ : how they said, Down with it, down with it, even to the ground.

[b]R.V. *Remember, O LORD, against the children of Edom the day of Jerusalem,* i.e. requite them for their savage exultation on the day of its fall. Obad. 10, 11.

8 O daughter of Babylon, [c]⌜wasted with misery⌝ : yea, happy shall he be that rewardeth thee, as thou hast served us.

'daughter of Babylon' = the city personified; see Ps. ix. 14.

[c]R.V. *that art to be destroyed.*

9 Blessed shall he be that taketh thy children : and throweth them against the stones.

As 'Babylon' symbolizes the world opposed to God (see Rev. xviii. 2 ff.), so her 'children' may be mystically understood to mean evil thoughts which must be destroyed before they gain strength.

PSALM CXXXVIII. *Confitebor tibi.*

An expression of Israel's gratitude to Jehovah for past mercies, and of confidence in Him for future support. The Psalmist speaks in the name of his people.

Probably written after the return from captivity.

Proper on Annunciation of B.V.M. [America].

I WILL give thanks [1]⌜unto thee, O Lord⌝, with my whole heart : even before the gods will I sing praise unto thee.

'before the gods.' In defiance of the imaginary gods of the heathen, I shall adore and praise Jehovah alone.

2 I will worship toward thy holy temple, and praise thy Name, because of thy loving-kindness and truth : for thou hast magnified [d]⌜thy Name, and thy word, above all things⌝.

[d]*thy word above all thy name.* By the fulfilment of His word of promise God has surpassed even the manifestation of His goodness which His Name, Jehovah, implied. Exod. xxxiv. 6, 7.

[1] Not in A.R.V., added in P.B.V. from Vulg.

3 When I called upon thee, thou heardest me : and enduedst my soul with much strength.

4 All the kings of the earth shall praise thee, O LORD : for they have heard the words of thy mouth.

'they have heard.' In the Psalmist's prophetic vision the knowledge of God's words and ways has already reached and won over the world's kings.

5 Yea, they shall sing [a]in the ways of the LORD : [b]that great is the glory of the LORD.

[a]R.V. *of.*
[b]*for.*

6 For though the LORD be high, yet hath he respect unto the lowly : as for the proud he beholdeth them afar off.

Cp. Ps. cxiii. 5.

'beholdeth afar off,' i.e. excludeth from His fellowship.

7 Though I walk in the midst of trouble, yet shalt thou refresh me : thou shalt stretch forth thy hand upon the furiousness of mine enemies, and thy right hand shall save me.

8 The LORD [c]⌜shall make good his loving-kindness toward me⌝ : yea, thy mercy, O LORD, endureth for ever; [d]despise not then the works of thine own hands.

[c]*will perfect that which concerneth me.* Cp. Phil. i. 6, 'He which began a good work in you will perfect it until the day of Jesus Christ.'
[d]*forsake.*
i.e. the 'works' of mercy which Thou hast hitherto wrought for Thy people.

THE TWENTY-NINTH DAY

Morning Prayer

PSALM CXXXIX. *Domine, probasti.*

The praises of God omniscient and omnipresent.

O LORD, thou hast searched me out, and known me : thou knowest my down-sitting, and mine up-rising; thou understandest my thoughts [e]⌜long before⌝.

[e]*afar off.*

2 Thou art about my path, and about my bed : and spiest out all my ways.

3 For lo, there is not a word in my tongue : but thou, O LORD, knowest it altogether.

4 Thou hast [a]fashioned me behind and before : and laid thine hand upon me.

[a]*beset*. P.B.V. from Vulg.

'laid thine hand' &c., i.e. ordered my actions.

5 Such knowledge is too wonderful and excellent for me : I cannot attain unto it.

'O the depth of the riches both of the wisdom and the knowledge of God! how unsearchable are his judgements, and his ways past tracing out!' Rom. xi. 33.

'excellent' formerly meant 'surpassing,' 'excelling.'

6 Whither shall I go then from thy Spirit : or whither shall I go then from thy presence?

7 If I climb up into heaven, thou art there : if I [b]⌜go down to hell⌝, thou art there also.

[b]R.V. *make my bed in Sheol.*

8 If I take the wings of the morning : and remain in the uttermost parts of the sea;

i.e. If I should fly from east to west with the speed of the sun's morning beams.

'the sea'=the west, the Mediterranean being the western boundary of Palestine.

9 Even there also shall thy hand lead me : and thy right hand shall hold me.

10 If I say, Peradventure the darkness shall cover me : [c]⌜then shall my night be turned to day⌝.

[c]R.V. *and the light about me shall be night;*

11 [d]Yea, the darkness is no darkness with thee, but the night is as clear as the day : the darkness and light to thee are both alike.

[d]R.V. *Even.*

12 For my reins are thine : thou hast covered me in my mother's womb.

'For.' Thou knowest me, for Thou hast made me.

'reins' (kidneys), regarded as the seat of the emotions; see Ps. vii. 10, xvi. 8. Put here for the whole inner man as 'frame' *v.* 14 denotes the outer form.

13 I will give thanks unto thee, for I am fearfully and wonderfully made : marvellous are thy works, and that my soul knoweth right well.

14 [a]⌜My bones are not hid from thee : though I be made secretly, and fashioned beneath in the earth⌝.

[a]R.V. *My frame was not hidden from thee, when I was made in secret, and curiously* (i.e. with care) *wrought in the lowest parts of the earth*, i.e. a region as dark and full of mystery as Sheol. Ps. lxiii. 10; Eph. iv. 9.

15 Thine eyes did see my substance, yet being imperfect : and in thy book were all my members written;

16 Which day by day were fashioned : when as yet there was none of them.

17 How dear are thy counsels unto me, O God : O how great is the sum of them!

18 If I [b]tell them, they are more in number than the sand : when I wake up I am [c]present with thee.

[b]*count.* P.B.V. 'tell' has this meaning.

[c]*still.*

19 Wilt thou not slay the wicked, O God : depart from me, ye bloodthirsty men.

Cp. Ps. vi. 8.

20 For they speak unrighteously against thee : and thine enemies take thy Name in vain.

21 Do not I hate them, O LORD, that hate thee : and am not I grieved with those that rise up against thee?

22 Yea, I hate them right sore : even as though they were mine enemies.

23 Try me, O God, and seek the ground of my heart : prove me, and examine my thoughts.

24 Look well if there be any way of wickedness in me : and lead me in the way everlasting.

'the way' of holiness and everlasting life.

PSALM CXL. *Eripe me, Domine.*

A prayer for deliverance from violent and crafty foes.

DELIVER me, O LORD, from the evil man : and preserve me from the [a]wicked man;

[a] *violent.*

2 Who imagine mischief in their hearts : and stir up strife all the day long.

3 They have sharpened their tongues like a serpent : adders' poison is under their lips.

Quoted in Rom. iii. 13, according to the Sept. See Ps. xiv. 5.

4 Keep me, O LORD, from the hands of the ungodly : preserve me from the [b]wicked men, who are purposed to overthrow my goings.

[b] *violent.*

5 The proud have laid a snare for me, and spread a net abroad with cords : yea, and set traps in my way.

6 I said unto the LORD, Thou art my God : hear the voice of my prayers, O LORD.

7 O Lord GOD, thou strength of my [c]health : thou hast covered my head in the day of battle.

[c] *salvation.* P.B.V. 'health' = well-being.

'covered my head' as with a helmet —'an helmet of salvation.' Is. lix. 17; Eph. vi. 17.

'the day of battle,' when the ungodly assailed me.

8 Let not the ungodly have his desire, O LORD : let not his mischievous imagination prosper, lest they be too proud.

9 Let the mischief of their own lips fall upon the head of them : that compass me about.

10 Let hot burning coals fall upon them : let them be cast into the fire, and into [d]⌜the pit⌝, that they never rise up again.

[d] R.V. mg. *floods.*

11 [a]⌜A man full of words shall not prosper upon⌝ the earth : evil shall hunt the [b]wicked person to overthrow him.

[a] R.V. *An evil speaker shall not be established in.*

[b] *violent.*

12 Sure I am that the LORD will avenge the poor : and maintain the cause of the helpless.

13 The righteous also shall give thanks unto thy Name : [c]⌜and the just shall continue in thy sight⌝.

[c] *the upright shall dwell in thy presence.*

PSALM CXLI. *Domine, clamavi.*

A prayer for self-restraint and a spiritual mind by one exposed to bitter persecution.

The evening Psalm (see *v.* 2) of the early Church.

In the American Prayer Book this Psalm forms the first of the Psalms for Evensong on this (29th) day.

LORD, I call upon thee, haste thee unto me : and consider my voice when I cry unto thee.

2 Let my prayer be set forth in thy sight as the incense : and let the lifting up of my hands be an evening sacrifice.

The gesture of prayer. Ps. xxviii. 2, lxiii. 5; 1 Tim. ii. 8. Perhaps the Psalmist was absent from Jerusalem, or otherwise debarred from attending the daily sacrifice.

3 Set a watch, O LORD, before my mouth : and keep the door of my lips.

4 O let not mine heart be inclined to any evil thing : let me not be occupied in ungodly works with the men that work wickedness, [d]⌜lest I eat of such things as please them⌝.

[d] *and let me not eat of their dainties,* i.e. let me not conform to their luxurious sensual habits.

5 [a]⌜Let the righteous rather smite me friendly : and reprove me.

6 But let not their precious balms break my head⌝ : [b]yea, I will pray yet against their wickedness.

[a]R.V. *Let the righteous smite me, it shall be a kindness; and let him reprove me, it shall be as oil upon the head; let not my head refuse it.* The chastisement and reproof of the good will be taken by me in friendly part and welcomed.

[b]*for.* May I be kept thus spiritually minded (*vv.* 2—6) for I am resolved to use no weapon but prayer against my persecutors.

7 [c]⌜Let their judges be overthrown in stony places : that they may⌝ hear my words, for they are sweet.

[c]R.V. *Their judges are thrown down by the sides of the rock; and they shall.* The Psalmist is assured that the 'judges,' i.e. the leaders of the wicked, will meet with condign punishment and that their followers will then appreciate and welcome his advice.

8 Our bones lie scattered [d]⌜before the pit⌝ : like as when one [e]⌜breaketh and heweth wood upon the earth⌝.

[d]R.V. mg. *at the mouth of Sheol.*

[e]R.V. *ploweth and cleaveth the earth.* In this time of persecution, the bones of the slaughtered servants of God may be compared to the clods or stones turned up by the ploughshare. In P.B.V. they are likened to the chips scattered by the woodcutter.

9 But mine eyes look unto thee, O Lord GOD : in thee is my trust, O cast not out my soul.

10 Keep me from the snare that they have laid for me : and from the traps of the wicked doers.

11 Let the ungodly fall into their own nets together : and let me ever escape them.

Evening Prayer

PSALM CXLII. *Voce mea ad Dominum.*

A cry to God for succour by one persecuted and abandoned by earthly helpers.

I CRIED unto the LORD with my voice : yea, even unto the LORD did I make my supplication.

2 I poured out my complaints before him : and shewed him of my trouble.

3 When my spirit was in heaviness thou knewest my path : in the way wherein I walked have they privily laid a snare for me.

4 I looked also upon my right hand : and saw there was no man that would know me.

'my right hand' where I would naturally expect a protector to stand. Ps. xvi. 9, cix. 30, cxxi. 5.

5 I had no place to flee unto : and no man cared for my soul.

6 I cried unto thee, O LORD, and said : Thou art my [a]hope, and my portion in the land of the living.

[a] *refuge.*

7 Consider my complaint : for I am brought very low.

8 O deliver me from my persecutors : for they are too strong for me.

9 Bring my soul out of prison, that I may give thanks unto thy Name : [b]⌜which thing if thou wilt grant me, then shall the righteous resort unto my company⌝.

'prison,' probably figurative for deep distress.

[b] *the righteous shall compass me about; for thou shalt deal bountifully with me.* Those who have hitherto held back (*vv.* 4, 5) will gather round me.

PSALM CXLIII. *Domine, exaudi.*

A servant of Jehovah appeals to Him for succour in a dark day of persecution and calamity.

The seventh of the Penitential Psalms.

Proper on Ash Wednesday.

HEAR my prayer, O LORD, and consider my desire : hearken unto me for thy [c]truth and righteousness' sake.

[c] *faithfulness.* Cp. 1 St John i. 9, 'He is faithful and righteous to forgive us our sins.'

2 And enter not into judgement with thy servant : for in thy sight shall no man living be justified.

Quoted freely by St Paul, Rom. iii. 20; Gal. ii. 16.

3 For the enemy hath persecuted my soul; he hath smitten my life down to the ground : he hath laid me in the darkness, as the men that have been long dead.

A figurative expression of a state of deep affliction.

4 Therefore is my spirit [a]vexed within me : and my heart within me is desolate.

[a] *overwhelmed.*

5 Yet do I remember the time past; I muse upon all thy works : yea, I [b]⌜exercise myself in⌝ the works of thy hands.

Cp. Ps. lxxvii. 5, 11, 12.

[b] *muse on.* P.B.V. has this meaning.

6 I stretch forth my hands unto thee : my soul gaspeth unto thee as a thirsty land.

See Ps. lxiii. 2.

7 Hear me, O LORD, and that soon, for my spirit waxeth faint : hide not thy face from me, lest I be like unto them that go down into the pit.

'waxeth'=groweth.

See Ps. xxviii. 1.

8 O let me hear thy loving-kindness betimes in the morning, for in thee is my trust : shew thou me the way that I should walk in, for I lift up my soul unto thee.

'the morning' of deliverance which will succeed the night of suffering. Ps. xlix. 14.

9 Deliver me, O LORD, from mine enemies : for I flee unto thee to hide me.

10 Teach me to do the thing that pleaseth thee, for thou art my God : let thy loving Spirit lead me [c]⌜forth into⌝ the land of righteousness.

[c] R.V. *in*

11 Quicken me, O LORD, for thy Name's sake : and for thy righteousness' sake bring my soul out of trouble.

12 And of thy goodness slay mine enemies : and destroy all them that [d]vex my soul; for I am thy servant.

[d] *afflict.*

THE THIRTIETH DAY

Morning Prayer

PSALM CXLIV. *Benedictus Dominus.*

Some ruler of Israel is represented as interceding for the nation oppressed by foreign enemies, and looking forward to a golden age of peace and plenty. The Psalm is mainly a compilation from earlier ones, with a conclusion (12—15) probably borrowed from some other source.

BLESSED be the LORD my [a]strength : who teacheth my hands to war, and my fingers to fight;

1, 2. Taken from Ps. xviii. 1, 34, 48.

[a] R.V. *rock.*

2 My [b]hope and my fortress, my castle and deliverer, [c]⌈my defender⌉ in whom I trust : who subdueth [d]⌈my people that is under me⌉.

[b] R.V. *lovingkindness.*

[c] *my shield, and he.*

[d] *my people under me.* For 'my people,' Ps. xviii. 48 has 'peoples,' i.e. the heathen nations. Here if the reading is correct, Israel is meant, submissive to its ruler through divine appointment.

3 LORD, what is man, that thou hast such respect unto him : or the son of man, that thou so regardest him?

Suggested by Ps. viii. 4.

4 Man is like [e]⌈a thing of nought⌉ : his time passeth away like a shadow.

[e] R.V. mg. *a breath*; cp. Ps. xxxix. 6, 12.

Cp. Ps. cii. 11.

5 Bow thy heavens, O LORD, and come down : touch the mountains, and they shall smoke.

5—7. Cp. Ps. xviii. 9, 14, 16, 45, civ. 32.

6 Cast forth thy lightning, and [f]tear them : shoot out thine arrows, and consume them.

[f] *scatter.* 'them,' i.e. the enemies of the Psalmist and Israel.

7 [g]⌈Send down⌉ thine hand from above : deliver me, and take me out of the great waters, from the hand of [h]⌈strange children⌉;

[g] R.V. *Stretch forth.*

[h] R.V. *strangers* = foreigners.

8 Whose mouth [a]⌜talketh of vanity⌝ : and their right hand is a right hand of [b]wickedness.

[a]*speaketh vanity*, i.e. falsehood ; cp. Ps. xii. 2, xli. 6.

The 'right hand' was uplifted in taking an oath ; cp. Ps. cvi. 26.

[b]*falsehood.*

9 I will sing a new song unto thee, O God : and sing praises unto thee upon a ten-stringed lute.

Cp. Ps. xxxiii. 2, 3.

10 Thou hast given victory unto kings : and hast delivered David thy servant from the peril of the sword.

Cp. Ps. xviii. 51.

11 Save me, and deliver me from the hand of [c]⌜strange children⌝ : whose mouth [d]⌜talketh of⌝ vanity, and their right hand is a right hand of [e]iniquity.

A repetition of *vv.* 7, 8.

[c]R.V. *strangers*=foreigners.

[d]*speaketh.*

[e]*falsehood.*

12 That our sons may grow up as the young plants : and that our daughters may be as the polished corners of [f]⌜the temple⌝.

The 'corners' of reception rooms in the East are ornamented with carved work brilliantly coloured and gilded.

[f]*a palace.*

13 That our garners may be full and plenteous with all manner of store : that our sheep may bring forth thousands and ten thousands in our [g]streets.

[g]R.V. *fields.*

14 That our oxen may be [h]⌜strong to labour⌝, that there be no [i]decay : no [k]⌜leading into captivity⌝, and no complaining in our streets.

[h]R.V. *well laden* with the produce of our fields.

[i]*breaking in* of foreign enemies.

[k]R.V. *going forth* either into exile (as P.B.V.), or to attack besiegers.

15 Happy are the people that are in such a case : yea, blessed are the people who have the LORD for their God.

PSALM CXLV. *Exaltabo te, Deus.*

A hymn of praise to God the universal King, all-bountiful and all-merciful.

This and the next five Psalms were probably specially written for liturgical use.

An alphabetical Psalm.

Proper on Whitsunday. Special in Harvest Thanksgiving [Ireland].

I WILL magnify thee, O God, my King : and I will praise thy Name for ever and ever.

2 Every day will I give thanks unto thee : and praise thy Name for ever and ever.

3 Great is the LORD, and marvellous worthy to be praised : there is no end of his greatness.

'marvellous' here is an adverb as in Ps. xxxi. 23.

4 One generation shall praise thy works unto another : and declare thy [a]power.

[a] *mighty acts.*

5 As for me, I will [b]⌜be talking⌝ of thy [c]worship : thy glory, thy praise, and wondrous works;

[b] *meditate.*

[c] R.V. *honour.* P.B.V. 'worship' has this meaning.

6 [d]⌜So that men⌝ shall speak of the might of thy marvellous acts : and I will also tell of thy greatness.

[d] *And men.*

7 [e]⌜The memorial of thine abundant kindness shall be shewed : and men shall⌝ sing of thy righteousness.

[e] R.V. *They shall utter the memory of thy great goodness, and shall.*

8 The LORD is gracious and merciful : long-suffering, and of great goodness.

So God revealed Himself to Moses. Exod. xxxiv. 6; cp. Ps. ciii. 8.

9 The LORD is [f]⌜loving unto every man⌝ : and his mercy is over all his works.

[f] *good to all,* not to man only but to all His creatures.

10 All thy works [g]praise thee, O LORD : and thy saints [h]⌜give thanks unto⌝ thee.

[g] R.V. *shall give thanks unto.*

[h] *shall bless.*

11 They [a]shew the glory of thy kingdom : and talk of thy power;

[a]*shall speak of.*

12 That thy power, thy glory, and mightiness of thy kingdom : might be known unto men.

13 Thy kingdom is an everlasting kingdom : and thy dominion endureth throughout all ages.

Cp. Dan. iv. 3.

14 The LORD upholdeth all such as fall : and lifteth up all those that are down.

Cp. Litany, 'That it may please thee...to raise up them that fall.'

15 The eyes of all wait upon thee, [1]⌜O LORD⌝ : and thou givest them their meat in due season.

15, 16. Founded on Ps. civ. 27, 28.

'meat'=food in general.

16 Thou openest thine hand : and [b]⌜fillest all things living with plenteousness⌝.

[b]*satisfiest the desire of every living thing.*

17 The LORD is righteous in all his ways : and [c]holy in all his works.

[c]R.V. *gracious.*

18 The LORD is nigh unto all them that call upon him, yea, all such as call upon him faithfully.

19 He will fulfil the desire of them that fear him : he also will hear their cry, and will help them.

20 The LORD preserveth all them that love him : but [d]⌜scattereth abroad all the ungodly⌝.

[d]*all the wicked will he destroy.*

21 My mouth shall speak the praise of the LORD : and let all flesh [e]⌜give thanks unto⌝ his holy Name for ever and ever.

[e]*bless.*

[1] Not in A.R.V., added in P.B.V. from Vulg.

PSALM CXLVI. *Lauda, anima mea.*

Praise to the LORD the One true Helper of mankind. Written after the return from the exile.

The first of a series of Hallelujah Psalms with which the Psalter closes.

Proper on All Saints' Day [America].

A. R. V. prefix *Praise ye the LORD*, mg. Heb. *Hallelujah.*

PRAISE the LORD, O my soul; while I live will I praise the LORD : yea, as long as I have any being, I will sing praises unto my God.

2 O put not your trust in princes, nor in any child of man : for there is no help in them.

'princes' = probably the Persian kings and governors; see Ps. cxviii. 9.

3 For when the breath of man goeth forth he shall turn again to his earth : and then all his thoughts perish.

'Dust thou art, and unto dust shalt thou return.' Gen. iii. 19.

4 Blessed is he that hath the God of Jacob for his help : and whose hope is in the LORD his God;

5 Who made heaven and earth, the sea, and all that therein is : who keepeth his promise for ever;

From Exod. xx. 11.

6 Who helpeth them to right that suffer wrong : who feedeth the hungry.

7 The LORD looseth men out of prison : the LORD giveth sight to the blind;

Metaphors for deliverance from spiritual evil; cp. Is. xlii. 7, lxi. 1. The former may have been suggested by the release from captivity.

8 The LORD [a]helpeth them that are [b]fallen : the LORD careth for the righteous;

[a] R.V. *raiseth up*; see Ps. cxlv. 14.
[b] *bowed down.*

9 The LORD careth for the strangers; he defendeth the fatherless and widow : as for the way of the ungodly, he turneth it upside down.

'strangers,' 'fatherless,' 'widow,' types of the helpless. Ps. xciv. 6.

10 The LORD thy God, O Sion, shall be King for evermore : and throughout all generations.

A.R.V. add *Praise ye the LORD*, R.V. mg. Heb. *Hallelujah.*

Evening Prayer

PSALM CXLVII. *Laudate Dominum.*

Thanksgiving to Jehovah the Lord of Creation, the Restorer of Jerusalem.

Perhaps written for the Service at the dedication of the wall of Jerusalem after the return. Neh. xii. 27 ff.

Special in Harvest Thanksgiving [Ireland].

[a]⌜O PRAISE the LORD⌝, for it is a good thing to sing praises unto our God : yea, a joyful and pleasant thing it is to be thankful.

[a] *Praise ye the LORD*, R.V. mg. Heb. *Hallelujah*.

2 The LORD doth build up Jerusalem : and gather together the out-casts of Israel.

'build up,' by restoring the walls and houses, and repeopling the city. 'the out-casts,' i.e. those that had been carried captive.

3 He healeth those that are broken in heart : and [b]⌜giveth medicine to heal their sickness⌝.

[b] *bindeth up their wounds*.

4 He telleth the number of the stars : and calleth them all by their names.

'telleth' = counteth. He who knows every star will assuredly be acquainted with the case of each of His people. Is. xl. 26—28.

5 Great is our Lord, and great is his power : yea, and his wisdom is infinite.

6 The LORD setteth up the meek : and bringeth the ungodly down to the ground.

7 O sing unto the LORD with thanksgiving : sing praises upon the harp unto our God;

8 Who covereth the heaven with clouds, and prepareth rain for the earth : and maketh the grass to grow upon the mountains, [1]⌜and herb for the use of men⌝;

9 Who giveth fodder unto the cattle : and feedeth the young ravens that call upon him.

Cp. Job xxxviii. 41; St Luke xii. 24.

[1] Not in A.R.V., added in P.B.V. from Vulg. which copies Ps. civ. 14.

10 He hath no pleasure in the strength of an horse : neither delighteth he in any man's legs.

10, 11. Cp. Ps. xxxiii. 15—17. God does not look with approval on those who rely on their own strength and resources.

11 But the LORD'S delight is in them that fear him : and put their trust in his mercy.

12 Praise the LORD, O Jerusalem : praise thy God, O Sion.

13 For he hath made fast the bars of thy gates : and hath blessed thy children within thee.

Probably there is a special reference to the setting up of the gates of restored Jerusalem. Neh. iii. 3, 6, &c.

14 He maketh peace in thy borders : and filleth thee with the [a]⌜flour of⌝ wheat.

[a] *finest of the.*

15 He sendeth forth his commandment upon earth : and his word runneth very swiftly.

15, 16. Cp. Is. lv. 10, 11.

'very swiftly' in accomplishing the errand on which it is sent.

16 He giveth snow like wool : and scattereth the hoar-frost like ashes.

17 He casteth forth his ice like morsels : who is able to abide his frost?

i.e. hail like crumbs of bread.

18 He sendeth out his word, and melteth them : he bloweth with his wind, and the waters flow.

See *v.* 15.
The snow, frost and hail, melted by the warm wind, flow away as water.

19 He sheweth his word unto Jacob : his statutes and ordinances unto Israel.

He who rules all nature by His word, has specially privileged Israel by giving it His written word. 'What advantage, then, hath the Jew?... Much every way: first of all, that they were intrusted with the oracles of God.' Rom. iii. 1, 2.

20 He hath not dealt so with any nation : neither have the heathen knowledge of his laws.

A.R.V. add *Praise ye the LORD*, R.V. mg. Heb. *Hallelujah.*

PSALM CXLVIII. *Laudate Dominum.*

A call to heaven and earth to join with Israel in the praise of God.

The Benedicite, the apocryphal addition to Dan. iii., is an expansion of this Psalm.

Proper on St Michael and All Angels [America]. At Matins, second alternative for Te Deum [Ireland].

A.R.V. prefix *Praise ye the LORD,* mg. Heb. *Hallelujah.*

O PRAISE the LORD [a]⌜of heaven⌝: praise him in the height.

1—6. The praise of heaven invited.

[a]*from the heavens.*

2 Praise him, all ye angels of his : praise him, all his host.

3 Praise him, sun and moon : praise him, all ye stars and light.

4 Praise him, [b]⌜all ye heavens⌝ : and ye waters that are above the heavens.

[b]*ye heavens of heavens,* i.e. ye highest heavens.

'waters' above the 'firmament.' Gen. i. 7; see Ps. civ. 3.

5 Let them praise the Name of the LORD : for [1]⌜he spake the word, and they were made;⌝ he commanded, and they were created.

6 He hath made them fast for ever and ever : he hath given them a law which shall not be broken.

7—13. The praise of earth invited.

7 Praise the LORD [c]upon earth : ye [d]dragons, and all deeps ;

[c]*from the.*

[d]R.V. mg. *sea-monsters.* Gen. i. 21.

8 Fire and hail, snow and vapours : wind and storm, fulfilling his word ;

'Fire'=lightning.

9 Mountains and all hills, fruitful trees and all cedars ;

[1] Not in A.R.V., added in P.B.V. from Vulg. which borrowed from Ps. xxxiii. 9.

10 Beasts and all cattle : [a] worms and feathered fowls;

[a] *creeping things.*

11 Kings of the earth and all [b] people : princes and all judges of the world;

11, 12. Man mentioned last as the climax of creation. Gen. i. 26.

[b] R.V. *peoples.*

12 Young men and maidens, old men and children, praise the Name of the LORD : for his Name only is [c] excellent, and his praise above heaven and earth.

[c] R.V. *exalted.* P.B.V. 'excellent' had formerly this meaning of superiority.

13 He [d] ⌜shall exalt⌝ the horn of his people; [e] ⌜all his saints shall praise him⌝ : [f] even the children of Israel, [g] ⌜even the people that serveth him⌝.

[d] R.V. *hath lifted up.*

[e] *the praise of all his saints.* God's exaltation of His people is the special theme of their praise.

[f] *even of.*

[g] *a people near unto him.* 'What great nation is there, that hath a god so nigh unto them, as the LORD our God is whensoever we call upon him?' Deut. iv. 7; see Ps. cxlv. 18.

A.R.V. add *Praise ye the LORD,* R.V. mg. Heb. *Hallelujah.*

PSALM CXLIX. *Cantate Domino.*

Israel restored from Babylon and new born as a nation, rejoices in its Divine King; and exults in the prospect of future victories over the nations. The Psalm, spiritually understood, foreshadows the conquest of the world by Christ.

Proper on All Saints' Day [America].

A.R.V. prefix *Praise ye the LORD,* mg. Heb. *Hallelujah.*

O SING unto the LORD a new song : let the congregation of saints praise him.

'a new song.' The new epoch of joy and hope calls for a new expression of thanksgiving; see Ps. xcvi. 1, xcviii. 1; Rev. v. 9, xiv. 3.

2 Let Israel rejoice in him that made him : and let the children of Sion be joyful in their King.

'that made him' a nation (Ps. xcv. 6, c. 2) and has now revived the national life.

3 Let them praise his Name in the dance : let them sing praises unto him with tabret and harp.

4 For the LORD hath pleasure in his people : [a]⌜and helpeth the meek-hearted⌝.

[a] *he will beautify the meek with salvation.*

5 Let the saints be joyful with glory : let them [b]⌜rejoice in⌝ their beds.

[b] R.V. *sing for joy upon*, i.e. let their rejoicing be in private as well as in public, *v.* 3.

6 Let the praises of God be in their mouth : and a two-edged sword in their hands;

7 [c]⌜To be avenged of the heathen : and to rebuke the people⌝;

[c] R.V. *To execute vengeance upon the nations, and punishments upon the peoples.*

8 To bind their kings in chains : and their nobles with links of iron;

9 [d]⌜That they may be avenged of them as it is written⌝ : Such honour have all his saints.

[d] *To execute upon them the judgement written*, i.e. To carry into effect the Divine will recorded in Holy Writ that all kingdoms shall become subject to God. Is. xli. 15, 16; Mic. iv. 13; Joel iii. 12; cp. Rev. xi. 15.

'Such honour' &c. i.e. the subjection of the world will redound to the glory of God's people.

A.R.V. add *Praise ye the* LORD, R.V. mg. Heb. *Hallelujah.*

PSALM CL. *Laudate Dominum.*

THE CLOSING HALLELUJAH.

A call to the universal praise of Jehovah.

As each Book of the Psalter ends with a doxology, so the concluding Psalm is solely a doxology.

Proper on Trinity Sunday [America].

A.R.V. prefix *Praise ye the* LORD, mg. Heb. *Hallelujah.*

O PRAISE God in his [e]holiness : praise him in the firmament of his power.

[e] *sanctuary*, here = heaven.

The 'firmament' of heaven which testifies to God's power.

2 Praise him [f]in his noble acts : praise him according to his excellent greatness.

[f] *for.*

'excellent' formerly meant 'surpassing,' 'excelling.'

3 Praise him in the sound of the trumpet : praise him upon the lute and harp.

4 Praise him in the [a]cymbals and dances : praise him upon the strings and pipe.

[a] *timbrel.*

5 Praise him upon the well-tuned cymbals : praise him upon the loud cymbals.

6 Let every thing that hath breath : praise the LORD.

A.R.V. add *Praise ye the* LORD, R.V. mg. Heb. *Hallelujah.*

INDEX

For EU product safety concerns, contact us at Calle de José Abascal, 56–1°, 28003 Madrid, Spain or eugpsr@cambridge.org.

www.ingramcontent.com/pod-product-compliance
Ingram Content Group UK Ltd.
Pitfield, Milton Keynes, MK11 3LW, UK
UKHW010731190625
459647UK00030B/300

* 9 7 8 1 1 0 7 4 4 5 7 6 5 *